UPROOTED WOMEN

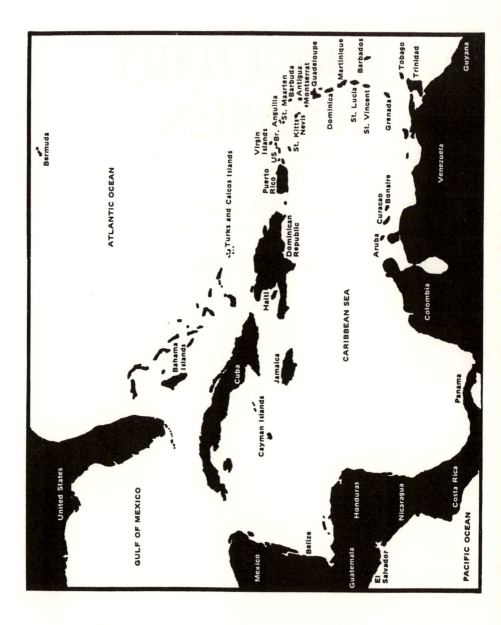

UPROOTED WOMEN

Migrant Domestics in the Caribbean

Paula L. Aymer

Westport, Connecticut
London

Library of Congress Cataloging-in-Publication Data

Aymer, Paula L.
  Uprooted women : migrant domestics in the Caribbean / Paula L.
Aymer.
      p.   cm.
  Includes bibliographical references and index.
  ISBN 0–275–95883–3 (alk. paper)
  1. Women alien labor—Caribbean Area.   2. Women domestics—Aruba.
3. Women alien labor—Aruba.   I. Title.
HD6110.A95   1997
331.4'8164'04609729—dc21   96–53939

British Library Cataloguing in Publication Data is available.

Library of Congress Catalog Card Number: 96–53939
ISBN: 0–275–95883–3

First published in 1997

Praeger Publishers, 88 Post Road West, Westport, CT 06881
An imprint of Greenwood Publishing Group, Inc.

Printed in the United States of America

∞™

The paper used in this book complies with the
Permanent Paper Standard issued by the National
Information Standards Organization (Z39.48–1984).

10 9 8 7 6 5 4 3 2 1

To my children,
Elise and Birch

Contents

Chapter 1

Introduction

In 1975 I moved to Aruba in the southern Caribbean. Whenever I went to Oranjestad, the island's capital, I noticed black women walking alone or standing in twos and threes at the post office, in the banks, or shopping in the bargain basement shops on the main street, Nassaustraat. These were women of childbearing age, and their hairstyles, simple dresses, and body language set them apart from the majority mestizo Aruban population, tourists, and the small numbers of local blacks. The women seemed strangely familiar to me; in fact, they strongly resembled women I had known during my childhood in Grenada in the eastern Caribbean. Moreover, they were out of place on the streets of Oranjestad. Why were they there in seemingly large numbers? I had to find out about them.

I began to get close to the women as they shopped. If they spoke English, I chose a right moment to interject and inquire about their purpose on Aruba. As women conversed with me, the pieces of the puzzle began to fit. During my childhood in Grenada in the 1950s, labor migrations from eastern Caribbean islands were common. Nearly everyone knew of someone or had a relative who had gone off to seek work in the oil lands of Trinidad or Venezuela, Aruba or Curaçao.

In 1975 as my inquiries deepened, memories from my childhood flooded my mind, filling in even intimate details. I realized that I had known several women—neighbors and relatives—who had set off to the oil lands. One of these women, my own childless, middle-aged spinster aunt (long deceased), had used her younger sister's passport to gain entry and meet Aruba's stringent age stipulation for migrant domestics. That first year on Aruba, I recollected how I had been very friendly with the children of another woman who had left them while she went off to seek wage work. This woman, a widow at the time, put her older children in charge of the younger ones and went to Aruba, where she remained for ten years.

Some mysteries from my childhood slowly became clear in 1975. I vividly recalled the puzzling influx of scores of well-dressed, silent children to my elementary school during those years. At last I understood. In the 1950s, these children of eastern Caribbean migrant workers and their parents had been repatriated from the oil lands: Venezuela, Curaçao, and Aruba. I recalled how, for a while, the children seemed lost, since they spoke and understood very little English.

By 1975 the oil-producing countries of the Middle East had already replaced the southern Caribbean oil fields in production and importance. Therefore, I was surprised to discover that the traffic in migrant domestics from the eastern Caribbean to the former oil lands had not ceased. Quietly, poor eastern Caribbean women had continued the pattern of female migrant labor begun by other women several decades before.

Standard Oil New Jersey has carefully and thoroughly chronicled its oil exploration and business enterprises in the Caribbean (Fanning 1950; Popple 1952; Wall 1988). The company's accounts make little or no mention of the participation of women in the oil economy it created in the southern Caribbean.

During my two years on Aruba, I began deliberately identifying English-speaking migrant domestics who had arrived since the 1960s, and since tourism and banking had replaced the oil economy. I came to know about twenty women fairly well. These women were between the ages of twenty-four and thirty-five, and were mainly from the islands of St. Vincent, Dominica, St. Kitts, Nevis, and Grenada. Among them were five women whom I recognized on sight—they were children in my village during my own childhood on Grenada.

My interest in the women intensified when I realized that an older cohort of former migrant domestics from the eastern Caribbean had become permanent residents on the island. These women were the remnants of the earliest female labor migration treks to the oil lands that began in the late 1930s and peaked during the early 1950s. Many of them frequented the Protestant churches in San Nicolas and Oranjestad, Aruba's main towns. These now elderly, worn-out women had made a restless peace with the society that had received them as migrant workers. Reluctantly, they had accepted Aruba as their final destination.

CHANGES IN MIGRATION PATTERNS

Since the 1930s, fundamental changes have occurred in the composition of the migration flow from the eastern Caribbean to the former Caribbean oil countries. For example, among the aging former domestics on Aruba, several women were originally from the island of Montserrat. However, in 1989 when I began searching in earnest, I could find no young migrant domestics on Aruba from that island, nor did the older Montserrat women know of any young domestics from there working on Aruba. It seemed too, that women from the island of Nevis were also no longer attracted to Aruba (Olwig 1993).[1] However, Aruba continued to be very attractive to women from the southernmost islands of the anglophone eastern Caribbean—Grenada and St. Vincent in particular.

A significant difference between the women of the age cohorts is the sense of temporariness and transience which pervades the lives of the younger women. If the women of the older age cohort had finally come to view Aruba as home, the women of the younger cohort were still footloose. They saw themselves and were seen in the community as uprooted women, still on edge, anxious to move on. These younger women were always in search of niches and on the lookout for better breaks, even when these entailed further travel to a more lucrative migration apex.

RATIONALE AND METHODOLOGY

I moved with my family to the United States in 1979, but could not erase the migrant women from my mind. As a U.S. immigrant, I was struck by the power of socioeconomic forces to impel workers to search for a better life, enticing them to forsake everything and take up residence in foreign countries. It was in the United States that I began to fully comprehend the meaning of social exclusion. Like the women on Aruba, I had become the immigrant, thrust to the margins of a society and looking in. On Aruba, I had lacked the contextual knowledge to formulate in-depth questions regarding the autonomous female labor migration and the female migrant labor experience. In the United States, endowed with some personal experience and much interest in the topic, I decided to look closely at the phenomenon of poor women who leave home alone in search of wage labor and a better life. The migrant domestics on Aruba became my research focus.

I had traveled to the United States from the Dutch Antilles and was fascinated by the unintended but enduring labor links and migration patterns formed between the impoverished islands of the anglophone eastern Caribbean and the semi-industrialized oil countries, including Aruba. For long after the oil speculators, engineering firms, and business mogols had made their profits, moved on, and forgotten the oil enclave (and Aruba's existence in particular), Aruba's labor link with the poorer eastern Caribbean islands continued.[2]

Such massive and intense incursions of workers and wealth into a formerly neglected region of the world surely caused drastic changes and had long-lasting socioeconomic repercussions. Even though demand for male migrant labor in the oil refining business weakened in the early 1950s, eastern Caribbean women continued to find ready employment as maids in Aruba.

Questions Arising

The story of intra-Caribbean female migrant labor flows provides a rich, informative addition to the female labor history of the area. There are unique characteristics of labor control and manipulation built into any migrant worker/employer relationship. However, when the migrant workers are female, and many are already mothers, their labor history makes special contributions to ongoing research on the organization of households and the family life of poor families.

What essential features of the migrant labor category makes migrant workers important to most modern industrial nation-states and their multinational companies? How is gender manipulated by political economies that make use of female migrant labor? How is racism constructed in the Caribbean? How do immigrant minority women express womanhood and practice motherhood in racialized receiving societies? How does the normative system in the sending society rearrange itself to support migrant women in long-distance mothering activities? How do migrant workers infiltrate and nullify nation-state boundaries?

Methodology

I returned to the Netherlands Antilles for three months in the summer of 1989 to do fieldwork among the anglophone eastern Caribbean migrant domestics. I visited St. Eustatius and St. Maarten in the Windward Netherlands Antilles before going to Aruba in June 1989.

I needed to understand the immigration and labor laws of all the Netherlands Antilles. The Dutch organized the Netherlands Antilles as a political unit with Curaçao as the seat of the colonial government that managed the affairs of all six islands. Immigration laws emanating from Curaçao were the same for all six islands with some minor modifications.

Language threatened to be an impediment in my research efforts on Aruba since the laws were written in Dutch and Papiamento, and I understood neither. To circumvent this, I located some English-speaking former residents who had worked and lived in the black community there. They became my interpreters as I worked my way through officialdom on Aruba.

During my twelve-year absence, women from the new sending countries of Haiti and Jamaica had poured onto Aruba. There they had joined other poor women from the Dominican Republic, Colombia, Venezuela, and the anglophone eastern Caribbean to find work. In 1989 women from the anglophone eastern Caribbean were still a significant group on Aruba and comprised about one-third of the 1,500 domestics living and working within the two-square-mile area of Oranjestad.

The women I knew during my earlier years of residence on the island provided my reintroduction to the maid community in Oranjestad in 1989. I was able to locate most of the elderly women I had known in the 1970s, but tracking down the younger women proved more difficult. They were a more transient population and turnover was high among them. I finally found three (one of whom died while I was there) and they helped me locate others.[3]

I walked the streets of Oranjestad daily and especially on Thursday afternoons (the maids' half-day), looking for women whose profile I recognized easily. I was seldom wrong. Occasionally I approached a woman who turned out to be a maid from the Dominican Republic or Haiti. Communication in these cases was impossible, as I could speak neither Spanish nor Haitian Creole. Once women appeared friendly and willing to converse with me in English, I would ask them to introduce me to their friends. I composed and handed out a flyer with my address that stated my own Caribbean roots and my interest in meeting English-speaking maids.

I explained my research focus to one of the chief librarians at the main library in Oranjestad, where I spent many hours during the heat of day. She passed out some flyers to her friends who employed maids. I also visited the Methodist church in Oranjestad which was attended frequently by migrant domestics from both age cohorts.

These combined methods generated an initial core of migrant domestics. I was able to meet about fifty women by a process of referrals through which women introduced me to their friends, sent women to visit me or sent me to locate them. Twenty-six of these women became the focus of my research effort. Over a three-month period, I met and walked through the streets of Oranjestad with many migrant domestics. Walking the streets with the women was part of a "getting acquainted" strategy; but the intent was always to have a long, preferably sit-down visit or a series of sit-down, shorter visits with each woman.[4] This involved inviting each woman to my apartment, or asking her to use her precious spare time (usually on Thursday afternoons) to meet me socially somewhere.[5] A woman's cooperation was usually generated by gaining her trust or because of some level of curiosity and inquisitiveness on her part. For a variety of reasons, follow-ups with many women became impossible after an initial meeting.

A woman was included in the twenty-six subjects on whom I focused if I had been able to spend at least four hours in her company and had managed to administer, through informal conversation, a prepared questionnaire concerning her life prior to and during her stay on Aruba.

There was much general similarity in the women's lives, but there were also marked differences and a uniqueness in the life experiences among those in each age cohort. All of the migrant women had been born into relatively poor families.[6]

The majority of them had been born into non-nuclear family and household arrangements. They had begun bearing children in their mid- to late teens. All of the women had arrived on Aruba because a relative or family friend had found a work sponsor for them.

There were strong differences in life experiences between the women of each age cohort. The twenty women in the study's younger cohort ranged from ages twenty-four to fifty-one. It was noteworthy that fifteen of these twenty younger women, who began arriving in the late 1960s, had left young dependent children in their sending islands. Only one of the six older women had been a mother (of a grown son) upon her arrival on Aruba.[7] Two of the six older women had married on Aruba, while only one of the younger women had married while on contract.

The women varied in their levels of education. Of the twenty younger women, eight had finished seventh grade schooling, which under the British colonial system was equivalent to one or two years of high school. The other twelve had reached various low levels of grade school. Of the older cohort (women who had arrived between the 1940s and 1950s), three had completed seventh grade and the other three had not finished grade school.

During the period of my data gathering, fourteen of the twenty younger women were live-in maids who worked ten-hour days, sometimes longer. All had followed a pattern of renewing their yearly contracts. Thirteen had fulfilled the mandatory five-year live-in period but had chosen to remain as live-in maids to save more of their wages.

It was easier to interview the older women who arrived on Aruba in the 1940s and 1950s and are now elderly, retired, and ailing. In 1989, the average age of these women was seventy. The smallness of their total number is explained by this group's dwindling numbers, and by whether the women were well enough and willing to allow me a home visit. Of the six in the study, five had retired. Four owned their homes and two were long-time renters. The six women invited me to their homes, and I was able to spend long periods with them.

I soon discovered in my dealings with the migrant domestics that my use of Grenadian dialect set them at ease. In telling their story, I have generally used the women's Caribbean dialect as I recorded it during our conversations. There are instances, however, when for the sake of clarity I have taken the liberty of replacing the dialect with more formal English. I have endeavored to retain the exact meanings of the women's statements in each instance.

The Caribbean: Location

The Caribbean islands stretch in an arc from the Bahamas just off the tip of Florida, to Curaçao, Bonaire, and Aruba. These southwesternmost Caribbean islands, the Dutch Leewards, lie just off the northwestern coast of Venezuela, South America. Over the last three or four centuries, the islands of the Caribbean have been fought over and prized as colonies by various western European nations. The United States began to invest in Caribbean agriculture only in the second half of the nineteenth century. For centuries, the region had been dominated by the British colonial presence.

Britain ruled its widely dispersed Caribbean colonies by creating manageable administrative blocks. Britain doled out investments, aid, personnel, and experiments in agriculture and education to colonies in each administrative block according to the ranked value of the territories viewed through the eyes of the British colonial office. Jamaica, Barbados, and later Trinidad, the larger islands, ranked highest in the British colonial hierarchy. This book focuses on some of the smaller islands administered by Britain—the Leeward and Windward islands—to trace female labor migration flows that emanated from them beginning in the 1930s.

The Caribbean region assumed new strategic and economic importance to the major international powers when oil was discovered in large quantities on Trinidad and Venezuela. Subsequently, U.S. companies and other international oil entrepreneurs made massive investments in extractive and refining businesses operated on Venezuela, Trinidad, Curaçao, and Aruba respectively. All during the twentieth century and especially since the 1940s, the Caribbean region found itself increasingly within the U.S. sphere of influence.

Labor migration from the Caribbean to the United States increased phenomenally with increased U.S. investments and presence in the region. The interest of the Caribbean people riveted on the U.S. mainland during the early twentieth century in response to the incursions of U.S. investments in fruit plantations, shipping companies, oil enterprises, infrastructural and construction operations in the region. Eastern Caribbean labor migrants, confined until the 1930s to intraregional job scouting, began to envision the United States as a new important migration apex.

Much has been written about Caribbean labor migration treks and how migration is a way of life for Caribbean people. Typically, accounts tell of Caribbean male labor migration that began almost immediately after emancipation in the 1830s. Whenever mentioned, the travels of Caribbean female labor migrants are generally subsumed under the neutral category of Caribbean labor migrants. Written records date significant Caribbean female migration treks as beginning only in the 1950s and 1960s, when women joined male labor migrants in the historic Caribbean labor migration treks to Britain (Gmelch 1992; Foner 1979).

In *Uprooted Women*, I contend that the initial labor migrations of eastern Caribbean women were intraregional. The book documents the labor migration flows of two age cohorts of eastern Caribbean women to the oil lands of the southern Caribbean—Trinidad, Venezuela, Curaçao, and Aruba—in response to calls for female-gendered labor. I present the massive incursions of U.S. investments in the southern Caribbean as an important precipitating regional event that propelled eastern Caribbean women into migrant labor.

In my efforts to explain the migration culture of the Caribbean, I make use of classical migration theories but treat them as inadequate. They highlight the "push" and "pull" of market forces emanating from industrialized countries as exerting great influence on labor migrations from poor countries (Lee 1966). Marxist economic class explanations must be stretched to fit labor conditions in predominantly agricultural settings such as the Caribbean, where the majority of the population entered the wage economy as late as the 1930s.

The World Systems Model (Wallerstein 1974) best explains the collusion of multinational companies with powerful nation-states, and how their concerted efforts effect easy penetration into foreign countries. But the focus of all these labor migration perspectives is on structurally induced and controlled labor migration flows. Industrialized countries are always the powerful actors.

Uprooted Women injects gender into existing labor migration theories, and views labor migration from migrant women's perspectives. Labor migration has become a major entrepreneurial activity for the women who refuse to be fazed by foreign nation-state boundaries.

The book is a sociohistorical and ethnographic account of pioneering anglophone eastern Caribbean women who signed up to be migrant domestics in the Caribbean oil lands. The book argues that this unprecedented experiment in female labor migration created a long-term relationship between black female migrant workers from the eastern Caribbean and "non-black" middle-class households on Aruba. Furthermore, wage-earning efforts of migrant labor in the oil enclave expanded and intensified female intraregional petty trading activities and stimulated the interests of eastern Caribbean women in new labor sites outside of the Caribbean.

Aruba, the site of a giant U.S.-owned oil refinery, became a major participant in satisfying western Europe's and North America's insatiable oil needs, especially during the decade of the 1940s and World War II. The island is singled out as a prototype of a twentieth-century industrial work-site that attracted female migrant labor. I argue that the female migrant labor flow to Aruba represented one segment of a wider intraregional and international labor trend, in a predictable international labor pattern.

During the twentieth century, women became the preferred labor migrant at many industrial work sites and urban centers. Demand for male workers slacks off in the second phase of foreign investments in poor countries. Women workers then migrate alone to be service workers. Women wage earners become main providers for themselves and their dependents (Momsen 1993; Glick Schiller, Basch, and Blanc-Szanton 1992; Sassen-Koob 1983).

The Oil Lands and Aruba

Among the surprises that awaited eastern Caribbean labor migrants to the oil enclave were the topography and climate differences between their sending countries and the new oil lands. Whereas most eastern Caribbean islands, including Trinidad, are at least partially lush and verdant, the

Caribbean coastlands of northwestern Venezuela, Curaçao, and Aruba (with a few other Caribbean countries) belong to a climatic category defined as a "tropical marine dry" subtype (Sealy 1992, 82). Much of the oil enclave (excluding Trinidad) is arid; sisal, cacti, and thorn bushes are the native vegetation.

Most eastern Caribbean migrant workers set out for Venezuela, Aruba, or Curaçao knowing little about these countries except that they were foreign and far away. They conjectured that the oil lands were peopled mainly by the descendants of West Africans, just as their sending islands were, and that these new people would speak some version of the official language of their European colonizers. Their population and language expectations were correct for Trinidad. However, Spanish was the language spoken in Venezuela, a former colony of Spain, and the descendants of African slaves were relatively few on Venezuela and Aruba early in the twentieth century. Furthermore, the native people of Aruba, Curaçao, and Bonaire spoke a native language, Papiamento.[8]

Papiamento is Aruba's mother tongue, even though Spanish rivals Papiamento as a language heard on the streets of Aruba. Dutch is the language of instruction in the schools, and all schoolchildren must also learn English, considered to be the language of commerce. Consequently, Aruban shops and streets are a babel of tongues, very unlike the streets of most English-speaking Caribbean islands.

Aruba's population reflects the island's colonial ties to the Netherlands and its geographical proximity to the South American mainland. The native Arubans are a mestizo people: they are the descendants of native Americans from Venezuela and Colombia, who interbred with small numbers of Spaniards, Portugese Jews, Dutch traders and civil servants, and Africans brought to Aruba during the peak period of African enslavement on neighboring Caribbean islands (Hartog 1961). Aruba's dry climate discouraged attempts at plantation slavery. Since the island was claimed by the Dutch in the seventeenth century, Aruba's sparse population eked out a living from fishing, planting guinea corn, cultivating the aloe plant, harvesting salt, and for a short period, mining limited gold deposits.

During the first decades of the twentieth century, many able-bodied males on Aruba and Curaçao left their impoverished islands to seek wage labor as migrant workers in the canefields of Cuba and the Dominican Republic. Many of these men headed home, especially in the 1930s, when both islands became important production sites in the oil enclave.

Then came the period of Aruba's booming economic prosperity, when its population and native way of life seemed to change overnight. From the 1930s until about 1960, the Lago oil refinery in effect became Aruba, and Aruba became the Lago oil refinery. San Nicolas, the oil boom town that had mushroomed under the shadow of the famous Lago oil refinery on the southeastern shores of the island, became the center of the island's economic activity.

Aruba's population increased and became diverse. From a mere 8,265, comprised mainly of mestizo Arubans in 1920, the island's population rose to 42,764 in 1945 (Hartog 1961). Thousands of black, English-speaking migrant workers from the Netherlands Antilles, especially from the islands of St. Maarten, Saba, and St. Eustatius, descended on Aruba. The presence of a small black population of former migrant workers and their offspring on Aruba can be precisely dated from the 1930s, when throngs of English-speaking Caribbean migrant workers of African descent began to arrive. Other black workers, eager to find wage labor, arrived or were recruited from impoverished British colonies in the Caribbean.[9]

A smaller and higher-status group of migrant workers also sought employment on Aruba during the island's years of intense population growth. Hundreds of whites, mostly from North America, South America and Europe, found employment in various capacities at the Lago refinery.

Migrant workers from the Netherlands Antilles (the Dutch colonies of St. Maarten, St. Eustatius, Saba, Curaçao, Bonaire, and Surinam) had a unique immigration status known on Aruba as "Dutch Rights." Persons with this privileged status could arrive on Aruba (or Curaçao) of their own volition and remain as long as they wished (Crane 1971, 100). These Antilleans, like Lago's white technical and administrative staff, were permitted family reunification on Aruba. Most other black male Caribbean migrant workers had few, if any, family reunification privileges.[10]

A mainly black and elderly population now lives in San Nicolas. Old men with Dutch Rights who decided to make Aruba their home, and retired migrant domestics, who severed strong ties with the anglophone eastern Caribbean, walk slowly and listlessly down narrow mazes that crisscross the village. Each tiny house is surrounded by rough concrete fences, rusting corrugated galvanized barriers, and shrubs. In the 1980s, a sympathetic local government began to renovate the shacks of these former migrant workers. However, when the government changed, the project stopped, and in 1989 there were still many houses without indoor plumbing. Native mestizo Arubans live, for the most part, in villages that dot the dry rolling countryside throughout the island.

Oranjestad, seven miles west of San Nicolas, has replaced that town in economic importance and is now the island's busy tourist and offshore banking center. The architecture, streets, and market scenes of Oranjestad, the capital, remain reminiscent of towns in Central or South America (Koot 1981, 139). Shop clerks are barely fluent in English; instead, Papiamento, Dutch, and Spanish are heard everywhere.

When San Nicolas was the economic center of Aruba, the oil refinery's expatriate administrators and technical staff settled in the exclusive area called "the Colony" on a ridge above the oil town. In the 1990s, Aruba's wealthy middle class—native Arubans, North American and European expatriate professionals—resides in and around Oranjestad. This is the privileged class that employs migrant domestics.

CHAPTER OUTLINES

Chapter 2 examines how the U.S. oil business investments in the southern Caribbean effectively weakened then displaced Britain's colonial Caribbean presence. The U.S. influence intensified through its defense efforts during World War II and the presence of its largest multinational corporation, Standard Oil New Jersey. One of this company's biggest investments was the Lago oil refinery on Aruba, which became host to U.S. big business, modern technology, and burgeoning throngs of migrant workers.

Until the development of an oil enclave in the southern Caribbean early in the 1900s, poor Caribbean women had only inconsistent access to wage labor through their own efforts in the informal economy. Chapter 3 examines how Caribbean women are crucial participants in Caribbean economies by their multiple money earning endeavors. However, economic theorists, planners, and policymakers ignore the women's contributions.

Chapter 4 explores the circuitous methods by which Caribbean women become foreign migrant workers in the oil lands. The entry of women crossculturally in the male-dominated migrant labor category has important social implications. The chapter shows how international entrepreneurs in the oil enclave, especially on Aruba, interpret gender and inculcate Caribbean women into labor migration.

Chapter 5 traces the changes in recruitment strategies used to attract two different age cohorts of migrant domestics. The older dwindling population of migrant women arrived in the 1940s, while the younger age cohort of migrant domestics began arriving in the late 1960s. These younger women are recruited to Aruba under chaotic and unstable socioeconomic conditions in their own islands while Aruba's economy is in transition from dependence on oil refinery to huge investments in tourism. The unexpected calls to work create great excitement for the women, who must mobilize family and community support to help take care of the dependents they leave behind.

Chapter 6 looks at poor eastern Caribbean families and households and the important place that women hold in them as chief providers and the unique kinds of mothering in which they become involved. In ethnographic accounts, the women tell about their lives as wage earners, mothers, and mates.

The migrant women exist in a world of work on Aruba. Many renew their contracts continuously and eventually become elderly while still under contract on Aruba. In Chapter 7 the women tell of their lives as live-in domestics, and their efforts to ward off exploitative relations with their employers and the authorities, while, at the same time, trying to eke out the best wages and work conditions.

Chapter 8 places the labor of the migrant women on Aruba within the context of the labor history of Caribbean women, their families, and Caribbean migration. The women's chances at bettering themselves involve access to petty trade, labor migration, and especially transnational relations with the United States.

Chapter 2

U.S. Oil Enterprises
in the Caribbean

In the years immediately after emancipation, eastern Caribbean men ventured out of their islands cautiously.[1] There was a survival logic to the earliest labor migration treks of these former slaves and their descendants. Poor Caribbean men practiced a kind of chain migration within the relative safety of neighboring British colonies. Until the mid-1880s, the British colonies of Trinidad and British Guiana (now Guyana) were the most attractive destinations for seasonal workers in sugarcane harvesting (Marshall 1982).

British Guiana declined as an important sugar-producing country, and by the end of the nineteenth century, it ceased to be a major receiving country for eastern Caribbean migrant workers. It was the island of Trinidad, with its mixed economy of agriculture and later oil, that continued to be inundated with labor migrants. Well into the first half of the twentieth century, thousands of single male laborers, and sometimes entire immigrant families from the smaller eastern Caribbean islands, poured into Trinidad (Marshall 1982; Brizan 1984; Brereton 1981).[2]

U.S. BUSINESS INTERESTS

In the decade prior to the U.S. Civil War, U.S. investors and politicians began to view the Caribbean as an area of strategic political significance that might prove valuable for exploration and extraction of mineral wealth. In the post–Civil War years, and as the nineteenth century ended, the United States made forays into the Caribbean, with contingents of its large modern navy designed intentionally to increase international trade and to establish itself as a world power.

The Caribbean was important in the emerging U.S. world view. The region served as an outer territorial boundary against the encroachment of any European power intent on rivaling U.S. hegemony this side of the Atlantic (Fernandez 1994; Langley 1989). To this end, the United States began aggressive economic incursions into the Caribbean area, especially the vulnerable Spanish-speaking Caribbean "rimlands" (Augelli 1962): the colonies of a shrinking Spanish empire.

The United States stood poised to usurp Britain's colonial dominance in the Caribbean and quickly imposed its hegemony there. By the end of the nineteenth century the United States routed Spain's colonial Caribbean presence and badgered Britain and other European powers that owned Caribbean colonies. U.S. foreign policy gave official recognition to Spain's restless Caribbean colonies and breakaway republics such as Panama, Colombia, the Dominican Republic, and Cuba. The U.S. strategy: to dazzle ruling dictators of these Spanish-speaking Caribbean rimland republics with U.S. investments, win their allegiance, and then receive carte blanche from them to set up branches of U.S. corporations in their countries.

By the end of the 1890s, the United States brought Spain's four-century-long Caribbean colonial presence to a quick end, acquiring or appointing itself political guardian of most of Spain's prized former Caribbean posessions. U.S. businesses began to oversee Cuba's highly lucrative sugarcane, coffee, and tobacco industries. The U.S. government, spurred on by big business interests, also had its eye on Mexico's oil resources, and oil speculators gained permission to search Mexican territory. The United States also replaced France as the industrial power engaged in the construction of the Panama Canal.

U.S. businesses made large investments in agricultural enterprises in Costa Rica, Nicaragua, Panama, the Dominican Republic, and Cuba. Investments were made in oil extraction in Venezuela, Trinidad, and Aruba, and bauxite mining in Jamaica and Haiti followed later. Plans were enacted to quickly transform chosen sites into U.S.-owned and -operated economic enclaves ensconced in Caribbean backwaters.

U.S. companies pulled in whatever they needed at their remote production sites: technology, bureaucratic forms of labor management, manufactured goods, forms of leisure, and foreign migrant laborers. However, there was no plan by the United States or its corporations to invest in the people of these Caribbean societies or to inaugurate any widespread socioeconomic transformation. The bottom line for investing companies was always expansion and maximization of profits (Sunshine 1994). By the first decade of the twentieth century, as never before, the United States viewed the Caribbean as part of its backyard. The mission to place the Caribbean region firmly within the U.S. sphere of influence had been accomplished.

Foreign Male Labor

Work sites mushroomed throughout the Caribbean in tandem with production and trade enterprises introduced by U.S. business interests. Foreign male workers—migrant laborers—became an important business investment at U.S. Caribbean work sites. Management usually determined that native, non-anglophone workers were either unsuitable or insufficient for the tasks. Besides, temporary foreign labor was the latest international labor experiment of that time.

In the nineteenth century, western European industrial economies had begun to experiment with varieties of foreign migrant worker arrangements (Miles 1993). Foreign migrant labor had replaced slave labor in nearly all former British colonies. A supposedly enlightened world view saw voluntary, contracted wage labor as an improvement on the labor relations of slave economies. Nation-states and employers viewed foreign migrant workers as a cost-efficient, short-term economic investment, especially during periods of unexpected economic transition and expansion (Castles 1989).

Labor scouts roamed the Caribbean hiring thousands of poor men who were then transported to labor in "foreign" (non-anglophone) Caribbean countries.[3] Eastern Caribbean males found intermittent employment, mainly as laborers, at construction sites in the Panama Canal zone, in the sugarcane fields of Cuba and the Dominican Republic, coffee plantations of Brazil, banana plantations of Costa Rica and Nicaragua, and in the mahogany forests of British Honduras (Richardson 1992; Brizan 1984; Marshall 1982).

When Britain declared emancipation for slaves in its colonies in 1834, most of its Caribbean colonies were already unprofitable producers of sugar. Cash flow in the colonies and wage-earning jobs were always scarce in the nineteenth-century Caribbean. Workers on the islands often went unpaid or received irregular cash payments for their labor (Brizan 1984).[4]

Poverty drove men to seek work under terrible conditions in foreign migrant labor camps within and outside of the Caribbean (Bolland 1992; Richardson 1992). In British colonies, labor relations still resembled plantation slavery. Male migrant workers labored in frontier conditions and disease-infested environments at foreign work sites in the Caribbean. Racist labor relations in the camps approximated those of the slave barracks at worst, and the harshest conditions of indentureship at best (Richardson 1992; Enloe 1990). Yet between 1904 and 1914, from the island of Barbados alone, about 60,000 men left for the Panama Canal zone (Marshall 1982, 8). Legend and mythology surrounded Caribbean male labor migrations; over the decades, these migrations assumed rite-of-passage significance—the poor man's initiation into maturity.

The former slaves and their descendants had hoped that emancipation would mean ready access to wage labor and opportunities to live on the land as self-sufficient, free citizens. Instead, postemancipation Caribbean blacks lived extremely unstable lives (Richardson 1992; Brizan 1984; Brereton 1981). At this time, eastern Caribbean women and the majority of people in the British colonies survived in relatively closed and impoverished island worlds (Mary Proudfoot 1954; Brizan 1984). The powers overseeing the Caribbean had few plans for the former British island colonies, and little hope that viable societies could be created from colonies that had been virtual slave-labor camps (Mintz 1992; Mary Proudfoot 1954).

Women and Children Left Behind

Between 1880 and 1920, the British islands experienced heavy population losses through labor migration (Marshall 1982, 8; Brizan 1984). Ideally, labor migration gave men access to the wage economy, and allowed them to be good providers. The women and children left behind survived as best they could, hoping that the men would remember them by sending monetary or other remittances, and return at last with accumulated savings to compensate for their absence (Richardson 1992; Crane 1971). No comparable foreign wage-earning opportunities existed at this period for eastern Caribbean women. Besides, many men failed to send remittances home or return.[5]

For decades, women and children formed the bulk of the population on some small islands where the shortage of adult males was very noticeable (Crane 1971; M. G. Smith 1962). People who remained behind tried to alleviate economic hardship through petty trading, constant male and some female labor inter-island migration. Richardson (1983) describes the popular form of inter-island labor migration, "speculating," when people migrate only to places within easy return of their home bases.

Women who could no longer find wage work as field hands in their villages set out on their own for urban areas, or traveled to neighboring islands to seek lower-paying but predictable wage-labor as housemaids (Colin Clarke 1986; Brizan 1984; Brereton 1981). It was obvious that many poor Caribbean women could perform well in better-paying but laborious male-type work. However, in each British Caribbean colony, a stipulated official wage offered women twelve to fifteen cents per day, while the going man's wage was twenty-five to thirty cents a day. Male and female wages remained fixed even when women did men's work (Brizan 1984; Brereton 1981, 78).

Field labor on slave plantations in the previous centuries was ungendered (Davis 1981). But, by the early decades of the twentieth century, gender mattered greatly in the procurement of wage labor, and Caribbean males were the preferred gender at regional British and foreign labor sites throughout the Caribbean islands and rimlands. Labor scouts who visited Barbados, Grenada, St. Vincent, St. Lucia, and Trinidad during the first decades of the twentieth century recruiting workers for foreign work sites, sent clear messages that women should not apply. Besides, family reunification was discouraged at work camps.

A trickle of women did leave to join migrant males—husbands and boyfriends—in Panama, Costa Rica, Nicaragua, and the Dominican Republic (Richardson 1992; Brizan 1984). Caribbean men had limited and precarious transportation to migrant labor camps. Communication between migrant laborers at work sites and relatives back home was unpredictable or often nonexistent (Malcolm Proudfoot 1954, 333); and hardy women who found their way to frontier-styled camps understood that their status was likely to be that of camp-followers. Women at male labor camps lived in austere, isolated conditions taking care of the housework while their menfolk worked for wages. Besides, migrant labor camps in the foreign Caribbean were considered to be temporary by employers and citizens of the receiving countries.

Women left behind by migrating men took charge, becoming skillfull in traditionally male-gendered tasks, and assuming both mothering and fathering obligations (Edith Clarke 1966). Women ensured the general upkeep of the family and other institutions. Forced to survive with minimal male labor input at home, they learned to depend on each others' support and to organize family life in extended households. Maternal kin, especially older women, became the repositories of practical wisdom (Crane 1971; Koot 1981; Rubenstein 1987; M. G. Smith 1962).

However, early in the twentieth century, powerful social and economic forces sweeping through the region enticed and released women to participate with menfolk in what, until then, had been viewed as highly risky male labor migration activity. The discovery of large deposits of oil in the southern Caribbean marked a drastic change in Caribbean migrant labor destination, composition, and workers' experiences and expectations.[6] By the 1920s, poor Caribbean men focused their labor sights on newly developing oil enterprises located in Trinidad and the "foreign" (non-anglophone) Caribbean countries of Venezuela, Curaçao, and Aruba (M. G. Smith 1962; Marshall 1982).

ENCLAVE FORMATION

Early in the twentieth century, European and North American oil exploration teams discovered large deposits of oil in the southern Caribbean.[7] Extraction of crude oil and some limited refining activities had already begun on the island of Trinidad during the last decade of the nineteenth century. These limited oil finds had already attracted large numbers of job seekers into Trinidad from the neighboring islands, when news reached the eastern Caribbean that rich oil deposits had also been found in Venezuela, South America.

Significant crude oil and asphalt deposits discovered in and around the southern peninsula of Trinidad were smaller than amounts predicted in

Venezuela. The oil deposits were located in a contiguous area along the southwestern shores of the island of Trinidad and the Caribbean coastlands of northeastern Venezuela in South America, less than twenty miles south of Trinidad (Pratt 1950; Zuloaga 1950; Popple 1952). Geologists confirmed that the Caribbean island of Trinidad and Venezuela on the South American mainland shared the same oil-rich continental shelf (Richardson 1992, 117; Martinez 1989, 10, 65).

Companies registered in Canada, the United States, Britain, Germany, and the Netherlands, played hardball with each other for the best bargains in oil shares of the Venezuelan oil finds (Wall 1988). In Trinidad, rival companies representing competing national interests frantically prospected and staked claims in the rural southern parts of the island.

The oil enclave that developed in the region was an interconnected subsystem of an ambitious and aggressive international oil economy, comprised of wealthy and influential multinational corporations. Industrialized nations in Europe and North America strongly supported and safeguarded their national oil interests in the Caribbean. Though affiliates and companies often behaved as distinctly separate companies, their competition was mostly marketing strategy, meant to heighten productivity and efficiency, and increase profit margins (Heroy 1950, 27). Highly interdependent systems of oil conglomerates shared technology, bought surpluses from each other, traded personnel, and especially during World War II, presented a united front in production and defense.

By 1939 three large refineries were operating in the Dutch Antilles: two on Aruba, one on Curaçao.[8] A few much smaller refineries were located on the island of Trinidad. The combined maximum production levels of these Caribbean oil refineries during the mid-1940s, were higher than any on the U.S. mainland (Heroy 1950, 34). Caribbean petroleum, geared specifically for western European markets, also augmented U.S. mainland outputs. From the late 1930s, and especially in the high production years of World War II and the economic boom that followed, the oil enclave in the Caribbean stimulated the weak economies of the southern and eastern Caribbean and poured wealth into the U.S. economic system.[9]

The booming oil industry that emerged in the region involved oil exploration, extraction, refining, and transportation of the abundant deposits of oil. The attention of international entrepreneurs, politicians, and scientists interested not only in oil and profits, but in transportation and aviation, zeroed in on the southern Caribbean, the world's newest and most promising oil production area.[10] By the mid-1950s, the Caribbean oil enclave's glory days were almost over, as the Caribbean oil market began to be eclipsed by Middle-Eastern (Gulf states) oil. However, this intense period of U.S. investment in the Caribbean would have significant socioeconomic and migration repercussions for the region.

Standard Oil New Jersey

Any story that recounts the expansion of U.S. corporations and especially of profitable U.S. oil investments abroad, must include the story of Standard Oil New Jersey and its enterprises in the southern Caribbean. It is the story of a powerful, U.S.-based, multinational corporation that constructed a massive oil extraction, transportation, and shipping enterprise in the southern Caribbean.

The company's major affiliate and most important producer, the Creole Petroleum Corporation located in Venezuela, was a business front for the parent company, Standard Oil New Jersey (Jersey). The official history of Standard Oil New Jersey calls Creole, "the principal source of crude; the industry's showcase; one of the most vital links in the Jersey circuit; the breadwinner" (Wall 1988, 396). The Creole Petroleum Corporation became Jersey's single most profitable operation until the mid-1960s (Wall 1988, 25, 396).

Through its affiliate, in April 1932 Standard Oil New Jersey purchased the Lago Petroleum Corporation. The purchase included acquisition of two important companies: the Lago Oil Transport Company Limited and the Lago Shipping Company Limited, as well as the completed plans for the construction of the Lago refinery complex on Aruba. The Lago refinery—"the giant"—would be the main recipient of Creole's crude from its vast Venezuelan oil deposits (Wall 1988, 25). This deal firmly ensconced the largest U.S.-based, multinational corporation of that period into the Caribbean islands.

The international oil interests were afraid of placing all of their investment eggs in the same Venezuelan basket (Taylor 1955, 17). The islands of Aruba and Curaçao provided the solutions to investors' economic political insecurities concerning their massive oil investments located in a foreign country. Royal Dutch Shell Company, the first major foreign oil company to have operations in Venezuela (Boue 1993, 14) chose Curaçao on which to erect the first giant Caribbean refinery. Heavy Venezuelan crude oil was piped into barges, then towed across the narrow stretch of water between Venezuela and Curaçao. Standard Oil New Jersey chose the island of Aruba for a similar offshore refinery.

Since Curaçao is a Dutch colony, Royal Dutch Shell Company was able to easily lease several hundred acres of land on Curaçao for the building of its refinery. However, the Dutch government had no similar interest in leasing their neighboring colony of Aruba to its country's most serious oil rival, Standard Oil New Jersey. Besides, a Royal Dutch Shell affiliate—Eagle Petroleum—had already erected a small refinery on Aruba's west coast.

U.S. pressure was brought to bear on the Hague, forcing the hand of the Dutch government. Several hundred acres of land on Aruba's east coast were leased eventually to Jersey, through its affiliate Creole. The foundations of the famous Lago oil refinery were begun in 1928 (Betancourt 1979, 36). Oil pipelines on the shores of Lake Maracaibo in western Venezuela soon began to pour crude oil into waiting oil barges and tug it to receptacles on Aruba to await the refining process (Heroy 1950, 27). The company's profits yielded $156.7 million in 1950, almost 40 percent of its worldwide total profits (Wall 1988, 25). By the 1930s, international oil companies, dominated by Standard Oil New Jersey and its affiliates had successfully established an oil enclave in the southern Caribbean.

Migration fever was rising throughout the eastern Caribbean. Many eastern Caribbean males without wage work or already employed at foreign regional labor camps, responded to the new labor calls and began heading for the southern Caribbean. All during the first half of the twentieth century, people of the eastern Caribbean came to know exotic place names associated with the enclaves such as: Lago, Aruba; Curaçao; Maracaibo, Venezuela; and Point Fortin, Trinidad. These names became bywords for optimism about wealth that could be acquired through back-breaking labor and sheer luck in the oil enclave in the southern Caribbean.

Socioeconomic Repercussions

U.S. economic expansion into the area introduced eastern Caribbean migrant workers to new ways of life. Male migrant workers from the back-of-the-beyond suddenly found themselves exposed to unheard-of aspects of modernity. News quickly spread throughout the eastern Caribbean that in the oil enclave, workers were receiving the highest wages that Caribbean migrant workers anywhere had ever made (Koot 1981; Larson, Knowlton, and Popple 1971). At certain periods, and especially during the expansion of the 1940s, the oil operations' demand for laborers seemed insatiable.

Between 1900 and the 1950s, labor unrest broke out intermittently throughout the enclave and often ricocheted throughout the Caribbean. Exposure to life and work in the enclave stirred workers in the oil lands to see the need for labor organizations in the Caribbean workplace. Ostentatious shows of wealth in the oil countries, strict bureaucratic labor relations that placed Caribbean workers on the lowest work levels, ranked access to housing, well-stocked commissaries, health care, and social amenities whetted workers' appetites and stimulated demands for fair wages. Workers' complaints revolved around racialization of jobs and wages. Caribbean workers exposed company policies of paying white laborers at higher wage scales than those offered Caribbean laborers involved in identical jobs. The people of the region had been given a vision of possibilities for a better life that made them restless.

Labor unrest first flared up in the enclave during the 1930s. It began in Venezuela, swept into the Trinidadian oil fields and up throughout the

British colonies as far as Jamaica (Brereton 1981, 178; Brizan 1984). Again in the late 1940s, oil worker unions stirred up workers to strike, especially in Trinidad and Aruba.

During the early 1950s, repatriated oil workers showed up in their eastern Caribbean sending countries full of organizing zeal and readiness to express their dissatisfaction with life in the islands. Labor unrest swept through the islands. This time workers' protests were couched in new language that requested political rights and adult suffrage; the end of colonial ties reverberated throughout the Caribbean (Brereton 1981; Mary Proudfoot 1954).

Oil companies were quick to safeguard their interests, and struck a telling blow to employees' expressions of work dissatisfaction fueled by vocal and charismatic black foreign workers. Company officials devised policies to limit union organizing and membership, and lessen their overall clout in the oil enclave. They sped up the mechanization of much of their oil operations and put thousands of foreign workers out of work. By the mid-1960s all unemployed foreign male workers on Venezuela, Curaçao, and Aruba had been repatriated to their sending eastern Caribbean islands.

COUNTRIES OF THE OIL ENCLAVE

Of the oil-producing countries of Trinidad and Venezuela, Venezuela was a substantially richer source of oil in the region.[11] But the Caribbean island of Trinidad was "the true pioneer of oil . . . [in that] the first well was drilled in May 1902" (Brereton 1981, 199–200).

Trinidad was not a "foreign" work site for eastern Caribbean labor migrants. The island holds the title for being home-away-from-home for thousands of "small islanders," as Trinidadians derogatively labeled the ubiquitous Grenadians, Barbadians, Vincentians, and others who constantly showed up on Trinidad to job hunt. An important entry point for Caribbean labor migration to the oil enclave, Trinidad, unlike the other countries in the enclave, was a British colony until the early 1960s. The United States used Trinidad as a bulwark against German destruction of oil supplies in the Caribbean enclave during World War II.

Aruba

From the late 1920s to the late 1930s, life in the formerly quiet backwater towns of the Caribbean oil countries swiftly took on a frontier atmosphere. Thousands of male migrant workers from across the world, especially the Caribbean, flocked to the region. Aruba in particular became a major, largely male labor outpost in the southwestern Caribbean (Koot 1981, 131; Crane 1971, 100).

The U.S.-based, English-speaking operators of the Lago refinery sought out and readily employed English-speaking migrant workers from the eastern Caribbean. English was unofficially declared the language of commerce and work relations at the Lago oil refinery complex (Hartog 1961, 369). English-speaking black migrant workers poured onto the island from the Dutch Windward Islands of Saba and St. Martin and from the English colonies of the eastern Caribbean. For several years the foreign worker population outnumbered the native Aruban population, and English became the language of commerce. A similar foreign invasion occurred on Curaçao, when the Royal Dutch Shell Company, operated mainly by Dutch expatriates, imposed Dutch as the language of operation in the refinery, although Papiamento is the mother tongue on the islands of Aruba, Curaçao, and Bonaire.[12]

Of all production sites in the oil enclave, Aruba was best suited to reveal important aspects of the U.S. presence in the region. The island was assigned the major role of host for an important subsidiary of the largest U.S. corporation of that time. During the oil boom of the 1940s through the 1950s and since, Aruba became a microcosm of international labor migration patterns and wage labor relations that construct and manipulate gender, race, and class inequalities.

Construction of the Lago complex created demands for ancilliary male-type jobs such as plumbing, pipe-laying, and electrical work. The refinery enlisted a retinue of subcontractors. These contractors depended on the labor of unskilled and semi-skilled eastern Caribbean male migrant workers. Male laborers were also in demand for road building, dredging harbors, manning the tugboats and oil-carrying barges, and unloading the constant fleet of cargo vessels which arrived daily. By 1940 a large, racially and economically varied community resided in the oil enclave in the southern Caribbean (Green 1974; Hartog 1961; Phalen 1977). The majority of male migrant workers hailed from the eastern Caribbean. Men often performed a series of work stints returning after each to their sending islands. Men arrived on Aruba alone, and with the clear understanding that their stay would be temporary.[13] At first, few if any females were welcome.

Slowly but steadily the oil corporations' vision for their major financial and technological investment in the southern Caribbean, and on Aruba in particular, revealed itself. Whether in Venezuela, Trinidad, Curaçao, or Aruba, the organizing model for the oil enterprise was that of an *enclave*; a modern industrial work site in the middle of preindustrial, agriculturally impoverished economies (Sunshine 1994). Each company purposefully arranged life at its respective production sites to promote the enclave vision.

The oil complex and its environs were physically and socially organized to become a home away from home, especially for white expatriate workers. For example, San Nicolas (if not Aruba) was to be a self-sufficient, efficiently run company town. In time, the most modern amenities were established, including company housing, commissaries, social clubs for various echelons of workers, golf courses, beaches, a chapel, fire prevention facilities, company police, and company schools complete with tutors from the Caribbean, South America, and the United States.

Labor at the Lago refinery was arranged as it was in any U.S. overseas army base. Aruba soon began to resemble any well-run U.S. army camp or prosperous company town. Facilities, built to enhance the lives of Lago's employees, also reflected the ranks of the companies' bureaucratically organized labor structure.

Oil Production in World War II

The Caribbean oil industry, and especially its operations at the Lago oil refinery on Aruba, became deeply involved in the Allies' war effort during World War II. Extensive construction projects undertaken on Curaçao and Aruba in the early 1940s installed new "cracking units." Through the innovative method called "cracking," North American and European scientists and engineers created the technology that converted heavy crude oil into its component parts. The process subjected crude oil to extremely high temperatures and pressures. This method produced an end product of light aviation fuels, crucial for use by the European Allied aircraft during World War II.

Demand for migrant workers soared during the war years (see Table 1), and the accounts tell of men—both white expatriates and black laborers—working day and night for the war effort (Philipps 1988; Wall 1988; Baptiste 1973; Fanning 1950; Zuloaga 1950). The population of foreign workers increased steadily in the enclave and by 1948, 13.5 percent of Curaçao's population was foreign born. In the same year, the foreign born in Aruba's population of 48,000 was 28 percent (Hartog 1961, 370). In 1940 the Lago refinery processed 228,007 barrels per day. By the next year, production had soared to 288,805. Employment numbers climbed with production yields during World War II, and both peaked in the early 1950s (see Table 2). All the production sites in the enclave, as well as oil-laden tankers bound for England during the mid-1940s, became targets for German attack during World War II (Wall 1988).[14] There was some initial international jostling about whose armed forces should be allowed into the area to protect the oil resources and where they should be stationed. The French, British, and Dutch had dispatched troops (too precipitously in the U.S. estimation) to the enclave to guard their respective oil interests (Hartog 1968, 358; Baptiste 1973). The United States refused to consign this important defense effort within its own sphere of influence to any of its European allies, who themselves had rival oil interests in the enclave (Baptiste 1973).

Increased production needs, protection of Caribbean oil, and the need for an allied victory in World War II strongly consolidated individual nationalistic efforts. Much allied cooperation developed despite business rivalries. European oil markets depended on the combined Caribbean oil output for their supplies. U.S. companies commanded the largest shares of these supplies.

Table 1
Lago Refinery Employees, 1941–1945

	1941	1942	1943	1944	1945
Expatriate employees	709	715	647	608	652
Caribbean employees	4,046	5,427	5,641	5,747	6,806
Totals	4,755	6,142	6,288	6,355	7,458

Source: Popple (1952, 225).

The strong defense posture of the United States during World War II ratified its regional hegemony and its position as a world power. During the war, the United States constructed and manned a string of army bases and outposts in the eastern Caribbean. A massive U.S. Army base erected on Chaguaramas, Trinidad centered the U.S. defense operations there (Williams 1964). This added incursion of U.S. technology and civilian and military personnel, combined with "can do" work habits, underscored the U.S. presence in the oil enclave and its dominance throughout the eastern Caribbean. U.S. oil enterprises in the enclave and the U.S. military in the Caribbean operated as an integrated whole.[15]

Migrant workers to the enclave considered themselves lucky if they found jobs directly in the oil businesses or on the military camps. Even during the economic boom during the war and immediately after, many workers could only find jobs with subcontractors to the oil industry. Others became self-employed. Foreign entrepreneurs from North America and Europe opened businesses in construction, banking, hotel services, and shipping.

The economic boom on Aruba spawned small businesses. Small-time entrepreneurs—the majority labor migrants—engaged in the informal economy. They sought to strike it rich in jobs such as water carrying, operating bakeries, tailoring, hairdressing, barbering, tutoring, and catering. Labor migrants from other Dutch Caribbean colonies had "Dutch Rights" status and could remain indefinitely (Crane 1971, 100). Even some temporary migrant workers from the British colonies were granted special job licenses to do business in areas of popular need.

Female Migrant and Aruban Workers

Female migrant laborers had no significant work presence in the labor hierarchy at the oil fields or refineries of the enclave, until the mid-1930s.[16] Aruban cultural customs confined Aruban women to non-waged work in their households. Foreign women, pulled in as service workers in the second tier of migrant labor hirings, could remain if they were sponsored by an employer or by the local government. Women did gendered work, as maids, nurses, or licensed prostitutes, and received wages much lower than any paid to male migrant workers on the island. Until the late 1940s, Aruban men could not fulfill the refinery's hiring criteria.

Arubans launched an effective lobbying and protest campaign against the hiring practices of the Lago refinery. The scene was set for a labor showdown and social unrest stirred up by native Aruban dissatisfaction. In the late 1940s, the Lago oil refinery made a major labor relations decision. The company's productivity and profit interests held sway. Temporary foreign workers were to be sacrificed for long-term economic stability of the oil companies' Caribbean investment. Lago's new labor policy concentrated on the hiring of native Aruban males. From the late 1940s, the refinery's training and hiring practices and its labor laws reflected its new labor preferences.

End of an Oil Era

As the decade of the 1940s ended, so did the Lago refinery's long-standing demand for male workers from the eastern Caribbean. Lago intensified its mechanization program begun in the early 1940s and by the end of that decade, the work contracts of eastern Caribbean male migrant workers at the Lago refinery complex became steadily unrenewable.

The men were repatriated in droves to their sending countries. Their jobs became defunct or were quickly taken on by native Arubans. The oil refinery's new hiring policy sought to place Arubans in management positions. The astute new labor replacement plan steadily replaced the high-waged, white expatriate workers with Aruban employees or employees from the Dutch Antilles. Many native workers were first sent abroad by the refinery to be trained; other Arubans were trained locally in programs set up by Lago. The refinery brought in foreign temporary tutors to the oil enclave to train the young sons of the native workers. (Wall 1988).

The heyday of oil refining, once the backbone of Aruba's economy, was over by the mid-1950s (Koot 1981; Hartog 1961). Aruba had no oil deposits of its own. Lago had depended on Venezuelan oilfields for its oil supplies. New labor legislation had the full support of Creole, the Lago refinery's parent body based in Venezuela. The emphasis on native workers pleased the Venezuelan government and people, who had been anxious for a long time to increase the employment of their own nationals, and so keep more of the profits from oil production at home. When a large refinery was built at Amuay on the western shores of Venezuela in 1950, it heralded the slow demise of Lago's operations on Aruba (Wall 1988).

Tourism steadily augmented and then replaced Aruba's oil economy. Native Arubans who had become politicians and businessmen engineered the redirection and diversification of the island's economic base. Aruban men who had received technical and managerial training in the refinery's schools, or had been sent abroad by the refinery to be educated, now used their expertise and money to invest in American- and European-owned hotels, casinos, and banks, or to start businesses of their own. Just as businesses had mushroomed in San Nicolas, Aruba's oil town from the 1930s to the 1950s, the island's formerly neglected capital, Oranjestad became its busy economic pulse after the 1950s.

By the 1950s, Aruba's native-born middle class had increased and consolidated. Without any legal means of employment, nearly all male migrant workers from the eastern Caribbean had been repatriated. Not so for female migrant workers. The presence of migrant domestics in any Aruban household declared that family's raised socioeconomic status. Just as white expatriates at the Lago refinery had done before the 1950s, Aruban households began demanding domestics from neighboring Caribbean and South American countries. Eastern Caribbean domestics became the maids of choice in many Aruban households (Koot 1981).

Table 2
Aruban Population

Year	Population
1910	9,357
1920	8,265
1930	15,687
1940	**30,614**
1941	**31,522**
1942	**33,853**
1943	**37,337**
1944	**39,318**
1945	**42,764**
1953	**57,303**
1955	55,483
1960	53,199
1972	57,905
1981	60,362
1991	66,687

Sources: Malcolm Proudfoot (1954); Green (1974); Hawley (1960); Hartog (1968); Eelens (1993).

Chapter 3

Eastern Caribbean Women:
Wage Workers

Persistent and pervasive poverty confront the people of the Caribbean. For a variety of socioeconomic and cultural reasons, Caribbean women see themselves and are viewed by their societies as main providers for their children (Massiah 1989, 966). Women and their dependents take the brunt of economic hardships.

Postemancipation Caribbean women struggled to incorporate themselves into the monied economy (Tinker 1994; Carnegie 1987; Abraham-Van der Mark 1983). Most women owned little of value in economic terms, except, perhaps their labor. For most of the twentieth century, no established economic structures existed that could deliver to households the basics for living, such as good housing, clothing, medical care, or consistent access to wages. Terrible conditions existed throughout the islands in the early decades of the century. Women faced unpredictable access to employment and hard cash. One of the now retired migrant domestics on Aruba explained her premigration predicament:

> It's not that we didn't have food in Grenada. Because as you yourself know, Grenada full of food. But if I have potatoes, everybody have potatoes. If I have bananas, everybody have bananas. Where ah going get money to buy shoes for my children? How ah going pay the school fee?

How do women and poor families participate in a monied economy? What macro- and microlevel structures must be in place to provide people with access to the taken-for-granted amenities of daily life? The "family wage" supported and elevated the status of white male workers in industrial societies and made them "good providers" for their nuclear families

(Bernard 1981; Collins 1990; Nakano-Glenn 1994). But only relatively few Caribbean males, members of the region's small middle class, ever managed to follow this family pattern. Created by the colonial powers around various forms of unfree labor, Caribbean economies have no built-in stimuli or profit rationale for propogating "good-provider" husbands and homemaker wives (Bernard 1981).

ECONOMIC THEORIES

A strident debate rages among social scientists and policymakers about the economic paradigm through which Caribbean societies could best be analyzed. The debate cannot be dismissed as merely "hot air," because economic analyses determine the focus of policymaking and influence funding agencies that provide financial backing for economic development planning.

Western industrialized countries present themselves as models of modernity, progress, and economic development for the rest of the world. And the neoclassical economic model predominates as the analytical tool that explains and predicts outcomes of economic processes in capitalist economies cross-culturally. The neoclassical economic model propogates the centrality of the market forces of supply and demand in labor procurement and in the production of goods and services. Simply put, the model states that left to operate freely, market forces would incorporate workers into wage labor at all levels of the labor market. Industrialization, the main engine in capitalist economies, would generate increased productivity, jobs, and wages. It has not happened in the Caribbean.

Classical Marxist economic theory makes class exploitation central to economic development in western industrialized economies. A small powerful class of capitalists (owners) buys the labor of a large proletariat (workers). An oversupply of labor—a reserve army of unemployed—keeps wages low and raises the profit levels of the capitalist employers. Inevitably, bloody class confrontation results unless redress of the inequities in existing economic systems occurs. Various corollaries have been added to the two main economic paradigms. Marxist scholars have reworked classical Marxist theories to reflect global socioeconomic changes. Neoclassical economic theory now includes a limited role for the state in affecting changes in the free market.[1]

The *World System Model or Analysis* developed around perspectives that refute the classical models of development, and augment Marxist economic theories (Wallerstein 1974). Leaning strongly toward the neo-Marxist paradigm, World System Analysis traces the integrative yet exploitative role that capitalism played over the past six hundred years or so, in creating a world economic system. It presents a picture of a worldwide interlocking system of trade, money markets, and multinational companies doing business with each other in core industrial centers. These companies have the integral support of national governments. The world economic system arranges and locates worldwide economic activities in blocks of countries depicted as three different economic strata: countries at the economic core, others at the semiperiphery, and still others at the periphery.

The very powerful core industrial countries are mostly western European and North American nation-states. Countries whose economies are partially industrialized such as Brazil, China, and South Korea would be on the semiperiphery, whereas poor, nonindustrialized countries such as the Caribbean would be located at the periphery of the system.

The world economy allocates the non-core—the rest of the world—to positions in the world economic system based on each country's political and economic standing vis-à-vis the block of core countries. Each core country holds financial, trade, and cultural—often colonial—ties with one or a group of non-core countries. Core countries maximize their own wealth, profits, and influence through trade and political and military incursions into countries located in the two peripheries (van Rossem 1996).

Core countries access the resources and exploit the labor of the peripheral countries during periods of colonization, imperialism, or warfare. Cross-culturally, market motives intermingle with deliberate racialized economic stratification in the operation of the world system (Miles 1993; Balibar 1991).

Caribbean Economic Development

Economic stalemate exists in the eastern Caribbean states (Paget Henry 1985). Not even in Puerto Rico, where the United States invested large sums in the 1950s in "Operation Bootstrap," (Ricketts 1985) did the neoclassical model of development work.[2] Despite their present political status of "independent nations," Caribbean states, called "mini-states" or "micro-states" by many because of their size, have always been economically and culturally dependent on core industrial centers for their survival.[3]

Dependency is a component of the World System model. Pantin writes from the *dependency perspective* to describe features of the dependency relationship between Caribbean countries and the industrialized core (1994, 61). He refers to a Caribbean "rentier mentality," in which each Caribbean state tries to outbid the others in its efforts to attract "renters" from the industrialized countries to exploit its resources at a negotiated price.[4] Paget Henry (1985), writing in the same paradigm, cites the tendency for Caribbean political elites to collude with foreign entrepreneurs, "central capitalists," in unwise and selfish economic deals that have little economic benefit to their states.

Caribbean economists, from a neo-Marxist perspective, introduced the concept of "plantation economies" to describe former colonies such as the Caribbean states (Best 1968; Girvan 1970; Brewster and Thomas 1967). Plantation economies develop unique, resilient, and wide-ranging ties to core industrial centers; the colonial powers that generated their existence.

Critics of the classical economic model and of economic development strategies emanating from this model, reject its positive projections of "trickle-down" economic development for countries in the economic periphery. They state that economic development schemes serve the interests of the investors and the core country. The Caribbean area stands as a case in point.

Since the 1980s, the World Bank and the International Monetary Fund have only supported development loans to the region contingent on strict structural adjustment policies. Economic analysis of poverty and underdevelopment downplays the centuries of economic neglect and underinvestment in the people of poor regions. Instead, investment and loan policies based on neoclassical models mandate that development would occur when poor countries make steady repayment of loans, cut their import spending, balance their budgets, raise productivity, and drastically shrink the role of the public sector as a major employer.

During the 1980s, Caribbean governments tried to comply with this neoclassical economic development strategy. Widespread cuts in social welfare and developmental goals undertaken by Caribbean governments took their toll on the region (Barriteau 1996, 146). So far, the economic plans seem to hold little promise of sustained economic growth.

If Caribbean politicians prophesy hopefully about projected economic growth, social scientists pinpoint the weaknesses of the two touted paths to economic growth. Caribbean states are small and poor. Politically weak states often comply with unfeasable imported political and economic models. For example, economies of scale make Caribbean-based industrialization, the engine that drove economic growth in the core countries, unprofitable. So far, although Caribbean states have shown willingness to accommodate foreign businesses, the bulk of Caribbean industrialization has been limited to a few assembly plant operations that employ relatively few workers, and pay very low wages.

Safa (1995) and Sen and Grown (1987) express little confidence in the economic predictions that project the Caribbean area as a productive and profitable site for either manufacturing or assembly plants. Abraham-Van der Mark (1993) examined the short-lived inclusion of women on the island of Curaçao in the late 1960s in U.S.-based light manufacturing and assembly plants. A growing number of social scientists and policy experts conclude that no development plan tried so far on any of the islands has been sufficiently labor intensive to meet the needs of the large numbers of unemployed. Neither have any group of foreign investors in the area committed to long-term investments in the people or the region for development sake. Profitmaking over the short haul remains the essential incentive for foreign investors.

Barriteau (1996), Safa and Antrobus (1992), McAfee (1991), and Massiah (1989) fault policymakers in international lending agencies for imposing on the region economic development schemes unsuited to the needs of the area, its people, and especially women. McAfee warns against the sinister intentions of foreign planners. However, even critics of the classical economic models seem to be searching for ways to insert the economic activities of women into traditional economic planning. But the labor contributions of poor women takes place mostly in the informal sectors of their countries' economies. And very few development planners have bothered to assess the economic role of informal economic sectors in poor countries. Could the existing economic paradigms be rearranged to recognize formerly excluded groups as active participants and contributors?

Women, Work, and Economic Development

The eastern Caribbean is a region of very high unemployment; averaging 25 percent in some states. Underemployment is always high. Men and women, families and households experience economic hardship. Many women have no "steady flow of income . . . and inadequate or non-existent financial support from male partners and kin networks" (Massiah 1989, 971). Whenever employment exists, however, males tend to be the preferred wage workers (Reddock 1994; Massiah 1989). And even when men and women engage in identical work, in many islands men still receive higher wages. Unrecognized and seemingly invisible, women earners involved in the formal and informal economies comprise between 40 and 50 percent of workers in most eastern Caribbean islands. Women head nearly half of all households in the eastern Caribbean, but still have no recognized place in the political economy. Female worker participation occurs as a residual of male employment.

Researchers disagree on how poor women and their money-earning activities should be studied. What is the best unit of analysis in studying poor societies? Poor Caribbean women express selfless, nonindividualistic reasons for their roles as breadwinners for their households. Maternal norms endorse their wage-earning efforts as contributors to a broad cooperative kin survival endeavor. Would research findings on Caribbean women and their families be better informed if the unit of analysis was individual workers, female heads of households, poor households that include women, women as co-working partners in a marital or non-marital union, or women as labor migrants engaged in kinship ties (Barriteau 1996; Stichter 1990; Massiah 1989)? This book focuses on women, migrant domestics, as wage workers and main providers for their dependents. Nevertheless, the image of women as non-wage workers still predominates.[5]

It is no wonder that neither established economic paradigm—classical economic or Marxist—seriously includes women as a category of wage workers in the formal economy. In the eyes of predominately male, white foreign economic planners, Caribbean female workers, if they are incorporated at all, assume the lowest rung of the labor bureaucracy. Even local elites minimize or disregard the women's significant economic contributions.

The formal and informal sectors of Caribbean economies overlap. The cash flow that women's labor generates not only provides economic stability to households, but also to weak local economies. However, economic planners consistently fail to include the economic contributions of women workers in their various economic development plans (Barriteau 1996; Massiah 1989). Part of the problem is that the so-called "informal economy," the economic niche in which poor women are most adept, does not exist in official economic paradigms, much less jargon and scholarship (Ward 1993). The economic irony is that poor Caribbean women, in theory, are allocated to positions of economic inconsequence by formal economic systems, yet these women's efforts make their countries' economies viable.[6]

Barriteau (1996) and Massiah (1989) report that studies on Caribbean women unequivocally reveal the historically central role that women take in the economic life of the Caribbean.[7] Reddock (1988, 120) records how early in the nineteenth century, as sugar production grew increasingly unprofitable, Caribbean slave women struggled to enter the monied economy. Using their garden plots and skills, women became engaged in the informal economy in a veritable outburst of "independent petty entrepreneurial activity." These economic activities straddled the formal and informal economies.[8]

Women managed to maneuver their work and production skills to find economic spaces unnoticed or neglected by the formal structures. Every time the male-directed, foreign-based economy swung into downturn, poor women took up the slack by increasing their economic activity in the so-called informal economy (Barriteau 1996; Abraham-Van der Mark 1983; Massiah 1989). Women's contribution to the political economy of the region remains a devalued economic constant and a taken-for-granted item by planners. Economic strictures imposed on the Caribbean states during the 1980s as prerequisites for loans and foreign economic investment hit the poor, and particularly women, especially hard. Because of imposed structural adjustments, women almost single-handedly became responsible for basic health care and education for their households; amenities that states had previously provided.

Ward faults World System Analysis for not finding a significant place for women's work in the world economic system model. According to her, World System Analysis' descriptive and analytical contributions have been helpful, though inadequate. She outlines the contributions that women make despite their relegation to the so-called informal economy, which she describes as "forms of work that do not provide direct incorporation into processes of exchange or accumulation" (1993, 56). I agree, but must augment her definition.

Caribbean economies would collapse without the financial input of local women's economic involvement at least at two levels. Women participate daily in local informal economic systems. Female labor migrants, through their wage work and remittances, have become significant participants in foreign informal and formal economic systems. Building on Ward's definition, I describe Caribbean informal economies as forms of work that do not receive formal recognition, but which subsidize established processes of exchange and accumulation.

Can poor women be included in economic systems designed by investors trained in the established economic paradigms of industrial countries (Ward 1993)? Caribbean workers in the informal economy generate cash in myriad—tiny economic ventures created by socioeconomic insensitivity and exclusionary strategies of the so-called formal economy. More important, who stands to gain by incorporating women's economic activities into the formal economic systems? Will not women's incorporation and formal recognition into economic systems dislocate local and international socioeconomic stratification systems?

What then are poor women and their dependents to do? How can women (and men) who live in countries on the periphery of the world economy, and in the backyard of the world's most powerful nation, benefit from economic systems that ignore them? How can poor women insert themselves as workers and producers in any of the economic paradigms emanating from industrialized countries?

Although invisible to the formal economic system, poor women in poor countries situate themselves at the center of economic activity. They energetically capitalize on the most insignificant and unfree economic relations left open to them, deliberately or inadvertently. For most of the twentieth century, eastern Caribbean women have used labor migration as an important economic activity. I believe women have deciphered that labor migration at all levels—rural to urban, regional and international, free and unfree—presents women with scarce economic spaces. I depend on feminist theory to elucidate on the female condition experienced in local Caribbean economies and the world economic system. I have supported the stand that the world economic system is deliberately racialized to control and exploit the labor of certain populations. I now argue that gender and class are used deftly in political economies cross-culturally to exploit female workers.

Class and Gender Inequalities

Bureaucratic labor systems at best tend to devalue women's work. At worst, they neutralize and manipulate gender, rendering women workers invisible. U.S. feminist scholarship has had to come to terms with the important ways that real or imagined differences of class and race confront various categories of women in the United States and cross-culturally. Socially established differences define women, regulate their lives and relegate them to varying life chances and work experiences. Universal sisterhood is not enough.

Social scientists expound on how racist labor relations regulate worker allocation in local and international labor markets (Balibar 1991; Satzewich 1991). Racist labor hierarchies are buttressed by gender and class barriers that intersect and unfairly influence the inclusion and allocation of workers cross-culturally. Specific groups, and certainly the females within them, experience inordinate labor disadvantages.

Most female labor migration treks to foreign countries are relatively unfree; organized and regulated to exploit the gender, class, race, and other vulnerabilities of women. I argue, however, that female labor migrants themselves fully exploit the economic opportunities given them. They grab opportunities, experience great hardships, and yet try to rearrange the relationships of power and infiltrate the barriers set up within the restrictions of their low worker status.

Pros of the Informal Economy

This book rejects culture of poverty analyses of poor societies. It suits the economic status quo in western industrialized countries and the Caribbean to view the poor as deviant. With their eyes firmly fixed on goals of access to wages, the migrant domestics in the study displayed economic ingenuity, innovation, and dogged persistence in the face of employment that offered wages in return for monotonous drudgery. My observations replicate those of other social scientists who study the poor (Stack and Burton 1994; Glenn 1994; Collins 1990; Rubenstein 1987).

Economic activity generated by workers in the informal economy stimulates entrepreneurial innovation and creativity, and frees workers from inflexible normative trade and business patterns. Unmarried women with dependents like the migrant domestics in this study, become traffickers, traders, street hawkers, and migrant workers. The lack of rigid social rules or official stipulations which would circumscribe their money-making activities allows low-status workers to engage in unconventional labor and discover productive niches even when the formal economy is in recession. However, independence from formal regulation comes with labels of deviance, low social status, and other disadvantages.

The informal economy directs women to economic activities debarred them by bureaucratic stipulations that make demands, such as: high educational levels, expensive licensing laws, costly merchandising and marketing outlays. Dressmaking, cake decorating, pastry and candy making, hairdressing and manicuring, needlework, fruit and vegetable canning, trading and vending, baby-sitting and artificial flower making comprise a short list of some of the many "aboveboard" skills practiced by poor Caribbean women.

I borrow the concept of *de-skilling* (Stichter 1990, 19) often used by social scientists to describe how structural changes—technological improvements—in the economies of industrialized countries render the skills of entire categories of workers redundant. I argue that a similar kind of de-skilling occurs to workers in informal economies in industrialized or so-called Third World countries, and that mere access to consistent wages may not constitute economic development for these workers. All labor migration—regional, international, and even rural to urban—may be de-skilling activities for the poor, and especially poor women.[9] Women in the eastern Caribbean islands live on small land bases. As such, Caribbean women have never been dependent solely on peasant farming for survival. Boserup (1970) and Stichter (1985) tell how during the twentieth century poor African women became tied to agricultural chores, and how at least initially, women's all-around labor responsibilities increased with the departure of African men into male labor migration and their entry into the wage economy. However, most eastern Caribbean women belong to large landless populations, who have no lengthy history of agriculture on long-established family farms or peasant settlements (Mintz 1992). Eastern Caribbean women's labor history took more varied forms.

Women in this study often complained that they missed using the skills that provided them with precarious livelihoods prior to their labor migration. Seamstresses missed working their sewing machines; "putting out brides," as a few boastfully described their sewing skills. Marjorie, a Grenadian woman who had been on the job as a migrant domestic only six months, bemoaned the fact that her little vegetable garden, from which she had made some cash and supplemented her diet, had gone to rack and ruin. Others told how back in their sending islands they made "little crochet things for sale."

Migrant women in unfree labor migration situations forego their former subsistence skills, sometimes forever. Labor contracts in the receiving countries regiment the women to particular job specializations. Drastic changes in the women's social and living conditions in the receiving society often rule out participation in former money-earning skills. Therefore, migrant domestics in this study could not, under threat of deportation, practice any of the home-grown skills they had honed in the informal economies of their sending islands.

Female labor migrants in some countries do find ways to combine their jobs in the formal economy with informal money-making activities (Kasinitz 1992). Caribbean labor migrants in more free labor migration situations in foreign countries manage to market their products to hand-picked customers in immigrant neighborhoods.[10] Such activities add texture and complexity to labor migrants' lives. Labor migrants who trade in the informal economy make contact with their immigrant communities. Such trade marks the tentative beginnings of ethnic group mobilization or even inclusion in the host society.

Negatives of the Informal Economy

Poor workers in most societies receive minimal protection from the state. But poor women who work in the informal economy engage in particularly isolated, exploitative labor; in jobs outside of the regulatory and protective powers of the state bureaucracy. Already devalued because of poverty, poor workers in the informal economy often skirt the edges of the law. Mostly on foot, hawking wares in public places, defying formal structures and on the lookout for "quick breaks," these workers have only nuisance value to the authorities.

Labor becomes gender neutral and extremely malleable in the informal economy. Men, the preferred gender in the formal economy, still work gender norms to their benefit in the informal economy. Gender is made to be easily interchangeable, so that service workers, at the employers' whim and fancy, may be made to ignore traditionally gendered attachments to various types of work. Female-gendered work in one period may be confiscated and performed by powerful, threatening males at another period. During harsh economic times in the Caribbean, men became the preferred field laborers. When men lose their jobs in the formal economy, social norms encourage employers to dismiss female workers or employ fewer of them. Women then become housewives or move into the informal economy as domestics, seamstresses, and launderers.

Ward suggests, however, that workers in the informal economy resist incorporation into the formal economy, especially through unionization and other forms of organizing. They understand the exploitative workings of the economy and suspect that incorporation would be merely peripheral and condescending. She details a variety of ways that such worker resistance occurs (1993, 56–57).

I agree with Ward that exploited female workers use various strategies to circumvent and negotiate myriad obstacles that confront them in labor relations. Social scientists have struggled to analyze the personal and group responses of exploited workers to their condition. A popularly held analysis suggests that, given the opportunity, poor workers would not only flee their restrictive conditions but completely reject the values and socioeconomic relations that formerly oppressed them and deliberately construct their own (Caulfield 1974). Mintz (1992, 254), in considering the personal and group plans of recently emancipated Caribbean slaves in the middle of the last century, wrestles with the same issue: "is it not possible to imagine that slaves, individualized by slavery, but not dehumanized by it, could conceive of a distinctive agrarian way of life for themselves?" He concludes that as free workers they may have "rejected *in their minds* (my emphasis) the future that was chosen for them."

I would add that the give-and-take of daily social interactions in any society, and especially those between workers and employers, have complicated and often unpredictable repercussions. As the following chapters show, resistance is only one of several strategies used by workers making efforts to manipulate the tedium of their work situations (Aymer, forthcoming). Gender, class, racial, and ethnic differences crisscross and entangle people of all levels in stratified socioeconomic relations; and much more than a meaningless mixing of people occurs (Mintz 1992, 254–55). Over time, workers' persistent efforts of negotiation, collusion, restraint, subterfuge, and resistance manage to affect and change, even incrementally, the terms of workers' social and labor allocation or incorporation. The synthesis or clash of cultures that must occur reshapes the work place, and gradually transforms workers and the host societies.

I observed women working tirelessly, attempting as they put it, "to better themselves," meaning they were on the constant lookout for better wages and safer, more predictable wage work. Frantic forms of labor migration stretching over one hundred fifty years clearly show that poor Caribbean people, women and men, desire to fully participate in the monied economy, or whatever established economic structure allows them fair and just wages for work done. In fact, labor migrants interpret their present harsh work conditions as a temporary positioning of themselves—taking the proverbial brunt of the hardships—so their children would experience more economic access in the formal economy in the future.

The accoutrements of modern materialism dazzle the poor, who represent clear numerical majorities in Caribbean populations, as well as the region's small middle class and its cadre of political elites. Increasingly and deliberately, states expose their populations to ostentatious shows of wealthy foreign and local life-styles. Weak and impoverished Caribbean states court foreign tourists, offshore banking businesses, and financiers from core countries. Local politicians and businesses hopefully tell of intentions to accomplish "the integration of the working poor into the changing political economy," (Ong 1987, 150) but often few substantive and consistent wage-earning opportunities exist. However, whether in informal economies locally or as migrant workers in foreign countries, women perform work feats of physical and emotional strength to procure the marks of mobility and modernity for their dependents.

Women, Wage Work, and Family Form

The demands of wage labor in both the formal and informal economies of any society exert considerable influence on workers' family arrangements (Zinn 1994; Stichter 1990; Joan Smith, Wallerstein, and Evers 1984). Poor Caribbean women use a variety of extended family arrangements as resources and for support. Women ensure provision of basic needs by extending emotional and economic reciprocity and making alliances. Women share, borrow and lend children, goods, cash, and services. People who are dogged by financial insecurity make sure that their worlds of work and home, their neighborhoods and their households, overlap. Poor women create support systems that co-opt friends, neighbors, and elderly kin, as well as young children (Pulsipher 1993; Gussler 1980).

Women depend heavily on the help, and economic and other support of children of all ages. In poor Caribbean societies, cooperative family arrangements depend on the work of even the very young. Poor children in the eastern Caribbean experience limited privacy and brief childhoods (Massiah 1989, 971). Middle-class concepts of childhood and its idealized advantages of a designated period, sheltered, play-filled innocence, and parental bonding with the young in the intimate privacy of the nuclear family household, would prove counterproductive to the needs of many Caribbean families (Olwig 1993).

Women employed in main low-wage jobs augment their inadequate earnings through incessant, ad hoc moonlighting (Burpee, Morgan, and Dragon 1986, 4). "Occupational pluralists," (Comitas 1964, 440) these women invest energetically in "occupational multiplicity," (Rubenstein 1987, 148) and in "independent petty entrepreneureal activity" (Reddock 1988, 120). Women, even those who have jobs in the formal economy, try to stabilize their economic situations by engaging in petty trading activity (Massiah 1989).[11] On any eastern Caribbean island, tenacious petty traders and their children stalk the streets and show up at public events, plying their wares. Women are aggressive participants in the informal economy; marketing their services in sewing, cleaning, hairdressing, and "under-the-table" trade in manufactured and home-produced foods and goods (Massiah 1989, 966). These activities have increased tremendously since the 1960s, and may be indicative of recurring economic recessions that leave poor women without other means of subsistence. But women also undertake laborious male-gendered work.[12]

In bleak economic times, Caribbean men increasingly compete with women for traditionally female sectors in the informal economy. Wage work as field laborers, once the most popular form of employment for poor Caribbean women, no longer attracts them.

Women began moving out of the labor category in the 1930s (Massiah 1989, 972). As field hands, many poor women expected to make men's wages whenever they signed up to do "day work." This entailed occasional uncontracted employment as day laborers or farmhands, often on large estates, alongside several other laborers. Tasks involved non-gendered work attending to one of the island's cash crops, such as sugarcane, cotton, or bananas. However, for decades the going government female wage remained one-third less than that of male co-workers.[13]

A female field laborer's wages were even less sure whenever women found employment with small neighborhood landowners (Gussler 1980; Rubenstein 1987, 136; Barrow 1993, 186). Sentiment and exchange obligations that fulfill "family status production work" operate in small communities (Massiah 1989, 970). In some arrangements, a woman would receive non-monetary rewards as payment for her efforts, such as food, used clothing, or a promise to teach the woman's child a skill (Brierley 1993; Sunshine et al. 1985).

Wage Work: Road Work

In the anglophone, eastern Caribbean, only the most indigent women work in road-building gangs, called in some islands by the old French patois name, "traveaux" (Rubenstein 1987, 147). In such a relatively non-gendered form of labor; workers' wages should be secure. Public works departments theoretically employed gangs of men and women for road-building and road repairs. In reality, local governments engaged subcontractors to oversee jobs, and women dealt with middlemen able to capitalize on the women's impoverishment. Every poor eastern Caribbean woman seeking work mending roads knew that jobs were difficult to find, always temporary, and could only be secured after the male quota had been filled.[14] Besides, low-status women who are hard pressed for cash become vulnerable to the sexual demands of male overseers or employers.

During the first half of the twentieth century, huge numbers of eastern Caribbean women worked as domestics. Only work as field hands rivaled "maid work" in female employment. In 1921 Grenada, when the entire population was 66,302, the female category of launderers combined with that of domestic servants, totalled 5,102 (Brizan 1984). This number was outdone in the same year only by 15,445 agricultural workers, the majority of whom were women. Many of these women flocked from the neighboring islands to the oil lands seeking employment.

Since the 1930s, growing numbers of eastern Caribbean women have been interspersing their home-based economic activity with labor migration treks—urban to rural, rural to urban, intraregional and extraregional—the women's latest, most concerted attempts to gain firm financial footing. Caribbean women treat labor migration as another item in their labor commodity package. In fact, labor migrants alternate and/or combine trafficking in produce or manufactured goods with sale of their labor.[15]

FEMALE MIGRATION

Social scientists doing macro-level analyses of the Caribbean agree that the 1930s marked a watershed in the former hegemony of Great Britain in the region (Maingot 1994; Reddock 1988, 182). Also during this decade, a vocal black middle class jostled with local white and mulatto business and landowning elites for political participation, inclusion in restructuring of the economy, and for justice in the labor bureaucracy (Paget Henry 1985, 81; Brizan 1984).

I argue that important changes also occurred at micro-levels in anglophone eastern Caribbean society that especially affected women. A distinct new pattern of economic activities that involved increasing numbers of women in labor migration began in the eastern Caribbean in the 1930s, intensified in the 1940s, and has since become established.

The oil lands—Venezuela, Trinidad, Aruba, and Curaçao—began to generate wealth and wage labor starting in the 1930s. Continuous treks of male migrant workers from the eastern Caribbean began moving between their sending countries and the oil lands. Not only did these workers remit cash to their sending islands, but they conveyed news of the job opportunities and ostentatious living in the boom towns of the oil lands. Reddock (1994) records intense economic activity in Trinidad during this period. Brizan (1984, 218) records that "during the 1930s and 1940s the majority of Grenadians migrated to Trinidad as usual." In this same account, Brizan tells that between 1928 and 1953 there were 77,169 departures from Grenada to Trinidad. Grenada's population numbered just over 80,000.

Men cashed in first on the economic boom. Trinidad's official labor records of the time downplayed the intensity of female wage-labor activity, and also failed to record those activities in the low-level sectors.[16] The official records show a decline in female employment during the 1930s. No surprise, because on Trinidad in the 1930s, black migrant domestics "were not accepted as 'real workers' " (Reddock 1994, 84). The official *Wages Advisory Board* of 1935 made no mention of domestics in its categories of official wage earners, although tens of thousands of migrant domestics had found employment, many with white expatriate staff hired by the oil industry (Reddock 1994).[17] Essentially invisible to census takers, domestics belonged to the informal economy, no matter their substantial numbers and economic contributions to their sending and host societies.

Trinidad's oil-rich economy of the 1930s generated social mobility, and caused improved labor and social allocation among groups usually left out in the island's racialized economy. In 1929 an employment bureau established in Trinidad by ladies from the emerging black middle class, the *Coterie of Social Workers*, advertised for "reliable governesses, needlewomen, housekeepers, darners, scrubbers, and yard boys," to meet the needs of this growing class (Reddock 1994, 83).

Social pressures encouraged the fad of *housewification* among middle-class and aspiring middle-class Caribbean women. Reddock states that Fabian ideology out of Britain swept the colonies and encouraged strictly gendered middle-class behavior. The housewification ideology touted that the true place of wives and real ladies was the private sphere. One must therefore ask, why call "decent" women to return to their households at this time in colonial Trinidad? Jobs were plentiful for local men, and this may have been the society's attempt to ensure that women did not undermine the male-dominated economy. No longer wage workers and safe in the households of wage-earning men, many women ratified their new aspiring middle-class status by looking for household help (Reddock 1994, 83). These new demands for the marks of social mobility created jobs for poorer women who could make no claims to wage-earning men.

For decades, Trinidad marked the overseas limits to which numbers of poor eastern Caribbean women traveled intermittently in search of cash and the added advantage of anonymity. Located only 80–100 nautical miles from the southeastern Caribbean islands of St. Vincent, Grenada, and Barbados, Trinidad was an overnight's journey by inter-island schooner to waiting friends and relatives who lived in run-down immigrant neighborhoods (Brizan 1984, 217; Richardson 1983, 88). In the promising economy boosted by oil production, poor female labor migrants from the smaller islands could "try their hands" at making quick cash as maids, seamstresses, food-sellers, or prostitutes (Brereton 1981; Brizan 1984).

Trinidad literally became the jumping-off point for ambitious labor migrants. From there, they could begin the migrant worker tour of the foreign oil lands. Intraregional sea travel accomodations increased somewhat after the 1930s, and especially between Trinidad and the other eastern Caribbean British colonies. The discovery of oil stimulated seagoing transportation within the oil enclave thus facilitating labor migrant treks.

The decade of the 1930s had all the makings of social uprootedness, unrest and upheaval. Only in a few specific locations in the southern Caribbean could work, wages, and wealth be accessed by the masses of eastern Caribbean poor. To get any part of this largess, men, and increasingly women, had to leave home and become labor migrants. For the promise of good wages, labor migrants showed great willingness to subject themselves to new and harsh forms of racism and work exploitation.

DOMESTICS INTERNATIONALLY

"Whiteness" stands at the apex of racial and phenotypical correctness, internationally. European colonial racism promoted an enduring racial model that essentializes moral and esthetically favorable attributes, and claims them for Europeans. So, from the racist perspective, qualities such as humanness, morality, and beauty become innate attributes of the white European phenotype, and are also naturally absent in people of other phenotypes. Complex combinations of skin shades and other physical traits, such as hair texture, receive ranked value according to their approximations to the idealized, composite European phenotype. However, most of the former European colonies, including the Caribbean, have predominantly dark-skinned populations.

The social values attached to racial, class, and gender phenomena overlap and help to allocate individuals and groups to high- or low-level ascribed positions in socioeconomic hierarchies in societies; so that individuals and groups experience most exclusion when they fail to meet the litmus test of social and racial acceptability.

Invisible but rigid political barriers restrict the work opportunities of women of color who are labor migrants. Racism and accompanying low social status make "maid work" a major category of female employment for poor, dark-skinned and/or native women in many industrialized and Third World countries (Parpart 1990; Bunster and Chaney 1985; Chaney and

Garcia Castro 1989).[18] These so-called ethnic women (or men) find employment in the households of local or expatriate whites, and lighter-skinned or middle-class employers (Hansen 1992; Romero 1992; Rollins 1985). Barriers of difference based on the women's phenotype or ethnic traits, such as religion, language, or dialect, debar them from legitimate citizenship.

The all-time standby job for poor women in poor countries such as the eastern Caribbean, continues to be the job that women call "maid work" or "servant work" (Bunster and Chaney 1985; Chaney and Garcia Castro 1989). Women in the eastern Caribbean know that this form of employment is often short-term, demanding, and nearly always described by the employer as "part-time employment." Domestics operate at the lowest levels of the labor hierarchy internationally, and perform repetitive household and other tasks on behalf of higher-status workers.

The ubiquitous household help is a cross-cultural social marker. The presence of a maid in a household in industrial and developing societies confirms the substantive and symbolic upper- or middle-class status of her employers (Enloe 1990; Philipps 1988; Abraham-Van der Mark 1983). Poor women employed as domestics in racialized societies know well that they hold jobs offering little hope for social mobility.

Migrant domestics are prime candidates for employer exploitation and permanent social exclusion. Maids, the proverbial insiders-outsiders, hold a problematic work status. These women, usually unrelated to household residents, receive wages in return for doing chores, such as food preparation and taking care of children, pets, and the elderly. Maids operate at intimate centers of family life. Employers try to erect social barriers with subordinate maids to establish and maintain secondary relations. Making use of the rationale that touts the need for worker/employer decorum and social class distance, employers see to it that women who help them run their households remain perpetual outsiders, if not outcasts.

The probability of workplace exploitation for the maid increases phenomenally when a foreign migrant domestic—a woman of so-called different racial and ethnic background—finds employment in the households of citizens. The migrant domestics' *otherness*—the womens' ascribed low social status, nebulous political status, and perceived ethnic and racial differences from the population of the receiving country or their employers—present almost insurmountable barriers to inclusion (Hansen 1992; Rollins 1985; Turrittin 1976). Eastern Caribbean migrant domestics on Aruba fit the profile for social and labor-related ostracism.

Incorporation of women into the labor economy always follows clear gender, class and race stratification dictates and patterns. Female labor migrants setting out for Aruba could be described from classical economic and labor migration perspectives. Poor women from poor countries respond to the "pull" and "push" of the labor market's demand. Or, migrant domestics could be presented as the emigrated members of the reserve army of international workers who find wage-earning opportunities at industrial sites created by corporations in core or peripheral countries of the world economic system. Thus ensues the proletarianization and commodification of labor.

The almost permanent allocation of poor and foreign women to the low-waged service sectors of the economy must not be explained away by structural/functionalist theories. Structural jargon, when demystified, reveals supportive ideologies of class, race, and gender inequalities, as well as nation-state and citizenship rights that establish hierarchical social interaction in macro- and micro-level social relations.

How do the labor migrants view themselves as they participate in wage-earning activities? How do they view the structures that demarcate the worlds of domestics from employers, citizens from foreign migrant workers, sending societies from host countries, woman from worker, and domestic from mother? How do the migrant domestics negotiate the socioeconomic and political structures?

THE FOREIGN OIL LANDS

In the 1930s on Venezuela and Curaçao, specially designed housing began to be constructed by the oil companies to accommodate white expatriate staff and their families. By the early 1940s, white expatriate families on Aruba began to arrive. News reached the eastern Caribbean that Spanish-speaking women were being employed as domestics in these households. Although eastern Caribbean women felt the strong enticement of higher wages to be earned in the foreign oil countries to the south, they had to build up courage to travel to Venezuela, Curaçao, and Aruba, which were foreign and far away.[19] The culture, location, and foreignness of the non-British Caribbean had been exaggerated by colonial authorities. Isolated for centuries from other Caribbean neighbors, British or otherwise, each British colony dealt directly northward, with Britain. The colonial masters had stoked feelings of competition and suspicion even among their colonies. The British rallied colonial allegiance through suggestions of the "otherness" of rival European colonial territories in the region.

No matter how direct the course of travel, from the closest British islands in the eastern Caribbean the foreign Caribbean oil lands were at least 400–500 nautical miles away. Besides, poor women setting out from Montserrat, the northernmost eastern Caribbean sending island in the study, had to be prepared for an 800–1,000 nautical mile journey. Travelers to the foreign oil lands during the 1930s journeyed via St. Maarten and Curaçao, or Trinidad and Curaçao. Sometimes more stops were included, and barely seaworthy transportation, changes of vessels en route, mandatory overnight stays, and dramatic cultural changes all made the journey tedious.

Much of Trinidad's attraction to "small island" labor migrants was the welcoming immigrant community. In the 1930s and early 1940s, no welcoming resident communities of female relatives or friends awaited women arriving in the oil lands. Travel to the foreign countries of the oil enclave was both daring and frightening for female labor migrants.

What kind of employers could the women expect to find? What did female labor migrants from the anglophone eastern Caribbean know about the ways of foreign, unknown whites? Eastern Caribbean blacks, numerical majorities on each island, had learned over the centuries how to negotiate the local racial and socioeconomic hierarchies. The local whites, descendants of the slave-owning and business class, had steadily intermingled with and inculcated the ways of life of the black majority population.

Local white racism received intermittent support from other sources. A small cadre of British expatriates could be found on each island: mostly colonial civil servants, eccentric educators, missionaries, and transient businessmen. (Paget Henry 1981; Karch 1981; Riviere 1981). And, in spite of cultural similarities with blacks, native white racism on any eastern Caribbean island displayed greater intransigence and variation when bolstered by visiting whites.

In the 1930s, the majority of eastern Caribbean women belonged to a distinct lower class. In the foreign oil countries, these women were sure to face the hurdles of new ostracisms evoked by their unclear political status as foreign black women and their inability to speak or understand the strange languages spoken there. Female labor migrants already faced the suspicion of their societies every time they set out alone for neighboring Trinidad on occasional wage-earning stints. Returning women were often badgered with accusations of loose living in the big city. How more intense would the whisperings be when the host countries were far away and foreign? In the midst of personal and political uncertainty, women needed the social approval of their sending societies before they could dare to set out for the foreign countries of the oil enclave. Eastern Caribbean women needed job offers desperately.

Family Comforts in the Enclave

Provisions of homelike comforts for high-level employees concerned the oil companies in the Caribbean. Rival companies used promises of higher wages and better perks to entice valued high-level employees to change loyalties. The companies encouraged family reunification, and began to invest effort and money to construct prestigious company housing located in secluded, self-sufficient, company-run complexes for valued employees. On Aruba, leisure comforts of private beach clubs and beaches, golf courses, commissaries, medical complexes, chapels, and schools were deliberately installed for the comforts of expatriate professionals prepared to endure the inconveniences of work stints in the Caribbean oil enclave.

Arrival in the Caribbean of expatriate wives and families suggested settlement and long stays. The families of the professional and administrative staff in the oil lands led busy social lives. Expatriate families seemed willing to add one more amenity to their tropical comforts. Their leisure and sports schedules demanded household help who could take care of repetitive menial chores (Abraham-Van der Mark 1983; Philipps 1988; Phalen 1977; Kalm 1975).

All during the decade of the 1930s, nurses comprised the only female eastern Caribbean workers let into Aruba and employed at the Lago refinery's hospital. But poor women in the eastern Caribbean soon became aware that their service labor, too, was in demand. It could be sold in the foreign countries of the enclave for consistent, predictable, and higher wages than they ever hoped to get in their home islands.

By the late 1940s, the eastern Caribbean migrant domestics had steadily ousted their Spanish-speaking competition brought in originally from the neighboring countries of Venezuela and Colombia. English-speaking maids from the eastern Caribbean gained the dubious status of being the preferred migrant domestics of North American and European families residing in the foreign countries of the oil enclave. At least for a while, the oil enclave in the southern Caribbean became, for migrant workers, the New York of the region.

Chapter 4

Foreign Temporary Workers:
Migrant Workers

For nearly three centuries, European immigrants to the New World and their descendants used West Africans as forced, nonwaged labor: slaves. By the end of the nineteenth century, the experiment in slave labor proved unprofitable. Britain, France, Germany, and Switzerland respectively made extensive use of imported foreign migrant workers throughout the nineteenth century. The use of temporary foreign workers provided both psychological and physical fillips to nation-state builders.

Voluntarily, impoverished foreigners did the economic bidding of citizens, expecting nothing but their wages in return (Miles 1993). As the economies of western Europe expanded, so did their demand for migrant workers from neighboring European and Mediterranean countries.[1] Former insular mercantilist markets of European and North American countries opened up to free trade. Goods and wealth moved across national borders, and so did workers.

The inclusion of foreign guest workers in western industrialized state economies reached a high point in the 1950s. In the post–World War II period of economic reconstruction, western European countries received migrant workers from the poorer countries of southern and eastern Europe and North Africa, respectively (Castles 1986).[2] In attempts to boost labor shortfalls in their agricultural sectors, Canada and the United States also employed foreign migrant workers during World War II and after.

The British imposed a semi-waged indentureship on emancipated slaves during the nineteenth century. It proved unworkable (Bolland 1992). European colonial interests then conspired to replace the unpredictable labor of their former slaves with foreign migrant labor. From the mid-nineteenth century, until the first few decades of the twentieth century, subjects of

European colonies (Asians—Chinese and Indians—and Portugese) were transported to European- and North American–owned plantations in the New World, Asia, and Africa. These foreign migrant workers, officially called indentured workers, contracted themselves for varying periods to work on sugar plantations vacated by former slaves. Indentures were bound by semi-wage work agreements that varied from colony to colony.

DEFINING THE MIGRANT LABOR CATEGORY

Labor migrants "are not granted the right to permanent settlement" in the receiving country (Satzewich 1991, 39). Instead, they are conscripted for well-defined periods to work on specific work programs in receiving countries. Denied the rights and obligations of citizenship, they remain essentially stateless in the receiving countries where they work (Miles 1993; Satzewich 1991). Impoverishment ensures their work readiness and accessibility.

Migrant workers helped to internationalize labor and capital. A special type of wage worker, the migrant workers' readiness to follow the job wherever, proved crucial to the growth of multinational companies and the world economic system during the twentieth century (Wallerstein 1974). Internationally owned companies neutralize state boundaries. Multinationals pride themselves in being able to mobilize and transport a "voluntary" labor force (a veritable international army of migrant workers) to construction and production sites anywhere in the world economic system. Migrant workers are often seen by investors as a malleable, low-cost labor commodity, and companies have no obligation to their cohorts of workers after the job contract expires.

MIGRANT LABOR IN THE CARIBBEAN OIL ENCLAVE

The category of "foreign migrant worker" technically included all the foreigners who arrived to work in the oil enclave. Caribbean men, discarded to the exigencies of market forces after emancipation, already had decades of practice as "voluntary," reserve labor when northern oil entrepreneurs arrived in the Caribbean to exploit its oil reserves. Men flocked into the enclave—laborers from the eastern Caribbean and South America, and engineers, architects, and chemists from North America, Europe, and South America—all essentially temporary guest workers (Larson 1971, 379; Hartog 1961, 318).[3]

Procurement of migrant workers posed few problems for the foreign oil businesses. Rich oil reserves were located in a region dominated by western European powers and the United States. Rival oil companies, cutthroat to each other over land claims and oil marketing deals, exerted ideological consensus regarding their concerted entitlement to the Caribbean resources. A "gentleman's agreement" of sorts operated among these otherwise archrivals. They could exploit the region's rich mineral resources and vast labor reserves almost with impunity.[4] National boundaries, maneuverable during large-scale multinational operations, shifted easily for the recruitment of regional and extraregional foreign workers.

What rationale—practical, labor-related, ideological, or otherwise—dictated the labor allocation of this polyglot throng of skilled and unskilled foreign guest workers pulled into the enclave? Citizens of Venezuela, locals and natives in the colonies of Trinidad, Curaçao, and Aruba expected to be first pick for employment opportunities. They were mistaken.[5] Foreign migrant workers were the preferred employees at all oil production sites, except perhaps Venezuela, which had a large native population.[6] The oil businesses preferred to make labor deals with non-locals as much as possible. Foreign workers created "a veritable babel of tongues and diverse backgrounds" at work sites (Larson 1971, 379). Short-term, contractual labor arrangements between employers and low-level foreign workers predominated.

Colonial racialized labor models surely influenced European and U.S. companies as they structured labor bureaucracies in the oil enclave. Europeans had placed foreign migrant workers at the center of their capitalist economies, in Europe and their colonies.[7] Besides, the United States (the most prominent foreign power represented in the Caribbean oil enclave) had been incorporating foreign free and unfree workers in its political economy for nearly three centuries. The oil enterprises simply transposed versions of their own racialized bureaucratic structures into the enclave.

RACIALIZATION OF THE ENCLAVE

The racialized bureaucratic labor model placed foreign whites—male administrators, scientists, technicians, and professionals—in its upper echelons (Girvan 1970). Large numbers of black workers, many from the eastern Caribbean, formed its base. Special privileges, such as family reunification and housing, delineated the higher rank of the skilled, white foreign workers from the low-status Caribbean migrant workers.

In the enclave, the term "migrant worker" came to be synonymous with black Caribbean workers. A variety of euphemisms, such as "advisors" and "consultants," often describe white temporary guest workers wherever capitalist "development" is introduced in the Third World. However, it was the otherwise derogatory term, "expatriate" that evolved into a benign and acceptable definition of the white, skilled, temporary foreign worker (Wall 1988, 403).

The oil enterprises operated the enclave as a free trade zone: an unofficial "supranational economic unit," (Miles 1993, 115; Balibar 1991, 43) deftly regulated by the oil corporations in response to market demands. All local governments and native people were at the mercy of this "transnational solidarity" (Balibar 1991, 62).

Companies exerted tight control over workers by fostering labor uncertainty at work sites. Oil companies manipulated migrant worker flows to the enclave, and sometimes contrived labor shortages. Workers, constantly subjected to the threat of instant deportation, fulfilled their companies' labor goals. Migrant workers were a ready, malleable work force. A subtle labor discrimination strategy used against native workers mandated English to be the official language for employment. In the eyes of foreign employers, native Spanish- and Papiamento-speaking workers suffered from a linguistic disability. The linguistic deficit of native males (and females) summarily lowered their job opportunities in the oil economy.

The oil companies behaved like extensions of their respective national governments. They used their colonialist or imperialist statuses to negotiate land leases and make migrant labor agreements with each other. Agreements between governments with oil investments in the region eventually reached Caribbean locals as "done deeds." Locally, oil companies defused labor and political problems by co-opting powerful local politicians. Influential elites (cooperative "middlemen," courted and rewarded by the foreign companies and governments) could be trusted to keep restive natives quiet.[8]

Foreign oil companies in the oil enclave saw themselves first as representatives of their powerful nation-states, but they shared strong secondary allegiances to each other. Rival trade strategies often changed from competitiveness to collusion, directed particularly against the weak, "occupied" young republic, Venezuela, and the vulnerable Caribbean region. Together, the industrial nations in the enclave affected a united posture of rescue. They had arrived just in time to save the region's land and mineral resources from dissipation; for the benefit of the world. They were on a justifiable mission.

Companies focused on doing the job efficiently and quickly, completing the project, and moving on. Minimum obligations and encumberances ensured swift leave-takings. In the case of emergency—for example, local political unrest or the discovery of new oilfields elsewhere—foreign companies demanded leeway to downsize or exit the country with maximum speed.

An atmosphere of temporariness and dispensability regulated social and labor relations. Native Arubans, allocated to the lowest levels of the racialized reserve labor army, were nevertheless the most invisible and dispensable of all, initially. For a while, eastern Caribbean migrant workers—foreign labor—were pitted against the native Arubans. Before long, the preferred would discover to their chagrin, that all Caribbean workers were dispensable and replaceable. The oil companies could dismiss and repatriate, train and relocate workers to suit their latest compelling economic interests.

The relatively small physical and demographic size of the Caribbean region, its demographic composition, weak colonial status, and proximity to the United States exposed it to successive onslaughts of racisms (Miles 1993; Balibar 1991).[9] Accustomed in their sending islands to intimate but racialized work relations, workers experienced a formal, insensitive, and racially stratified labor bureaucracy in the enclave. Caribbean migrant workers and the natives in the oil lands knew assuredly that intensely strange influences had entered their lives.

Using the most modern methods of science and technology, the transnationals determined that a very tiny region of the world was economically important and they penetrated it. They did not declare war and there was no attempt at the type of colonization involving genocide and enslavement that had occurred in the region beginning in the sixteenth century. However, the industrialized nations, through their multinational oil companies, literally churned up the region and imposed on it their economic and political will. Naively, the powers expected no enduring immigration and labor repercussions or cultural attachments to result.

The intense presence of the industrialized nations in the Caribbean, by way of the oil industry and defensive activities during World War II, had significant resonances. It racialized the migrant labor category. The oil enterprises destroyed the uniformity of the Caribbean migrant labor category, and stimulated intramigrant worker ethnic differences. The vertical racialized relationship between the colonies and core industrialized countries remained. A pattern of unpredictable spurts of economic attachments between the United States and particular eastern Caribbean territories began.[10]

The oil enterprises clearly established a pattern of economic imperialism. International corporations could bargain for and access the region's resources without much opposition from Britain or other colonial powers. The oil enterprises and their importance to western industrialized nations during World War II permanently shook and uprooted Britain's colonial Caribbean boundaries. The active presence of several industrialized nations in the oil enclave also had unintended geopolitical consequences.

International economic activity in the Caribbean during the first half of the twentieth century had steadily, if unintentionally, eroded the national borders of the European and U.S. nation-states. New forms of "exteriorization of the interior" had occurred between the Caribbean and the industrial countries at the colonial and nation-state levels (Balibar 1991, 43). Caribbean labor migrations to Britain, Canada, and the Netherlands took off.[11] The Caribbean region began to fully appreciate its "backyard" status and settled into a special and permanent labor migration relationship with the United States.

"UNFREE" MIGRANT LABOR

Eastern Caribbean migrant workers possess archetypical characteristics that make them susceptible to incorporation into migrant labor. The political status of these descendants of enslaved Africans improved little with emancipation. They were a stateless people, allocated to the bottom of local and international economies. Caribbean migrant workers at foreign regional work sites fit firmly into the category of "unfree migrant labor" (Satzewich 1991, 52). Yet, this form of wage work provided Caribbean males with relative freedom from the hardships of their local societies (Bolland 1992).[12]

Satzewich's arguments regarding "freedom" revolve around the political terms under which migrant workers are hired, repatriated and included into racialized host societies. He argues that the international labor market uses racism as its main labor regulation and allocation strategy. He charges further, and supports with much evidence, that for most of the twentieth century, Canada has operated very "unfree" migrant worker schemes. Therefore, the applications of German prisoners of war received quick attention and favorable labor allocation, while Caribbean migrant workers languished through multiple rejections. His warning: that free labor markets cannot be measured by the receiving country's theoretical claims to having a democratic form of government. Freedom, operated through policy, is devised by a stratified political economy. It is always relative, contextual, experiential, and "historically specific" (Satzewich 1991, 53), even in modern, so-called democratic nation-states such as Canada.

Bolland (1992) centers his discussion of worker freedom in the context of the work lives of emancipated Caribbean slaves, during the decades immediately following full freedom. Many former slaves and their descendants frantically sought freedom by leaving their homes in the British Caribbean colonies to become "unfree" migrant workers. A seeming paradox—why exchange one unfree labor situation for another?

Bolland supports Patterson's (1982) theory that the meanings of freedom are developed under the shadows of a menacing, endangering threat (Bolland 1992, 140). Patterson theorizes that the meanings of freedom changed for western slave-owning societies, precisely as those same societies perfected a terrible system of chattel slavery on Africans and their descendants. Slave-owning classes observed and understood well, the absence of freedom. This engendered in them the unique western appreciation and interpretation of freedom displayed in personal, individualistic, independent decision making (Bolland 1992, 141).

Bolland suggests that oppressive as migrant labor might seem to the observer, for stateless, impoverished former slaves, "submission . . . to the impersonal forces of the marketplace seemed like a new and perhaps worse form of domination" (Bolland 1992, 143). He joins Scott (1987, 576) in highlighting the relative and nuanced implications of freedom for people who have experienced group injustice. For such, they suggest that a range of family and community goals may supersede individual autonomy and "control over one's own pace of work." Foner also warns that "what seem like miserable conditions and a downtrodden lot to an observer often represent definite improvements to . . . migrant women" (1986, 142).

I would add that freedom is multifaceted. Workers experience levels of freedom, or the lack thereof, at local, community, and household levels, too. These macro- and micro-level freedoms intersect and overlap, especially around interpretations of the gender and class statuses of workers. The free market is only as free as the structural supports and the checks and balances that make it relatively just. Analyses of freedom must expose for examination, the supportive features of freedom experienced at the ideological, normative, institutional, and personal levels.

Freedom for the Caribbean migrant domestics in this study signifies *anonymity*. The women came from societies and households where intimate relations and traditional work expectations oppressed them. They found some freedom as labor migrants in concerted work activities done for wage returns, and for employers to whom they had no community ties or societal obligations. Distance from kin and social exclusion in the host society allowed the women independence from sexual and maternal demands. They lived in relatively *anomic* social situations. In the low-status social space allotted them, the foreign women experienced limited but increased levels of personal freedom in which to interpret gender relations, express their sexuality, and decipher social class differences.

At the macrostructural level of labor relations, the migrant domestics experienced freedom as *predictability* in the labor relationship. The terms of hire, duration, wages, and conditions of termination offered in the labor agreements provided emotional and financial stability and wage-earning consistency that the women cherished. They took on their breadwinner status as a career or an intensive, short-term investment. They now had freedom to handle the purse strings and consistently provide for their dependents (Foner 1986).

Freedom, even in societies that practice slavery, is a contested condition. Migrant workers treated the harshness of the category under which they were given work, "unfree migrant labour," (Satzewich 1991) as a temporary condition. They were prepared to take the chance—to "try their luck," as they put it. From observation and migration myths, migrant workers knew that the harsh "unfreeness" of the migrant labor category might merely be an initial stage of the immigration process. But it could also entail a continuously contested relationship with those who held power. Incremental changes, even over a protracted period, become acceptable to labor migrants as they wait for the political winds to shift. This situation describes the historical labor relationship that Caribbean workers have always had with their employers.

These various attributes of freedom must be compared with the migrant workers' prior experiences of intermittent and unpredictable wage labor in their sending countries. The latter made for uncertain and precarious living. The workers' limited leeway to maneuver for wages, their hopes for better conditions, and the limited work options represented more than they had in their sending countries.

I choose to view the categories of *free* and *unfree* as socially dynamic, influenced significantly by life in society. Labor and immigration categories, constructed through testing the political winds of public opinion and popular demand, can be changed. Even the most unjust migrant worker policies are susceptible to negotiation, contestation, and amelioration (Omi and Winant 1986). However, Satzewich (1991) and Miles (1993) place the racialization of political economies as the centerpiece of all labor migration flows.

Their contributions question classical migration theories. They suggest that entrenched racist ideologies have always gerrymandered, fixed, and skewed labor migration flows and the allocation of workers in political economies. Miles (1993) states that racialization of economies provides the fuel for nationalistic fervor, and helped fashion the ideals of the European industrial nation-states. Nation-states depend on labor migrants and migrant workers to inject patriotic feelings in citizens. Even the most democratic states are suspect (Satzewich 1991). Both authors argue eloquently that racialization remains the salient feature in migrant labor hierarchies, and ultimately of many political economies. The free and just working of the labor market depends on the unjust and self-serving policies and behavior of the people who control it.

But labor migrants are far from powerless; they too have agency to infiltrate and influence labor markets and change the culture of political economies.

INSIDE THE MIGRANT WORKER CATEGORY

Immigration laws are demographic instruments. In the hands of skillful policymakers, the laws may deliberately manipulate the growth, dispersion, and composition of a country's population or its work force. Countries utilize immigration policy to create or bolster ethnic, racial, gender, and socioeconomic differences in hierarchically organized societies. If states are "gatekeepers," determining who may be included into a receiving country (Satzewich 1991, 35), then immigration policies are the gates. The gates may open widely, narrowly, or not at all, to prospective labor migrants. The terms of entry offered migrant labor categories at the gates effectively, maybe permanently, thrust them to the edges or the bottom of the receiving societies.[13]

The migrant worker category cuts widely across the foreign labor immigrant sector. Southern European workers imported to rebuild London or the cities of Germany in the late 1940s, Haitian or Jamaican laborers employed seasonally in the sugarcane industries in the Dominican Republic and Florida today, and women brought into the United States to work as maids or au pairs from the Caribbean and Scandinavian countries, respectively, would all fit into the broad migrant labor category (Castles 1986; Griffith 1986; Soto 1987). However, the foreign imported labor sector is racialized and, therefore, stratified.

Each receiving country creates and interprets the migrant worker category to suit its national economic needs and stratification ideologies. The race and gender of workers, and the geopolitical status of their countries of origin, are all taken into careful consideration. Therefore, the immigration policies of receiving countries may target particular sending countries and groups in those countries for allocation in specific migrant labor schemes (Kritz et al. 1992, 5; Satzewich 1991). For its au pairs, the United States contracts with a few western European countries. Au pairs, for example, are a preferred category of household and child care helpers. When compared with eastern Caribbean migrant domestics in Aruba or women brought from Jamaica to be live-in nannies in New York suburban households, au pair contracts offer safer, more lenient, more humane, and therefore freer conditions that include greater benefits than those extended to maids from poorer sending countries.

The term "migrant worker" has been stereotyped to conjure up images of poor, foreign males with limited bargaining leverage, bound by exploitative work contracts. The migrant worker mythology tells of hard-working men, in particular, driven by their desire to provide for distant dependents and their hope to eventually return home to waiting families.

The term "migrant workers" also connotes the movement of workers out of the migrants' own country into a receiving country, and that many migrant workers are typically foreign labor. In fact, some migrant labor treks take workers from rural to urban regions of the same country. Political economies, directed by racist ideologies, may simply designate groups of their own citizens to be non-citizens or treat them as second-class citizens. Poor or ostracized groups within a country—theoretically citizens of that country—may be forced to subsist on migrant labor which takes them on seasonal migratory treks within their country's own borders (Chaney and Garcia Castro 1989; Bunster and Chaney 1985; Rollins 1985).[14]

Racialized labor bureaucracies manipulate workers in the unfree migrant labor category. In its most unfree manifestations, employers dispense with the niceties of gender or may interchange gender expectations. Those in power may eschew traditional gender norms and superimpose new gender meanings on social situations involving the subordinate. For instance, eastern Caribbean migrant domestics registered shock when required to clean pet menageries, bathe and walk unruly dogs, and wash cars—all masculine activities in both the Caribbean sending and host societies.[15]

All during the twentieth century, for a variety of economic reasons, young single women have been the preferred gender at industrial work sites and in urban centers of the global economy (Layton-Henry 1992; Chaney 1987; Sassen-Koob 1983; Nash et al. 1983). Widespread inclusion of females into the formerly all-male migrant worker category has significantly changed the meanings of the labor category.

Foreign female workers participated in the formal and informal economies of the oil enclave and in the tourist economies that developed later.

Yet, few written accounts exist that disclose the employment of these female migrant workers. Few official records tell that they endured sometimes very similar, but often markedly different labor, immigration, and travel experiences from their male counterparts. Luckily, a reliable oral tradition, ethnographic accounts, and official demographic data of female migrant workers exist.

IMMIGRATION LAWS AND FEMALE MIGRANT DOMESTICS

Immigration and labor laws control and manage foreign migrant worker flows into a receiving country. However, demographic, racial, and sexist policies of the country may underscore migrant workers' rights in tedious, clearly spelled-out legislation that attempts to micromanage the social, sexual, and political activities of the workers. The intent is to thwart the workers' attempts at socioeconomic mobility and prevent unwanted competition with citizens in the open job market.

Immigration laws try to ensure that migrant workers never become an economic imposition on the host society.[16] So micro-level immigration and labor laws circumscribe guest workers' lives while they remain in the receiving country. Host societies implement various monitoring strategies that ensure compliance with work and residential regulations throughout the workers' stay. Dismissed or laid-off workers are subject to almost immediate repatriation.

Migrant workers are deemed unfit by the receiving society for inclusion into full citizenship. Ethnic or racial differences rationalize and separate low-status foreign workers from legitimate citizens. Receiving countries make it very difficult for migrant workers to acquire citizenship rights and political inclusion, even after they become eligible for full citizenship. Janet, a retired domestic originally from Montserrat, had been working in Aruba for more than twenty-five years when she tried to renew her Montserrat passport. When the immigration officer intimated that she was eligible for a Netherlands Antilles passport, Janet was pleased, surprised, and angry all at once. She mused:

> All the time you walking back and forth to the immigration for this or that, or they seeking you out to interfere with you. Not once in all those twenty-five years did anybody say, "Janet, fix your papers."

Age at Entry

In economies where labor is plentiful, employers can manipulate age limits for entry of foreign workers to increase or decrease the flow of migrant workers. Since the 1940s, the authorities on Aruba have changed the stipulated age for migrant worker entry several times. For example, in

1949 the upper age limit for entry of a migrant domestic was fifty. A 1953 law set a much lower age limit of twenty years at entry, and retained the upper age limit of fifty for migrant domestics seeking jobs on all the Dutch Antilles (Philipps 1988). Since the late 1960s, that upper age limit has been lowered—no woman above age thirty-five need apply.

Clearly, policymakers have changed their minds about welcoming more mature migrant domestics. What could be the rationale for putting in place immigration laws which lower the upper age limit for female migrant workers' entry into the country? Attempts to keep out older women may reflect a slackening off of domestic worker demand or a continued glut of women.

Aruba's immigration policy intends to contract only young women. Younger women, likely to be stronger and healthier, would not become liabilities to their employers and the island's health care system. Besides, younger women tend to be restless, want to return home to find mates and begin having children, or move on to other, more promising, destinations. The host country thus avoids having to deal with elderly, retired former migrant domestics.

Whatever the rationale, since the 1960s, poor women in the eastern Caribbean have had a briefer period in their life cycles for labor migration decision making. This might explain the urgency they felt to grasp the wage-earning opportunity once it came. Most migrant workers, "literally at the receipt of a telegram[,] would take off " (Miller 1986, 882) for the foreign country.

Immigration Niches on Aruba

Few public policies are so watertight that people who really want to find a way around them cannot discover loopholes; and some loopholes it seems, have existed since the 1940s and 1950s. Migrant domestics described matter-of-factly how they found ways around the labor and immigration laws.

Janet, a retired maid, explained how she arrived on Aruba in 1943, weak and tired after a three-week journey from Montserrat, on an inter-island schooner, the "Ruby." She, and her relatives waiting to receive her, knew that her sponsor was fictitious. Her documents said that she was a cook who had arrived to work at the house of a Jewish businessman on Main Street in San Nicolas. According to her:

> My brother used to do business and work with a Jewish businessman who ran a big business place on Main Street in San Nicolas. He get the businessman to sign the paper and sponsor me. But nothing go so. He lend my brother the money and sign the paper. When I get here, for the first week or so I pretend that I had a job there, but really I was on my own.

Because she had no sponsor, the plan was that she would move in with her seven male cousins who lived in a long, spacious shack—a kind of barrack—outside of San Nicolas. According to Janet, life was tedious and boring during those first weeks of lying low, without a job. Living with her male cousins was difficult because they were overprotective and wanted to run her life, all becoming involved in the job search on her behalf. In the meantime, she was in virtual hiding from the authorities.

Ivy, another of the older retired women, from Nevis, told how at age twenty-five she was already married, but poor and unhappy, and wanting some excitement in her life. Most of all, she wanted some hard cash, which her husband was unable to provide. As a married woman, she was ineligible for work as a domestic on Aruba and could not legally seek a sponsor. However, she was in contact with her father, whom she had never met because he had left home many years before to comb the Caribbean as a migrant worker when she was only a toddler. He moved to Aruba after working in the Panama Canal and the oil fields of Venezuela, gaining permanent residence by marrying a woman with Dutch Rights. Ivy applied for a tourist visa to visit him. The year was 1944, during the boom years of oil production and population increase on Aruba.

This ambitious woman then proceeded to implement a careful plan—once on Aruba, she would lie low for a reasonable time, then find a sponsor:

> It is true that when I leave for Aruba I was already married. But me and my husband was not getting on, we were not making it. We were fighting all the time. So my grandmother write my father who was working in Aruba and encourage him to send for me. My father did know that I was married, because is he self send me my wedding outfit—a beautiful wedding outfit from Aruba. But my father, too, seem to agree with me leaving the miserable man, because he never send any passage money for him, and when I get to Aruba he never enquire about him, or encourage me to send back for him. When the immigration authority find out two years later that I was still in Aruba, they give me a lot of trouble. They come asking me why I didn't tell them that I was a married woman. I tell them that they didn't ask me. Besides, I did fill out the immigration form. The form had everything on it if they had only read it.

The woman's father had proceeded to collude with his resourceful daughter in a plan as old as the formation of nation-state boundaries, citizenship rights, the issuing of legal travel documents, and the creation of illegal immigrants. If she played her cards right, her presence and marital status would be overlooked, she could remain on Aruba indefinitely, and then find work as a migrant domestic, even though her immigration status as a married visitor made her ineligible for the job.

After lying low for almost two years, Ivy emerged, applied for a job in the prestigious Colony, and got it. The desired loophole in the immigration laws had been found and used effectively. But her immigration vulnerability would later return to haunt her.

Sponsorship and Residency

The laws concerning legal entry and sponsorship of migrant workers have grown more strict over the years, while residency laws have become somewhat more lenient. For example, in the Dutch colonies of the enclave in the 1940s and 1950s, migrant domestics had to remain as live-in domestics for the duration of their stay. Each woman still must live for a mandated period as a live-in maid, within the employer's household and not in rooms attached to the employer's residence.[17] However, over the years, several changes have been made to the length of the mandatory live-in period; in 1989, it was lessened to two years, after which the women could find their own lodgings, if they so desired.

Employers assume full responsibility for domestics' public and private lives. All the migrant domestic's board and lodging needs must be provided by the employer, who also provides health insurance for the domestic living under her roof. Intense social control is exerted over the migrant women's reproductive capabilities. Women may not cohabit, become pregnant, or be joined by their dependents—except those who are vacationing—while employed as migrant domestics. Even when a woman lives on her own (she may reside too with a female relative or friend), spot checks are conducted by immigration authorities at each of the little rented rooms inhabited by the small number of "free-signing" women, to ensure that they do not break the law.

Migrant domestics had to avoid being charged as public nuisances. The term "social disturbance" was interpreted very broadly by Aruban residents, and usually in the Aruban community's favor, whenever it referred to migrant domestics. They might be accused of causing a public disturbance for having affairs with the husbands of citizens, being rude to citizens, causing a private disturbance in the households where they are employed, breaking any law, or inconveniencing a citizen in any way.

Each woman I interviewed gave examples of how broad and unfair these interpretations could be. Several of the women recounted a bizarre alleged incident in which a maid had quarreled with her mistress and they came to blows:

> The girl say that the mistress slapped her on her mouth and she let her mistress have a hard slap on her mouth. Well, the immigration came to the house, grabbed her as she was, took her to the airport, and put her on a plane, even though she was wearing slippers and her work clothes, and her hair was in curlers. They promise to send her belongings to her later.

A strange formal complaint and redress procedure was practiced by the women in case of any trouble between a migrant domestic and an Aruban citizen, resident, or employer. According to them, an aggrieved maid always had to hurry to the immigration office and make certain that her complaint was heard first by the authorities. For, the migrant domestics said, the person making the earliest complaint was usually most likely to be viewed favorably and declared to be in the right.

Free-Signing Status

After having been a live-in domestic for the two-year prescribed period, a woman could choose to live on her own. She then received the new status of "free-signing" from the authorities. Free-signing was a troublesome category for labor and immigration authorities; the woman's pseudoindependent life-style threatened to change her predominantly unfree status of migrant worker to another, less clear. This new status obscured the state's single, work-related purpose for allowing her entry into the country.

However, the new and nebulous status of free-signer did release the domestic from the watchful eyes of the employer. The free-signing migrant domestic managed her own time. She could socialize a little, and also had oppportunity to moonlight; the closest women ever got to anything resembling their petty trading activities in the informal economies of their sending societies. But the authorities carefully delineated moonlighting jobs to make them resemble the service chores women performed as live-ins.

Women exposed themselves to serious disadvantages in the "free-signing" work arrangement. They sacrificed much for what seemed to be very limited freedom in the form of relative independence and anonymity. The women liked expressions that suggested chance-taking, gambling: "I trying my luck." Free-signing represented the women's decision to gamble. Faced with options of either the living-in status which had some security, or free-signing with all its risks, many women chose free-signing.

Once granted the free-signing option, women became totally responsible for all their needs; even their expensive health insurance payments. Free-signing could be a danger to the ambitious woman's health, too. Several women, anxious to increase their earnings, worked tirelessly. They engaged their labor out to so many clients that they spent almost every waking moment working. There was much about the free-signing domestics that resembled the wage-earning activities of freed slaves during slavery—people declared free to sell their labor, but whose freedom was severely constrained by an overarching, unfree social system. The domestics' choice of free-signing with all of its problems also closely resembled the freed Caribbean slaves' definition of "freedom" after emancipation (Bolland 1992). Freedom for former Caribbean slaves meant becoming migrant workers, and taking a chance on the unknown—the proverbial devil they did not know. They outright rejected the option to remain and work with the plantation owners—the devils—they knew too well.

Gender and Female Sexuality

The labor and immigration policymakers' desire to control women's sexuality and their reproductive powers reached the level of obsession (Philipps 1988). The old sexual double standard obtained. Male workers—sexual creatures—were expected to make use of local brothels. Female workers should be asexual, if not celibate. An elaborate pretense vacillated between reducing female migrant workers to the level of asexual work automatons, while at the same time portraying them as oversexed hussies who had to be watched constantly, and whose sexuality needed to be restrained.

Powerful groups in most societies create sexual myths and taboos around concocted charges of deviant sexuality of low-status groups in the society (Hansen 1992). In cases where female foreign workers outnumber male workers, mating between migrant females and local males is often strongly discouraged and controlled by ideologies of racial endogamy. However, Aruban men do marry lighter-skinned migrant domestics from Colombia, Venezuela, the Dominican Republic and even the Philippines (Eelens 1993). Racial phenotype matters on Aruba. If eastern Caribbean domestics marry, and few ever do, their mates are usually black Arubans, not native mestizo Aruban men (Phalen 1977, 223).[18]

Cross-culturally, employers find female workers' biological ability to get pregnant and bear children, and the consequent possibility of interrupted work contracts, inconvenient and aggravating (Ong 1987, 154). Unfree migrant worker schemes, such as those operating in the Netherlands Antilles and Aruba in particular, repatriate pregnant migrant domestics once their pregnancy is discovered (Philipps 1988). The pregnant worker's perceived innate health issues and the ensuing duties of child care compound the "woman problem" for employers. Besides, host countries shun responsibility for the "social reproduction" of their migrant workers' children.

Migrant workers, like the poor in most countries, are deemed unfit for full citizenship, and must be prevented from bearing burdensome children. If the children of poor citizens have reduced rights and privileges in many societies, the migrant workers' children are even more of a drag on the host country's resources, and an adulteration of its racial makeup. Unfree host countries also prevent migrant worker family reunification.

Continuous treks of full-fledged migrant workers keep showing up in the host country. Nevertheless, receiving countries like Aruba take no responsibility for the social or biological reproduction of this category of employees, whose work benefits the host society. The lack of interest suggests that unfortunately, nation-state boundaries clearly define and limit each state's social obligations. Social and biological reproduction remains the burden and responsibility of the impoverished sending countries (Glenn 1992, 2).

Labor Migrants Who Stay

Labor relationships formed between better-off receiving countries and poor sending countries continue long after the migrant worker projects cease. An unwritten, and seemingly inevitable, law of foreign migrant worker schemes is that some of the foreign guest workers remain permanently in the sending countries (Castles 1986, 169). The migrant worker projects that attracted eastern Caribbean people to Trinidad, Venezuela, Curaçao, and Aruba early in the twentieth century have ended. But social and labor relations between the former sending and receiving countries remain.

Some labor migrants find ways to renew contracts and remain indefinitely in host countries. Temporary guest workers remain illegally by simply getting lost and merging into the host population. The ghettos and urban ethnic enclaves of many large cities hold secrets about former boom times and heavy labor migrations. But temporary migrant workers find legal niches in the migrant labor laws, too. Marriage to a citizen is often the definitive loophole that ensures the worker's stay and may offer social inclusion. The ability of labor migrants to find husbands indicates the level of freedom in the host country's labor migration policies.

The more free a migrant labor system, the greater its sensitivity to balance its ratio intakes of foreign male and female workers. It would also allow some form of family reunification. Migrant domestics arriving from Ireland and western Europe in the decades between the 1860s and 1880s found husbands in the United States and remained.[19] In the decades before this, racialized immigration and labor laws in the United States showed little generosity to Chinese migrant workers. An unfree labor migrant policy controlled the Chinese migrant worker flow into the United States, debarring Chinese females from entry and preventing family reunification. On Aruba, the migrant domestics' contracts set stringent limits that resemble those offered male Chinese workers in the United States during the nineteenth century. Since the 1950s, the majority of migrant domestics on Aruba remain unattached, single workers for the duration of their stay.

Marriages in the migrant worker population were more possible and occurred more frequently during the 1940s and 1950s, when the ratio of female to male migrant workers was more even. However, there are practical disadvantages in marriage between migrant workers. According to Aruba's immigration laws, upon marriage, the migrant domestic assumes the immigration status of her husband. Whenever a male migrant worker lost his job or was being repatriated for any reason, the man's wife was also legally bound to accompany him and leave Aruba (Kalm 1975, 167; Koot 1981, 132).

Migrant domestics and their spouses discovered the disadvantages of marriage during the late 1940s and early 1950s, when the majority of eastern Caribbean male migrant workers were repatriated.

Ivy, the migrant domestic from Montserrat, who in 1989 had been living for forty-five years on Aruba, painted a stressful picture depicting the precarious life of married migrant workers:

> For all the years we lived in Aruba, I always had five well-packed suitcases under my bed, ready and waiting to take off at the drop of a hat. My husband was never lucky to find employment with Lago itself, always with a contractor and every time the job end we back to worries. I never know when the knock would come in the night and we have to pick up and leave. I never take out Dutch Rights and its only since he died that I stopped worrying.

They knew the law. If her husband was without employment for a month, the entire family would have to leave.[20]

Eastern Caribbean women in the oil enclave found work, even as the factories mechanized, forcing the repatriation of male migrant workers. On Aruba and Curaçao the majority of domestics left on their own volition (Philipps 1988). However, a relatively large number of unmarried migrant domestics chose to renew their work contracts, and remained indefinitely.

U.S. LABOR SCHEMES

Aruba's labor and immigration laws developed with the strong collaboration of the Lago refinery, the chief employer of migrant labor. To fill what it saw as Aruba's labor shortage, the oil conglomerate looked to the rest of the Caribbean.

The local governments in the Dutch islands had no experience in regulating large-scale migrant labor flows, but the U.S. immigration authorities did. In fact, U.S. oil and agricultural businesses were directing three massive migrant labor flows simultaneously. During and immediately after World War II were the peak years for use of migrant labor by U.S. businesses. Workers flowed over the Mexican borders and into U.S. farms under the aegis of what was called the Braceros labor scheme. Caribbean workers moved into the United States to work on farms along the eastern seaboard in the H-2 program and migrant workers poured into the oil enclave in the southern Caribbean.

The H-2 migrant labor program resembled the Braceros labor scheme. Both strongly male-gendered labor migration schemes permitted migrant workers into the United States to do seasonal agricultural labor for specific periods (Briggs 1986; Reimers 1985). Labor policies in the oil enclave closely resembled the Braceros worker program.

Local governments on Aruba and Curaçao seem to have depended heavily on foreign-owned oil companies for assistance in forming local immigration policy. Immigration policy devised for Curaçao and Aruba eventually translated into laws for the entire Dutch Antilles. The enactment of such laws varied slightly from island to island.

Aruba was an ideal experimental site for a multinational corporation to try out labor and migration policies already in use on the U.S. mainland. Any immigration and labor controls exerted against Mexican workers entering from points along the long Mexico/U.S. border could be applied more effectively on Aruba: a small island, relatively flat, almost bare of vegetation, and obviously accessible only by sea and air.

Thousands of temporary foreign workers could be pulled in, closely and continuously monitored, and moved out with ease as labor demand warranted and labor and immigration policy directed. Besides, Aruba's small mestizo population made recognition and differentiation of natives from foreign workers easy.

In devising their respective migrant labor policies, nation-states copied and borrowed ideas from each other. Germany's 1938 harsh *Foreigner's Police Decree* allowed migrant workers to stay in Germany as long as their personality and the purposes of their stay "made them worthy of hospitality" (Castles 1986, 522). Britain based its *European Voluntary Worker Scheme* (1945–1951), which imported European laborers to help in post–World War II reconstruction, on Germany's Foreigner's Police Decree. And Britain involved some of its colonies—Canada, Australia, and New Zealand—in accepting European refugees as migrant workers (Satzewich 1991, 86–91). These British Commonwealth countries depended heavily on the mother country's migrant labor laws for guidance in devising their respective immigration policies.

Similarity in migrant worker schemes partly reflects the core design intent of all the immigration policies. European and North American nation-states have developed and exported ideologies of citizenship, strongly reasoned within a very similar logic based on premises of racial superiority, privilege, and entitlement. From this persepctive, any labor immigrant or migrant—free or unfree—is suspect. At their worst, varieties of unfree migrant worker laws seek to exert optimum control, often just short of enslavement, on workers' lives.

Positives of Migration Policies

Strict codification of the migrant labor laws provides the women with some recourse to the law. Immigration and labor laws delineate the rights, privileges, and obligations of employer and migrant domestic. In fact, in the absence of an official ombudsman, the immigration laws and officers become the women's only advocates (Philipps 1988).

The laws prevent the domestics from being at the mercy of their employers, ensuring that they have the security of board and lodge, and assuring them of an official basic wage which can be increased but not lessened. By law, and usually for the first time in their lives, the migrant domestics are provided with full health insurance coverage by their employers. It is true that the women's work lives are strictly circumscribed by law, but that same law declares each Thursday as the "maids' half-day off," during which domestics are given time to socialize and run their personal errands. Domestics are also given by law two unpaid vacation weeks each year, as well as two hours on Sundays to go to church. Never before have most of the women had their waking hours so apportioned: both bane and blessing to women whose public and private lives in their sending societies had merged imperceptibly.

Chapter 5

Migration Decision Making

W hen women began leaving the Caribbean in the 1930s to head for employment in the enclave, they had no way of knowing that they were part of an army of workers involved in a massive international operation. They had received word that their service labor had "use value" and was worth wages higher than they had ever received, either in their home islands or on neighboring Trinidad, where wage-earning opportunities were more diverse and lucrative. Was the call to labor in the oil enclave a classic case of the strong "pull" of labor demand at industrial centers, attracting surplus labor from the impoverished hinterlands and creating wage and labor equilibrium in the world economic system?

DEPENDENT BRITISH COLONIES

As the twentieth century dawned, a corporate economy with financial centers in North America and Europe had begun to expand its entrepreneurial interests into mineral extraction in the Caribbean. Powerful parent companies that organized international businesses through vertically integrated subsidiaries were replacing existing colonial mercantilist business arrangements. Labor, production, and trade relations that had been in place for nearly two centuries, and had fostered complete economic dependence of colonies on the colonial powers, had outgrown their economic and political usefulness. Multinational firms were ready to capitalize on improved technologies and the growing demand for what were seemingly abundant and accessible supplies of raw material, adequate supplies of labor, and modern methods of transportation (Girvan 1970, 493).

By the beginning of the nineteenth century, Britain had conceded that the bottom had fallen out of sugar production derived from sugarcane, the major crop grown for export in its British Caribbean colonies. Low production yields and high production costs had thrown many estates into bankruptcy, and as the nineteenth century began, the newer British colonies (the virgin soils of Trinidad and Guyana) had become Britain's only dependable sugar sources. The majority of Britain's Caribbean colonies had ceased to be serious players in the world economic system, and the people of the colonies were left to survive by using their wits. Once slavery ended in 1834, the former slaves and their descendants were virtually abandoned and left to their own economic devices. Put bluntly, as the twentieth century began, "the social conditions of the people of the Caribbean colonies had not improved from that of the early days of slavery and in many cases had worsened" (Claypole and Robottom 1981, 101).

A hundred and fifty years after emancipation and centuries of financial and economic relations with Britain, the Commonwealth countries of the Caribbean were still poor and dependent. Caribbean economies were not self-sufficient in food production. High food importation costs have always plagued the economies of the islands. The importance of almost every island for Britain was the cultivation of one or two unprocessed export crops that were produced without consideration for the food needs of the local people. Nearly 80 percent of the British islands' food consumption needs have always been met through imports from North America and Britain. The islands' histories of large landholdings (dedicated to export crops, owned by white expatriate or wealthy white planter-class families and cultivated by forced labor) prevented the development of a large black landowning peasantry.

Inter-island export trade in food, or political and economic cooperation was never nurtured by the colonial government and remained precarious. Each colonial territory had been organized to have vertical relations with British merchant houses and Britain's colonial office, to the detriment of inter-island commerce and cooperation.

The findings of the Moyne Commission, sent out in 1939 to investigate the cause of riots which swept through the islands in the mid-1930s, sought to impress upon the British public the stark conditions of poverty and neglect under which the vast majority of people in Britain's Caribbean colonies were living. The commission blamed the colonial government and its lack of oversight for the appalling conditions under which people worked, when they could find work.

> In the worst cases, city shop-girls worked for wages less than twenty shillings [about 5 U.S. dollars in today's currency] a week, and female domestics worked seven days a week from 6 A.M. to 9 P.M. for as little as six shillings [a day]. When food was provided the wages were reduced to about one shilling and six pence per week! No laws had been passed to insist on standard

allowances for sick leave, annual holidays or time off. Many women did manual work for a few shillings a week. Some weeded and manured fields, others loaded and unloaded barges with sand, coal or heavy banana stems. The poorest broke stones or worked at road building for as little as nine pence a day. (Claypole and Robottom 1981, 104)

After the initial flurry of shock and concern, and the recognition that social and economic changes would involve large sums of money, long-term planning and investment in the region, the task was assessed to be formidable, if not impossible. However, as the Moyne Commission was returning to Britain, the country was already engaged in World War II, a war which overtaxed the economic and political strength of Great Britain. As a result, the Moyne Commission's findings were not made public until 1944. However, in 1942, in the midst of the war effort and even as migrant workers were beginning to pour into the oil enclave, a strange conglomeration of western European and North American governments formed the Anglo-American Caribbean Commission. Until it was disbanded in the mid-1950s, this mainly research and advisory body looked into a variety of means to improve the socioeconomic condition of the Caribbean countries.

DISORGANIZATION MODEL OF SOCIETY

How did many in the industrialized world explain the economic and social malaise that overtook the postemancipation Caribbean? They theorized using controversial "disorganization models" to analyze so-called Third World societies. These models focused on the societies' economic underdevelopment, instability, weakness of institutions, and overpopulation; and concluded that the people had brought on themselves the persistent and pervasive poverty that their societies experienced (Glissant 1989; Cudjoe 1988). Structural factors connected with a colonial history of neglect and exploitation hardly entered policy discussions. Besides, little recognition was given to the significant contributions that the slave labor of millions of Caribbean people had made to the wealth and industrial successes of the so-called developed world (Williams 1944).

A very popular explanation held throughout the industrialized world concerning persistent poverty is that weak economic conditions, such as existed in the Caribbean at the turn of the century (and still exist), are due to the innate deviant, immature personality types (McClelland 1961; Inkeles and Smith 1974). According to this view, Caribbean poverty and underdevelopment were definitely psychological in origin, because blacks have "a marked dislike of certain types of manual labor; a lack of perseverance in labor of any kind" (Mary Proudfoot 1954, 71).[1] Not much hope was held out by the colonial masters that their former slave colonies could become viable societies. It is no wonder then, that men and women of the anglophone eastern Caribbean were heading for the oil enclave during the height of World War II conflict in the hope of finding wage labor that was non-existent in their societies.

U.S. INVESTMENTS IN THE CARIBBEAN

The slave plantation economies of the eastern Caribbean had been developed as economic experiments by the colonial powers. However, by the late nineteenth century, plantation economies that made use of waged migrant workers had been introduced into the Spanish-speaking Caribbean and Central American countries. They were created by U.S.-based multinationals, and were perhaps the earliest examples of the corporate, postemancipation firms in the region. The companies dealt in mineral extractive enterprises: oil, natural gas, and bauxite marked the expansion in this new type of colonial entrepreneurial investment in the Caribbean (Sunshine 1994; Sealy 1992).

Through their subsidiaries, multinationals, inject massive amounts of finances, research, technology, and labor into areas of the nonindustrialized world by way of the international corporate firm. This model of business enterprise is designed to promote growth in the corporation, and is hardly concerned with creating widespread horizontal development in the region where, for example, its extraction and production sites might be located. If, in the mercantilist trade arrangement with Britain, the Caribbean colonies had been controlled through colonial allegiances to the British crown and its trade houses while receiving little benefits in return, not much more could be expected in this new entrepreneurial arrangement with multinationals based in the United States. In this kind of investment, the parent company is "better integrated with its subsidiaries' needs, and market demands that come from the outside world, rather than with the economic needs of the host economies" (Girvan 1970, 512).

A "delicately balanced partnership" exists between the local government of the host country and the multinational subsidiary within its borders (Girvan 1970, 517). It was well understood by everyone that the mercantilist trade arrangements which existed between metropoles and their colonies were as strongly political as they were economic and cultural. However, multinationals are permitted to affect an apolitical stance with the countries in which they operate plantations, mines, or factories (Best 1968). Inevitably, however, the local economies become completely dependent on, if not absorbed by, the multinationals that are their highest taxpayers and largest investors.

Eastern Caribbean labor migrants were simply "trying to better themselves," when they began seeking wage labor in the oil enclave in the southern Caribbean. Male workers had gained the reputation of providing valuable migrant labor at intraregional labor sites. However, when female-gendered labor demand in the enclave pulled in women, this new female labor presence and contribution to the enclave's productivity remained invisible and unmeasured. The oil enterprise and local governments were hardly interested in a formal measurement of the migrant women's labor contributions to the oil economy, or the socioeconomic effects that the enclave exerted on the women's sending societies. Besides, in the 1930s there was cross-cultural invisibility and downright indifference to the economic contributions of women to local and international economies (Stichter 1990; Boserup 1970).

MIGRATION LIAISONS: FEMALES

In 1989, as in 1943, to arrive on Aruba as migrant domestics, the women of both age cohorts in the study made serious contact with a person or persons—male or female—on Aruba who stimulated and encouraged their migration interest. However, when asked, many women defiantly denied that they had been liaisons for other women. A common retort was, "Me, I wouldn't bring my dog to this hard life over here."

It was not unusual to hear mixed emotions in the answers the women gave to questions about their unofficial roles as labor scouts, for labor scouting suggested collusion with Aruban householders. Once the reality of the harshness of life sets in, it seems that the women lose some of their positive attitudes toward their migration and begin to doubt whether it was wise after all. Questions about encouraging friends to join them on Aruba evoked some retorts of denial and deprecation, disillusionment, embarrassment and even combativeness: "I would never stop anybody from trying their luck if they want to, but I won't bring anybody here to suffer in this hard life."

But the domestics on Aruba are efficient labor scouts. As soon as women settle into a job, they begin remembering needy friends and relatives they left behind in the sending societies. Some women admitted their active participation in job searches. For example, I found two sisters working for the same sponsor; the elder had referred the younger to her employer. In another case, I met five women "cooling out" one moonlit night on a side street in Oranjestad. I discovered that the forty-five-year-old woman who was sitting on the pavement was mother to two young daughters who were part of the group. According to the mother, her daughters had started making babies back home while she was working hard to support them, so she found them jobs.

In 1989 Eliza, who had worked on Aruba for eighteen years as a migrant domestic, called her niece Inez, another young domestic from St. Vincent, to a job. The younger woman left two very young children in St. Vincent and responded immediately to her aunt's call. Maybe the move was too hurried and she felt concerned about her newborn baby, for after only four months and changing employers three times, Inez broke her contract. She quit the job and returned to St. Vincent. However, hardship and need began to bite the young mother and she importuned her aunt to find her another work sponsor on Aruba. Quite disgusted with her niece's erratic behavior, Eliza did find her another sponsor, one year later.

One of the young women from my own village in Grenada, with whom I had renewed acquaintance on Aruba in the late 1970s, had been responsible for bringing in four of her friends. Two of these five women found employment at the same residence. Veronica, a retired maid from the older age cohort, readily admitted her activities as a labor scout. She expounded on her labor scouting with pride:

> I find work for at least four women. I bring them in here. Some prove ungrateful; others can't thank me enough. Besides, I help a lot to find a place when they change from one mistress to another.

It is noteworthy that the women's denials about being job liaisons became more strident when asked if they intended to find sponsors for their young daughters to join them as migrant domestics on Aruba. Many women reacted with rueful laughs which mimicked disgust; and they pretended that the question was an affront to their dignity.

Eliza elaborated on the feelings of effrontery that the question evoked. An employer had promised to get relatives in the United States to invite one of Eliza's three unemployed daughters (all of whom were still in St. Vincent) to be their housemaid. According to Eliza, she was shocked and disgusted when upon reminding her mistress of the promise, the mistress suggested that she had a job waiting for the young girl in the household of one of her friends on Aruba, and that Eliza's daughter should come and take it. Eliza sneered, "Me, I taking this hard life so my children wouldn't have to do it. Me, I don't want any of my daughters to push a broom in anybody house." In the minds of labor migrants plodding the stepping-stone migration path, the status of the domestic improves automatically in the desired migration apex. In the meantime, domestics on Aruba continued to collude with immigration authorities and Aruban households. Their concerted efforts kept the labor connection between employers in Aruba and poor eastern Caribbean women viable.

FEMALE TRAVEL TO ARUBA (1940s–1950s)

During the 1940s and 1950s, a large migrant worker community comprised of people from the anglophone eastern Caribbean, many related to each other, welcomed a continuous flow of new migrant domestics. In the typical boom-town economy that existed on Aruba at the time, cash-earning opportunities abounded. This peak employment period assured male and female migrant workers a choice of employers. Workers could enhance their economic positions by pooling resources with relatives. Women could take a chance at improving their financial and social status by marrying male migrant workers whose wages were much higher than theirs (Abraham-

Van der Mark 1983; Philipps 1988).[2] No wonder then, that all roads in the eastern Caribbean led to the enclave, as people tried to get in.

The people of the area have tried to deal with the social and personal disruption that migration causes by inculcating migration behavior into the normative structure of eastern Caribbean societies, and making it seem natural and inevitable. But if first-time migration was a frightening, formidable experience for men, it was (and continues to be) doubly nerve-wracking for young, unsophisticated women traveling alone.

Labor migrants traveling to the oil enclave from the eastern Caribbean crossed several cultural, racial and national boundaries in a few hours, while still remaining geographically within the Caribbean (Levine 1987). The migrant women and their families have an exaggerated sense of the distance between the sending eastern Caribbean islands and the receiving country, Aruba. This might be the result of indirect travel routes from the eastern Caribbean. Certainly, the necessity to "island hop" to destinations helps complicate travel to Aruba even in the 1990s.

Undeveloped and nonexistent intraregional transportation and communication facilities hindered easy travel within the Caribbean during the 1930s and 1940s. Entrepreneurial activities in the enclave itself had quickly stimulated sea and air travel, and telecommunications. However, it was easier to communicate between the countries of the enclave and from oil operation sites to the North American mainland and Europe than between the rest of the eastern Caribbean. Carefully circumscribed forms of development obtained on Venezuela, Trinidad, Curaçao, and Aruba. On Aruba, San Nicolas portrayed an interesting mixture of rough boom-town and modern facilities, over which the oil complex loomed. The rest of the island, as the rest of the non-enclave Caribbean, remained undeveloped. Few, if any, ethnographic accounts exist of the grueling journeys undertaken by male migrant workers to any of the Caribbean sites, at which thousands found intermittent employment from the end of slavery until the 1950s. The elderly women from the first cohort of migrant domestics vividly recall their pioneering journeys to the foreign countries of the enclave.

People who traveled to Aruba in the 1940s did so at their peril. The older women, now nearly all retired, who arrived on Aruba during the World War II years, recalled their trying journeys. Most traveled to Aruba via island schooner, and Caribbean waters around the oil routes were alive with Nazi German submarines (Baptiste 1973; Wall 1988). The Dutch airline KLM began flights out of St. Maarten in the mid-1940s, but many poor women could not afford the airline fare. Besides, people were still wary of the newfangled form of travel.

Women setting out for Aruba from the island of Montserrat, northernmost of the eastern Caribbean islands in this study, were in for a circuitous journey. They traveled southward first, by small schooner from Montserrat to St. Kitts or St. Maarten, then via Curaçao to Aruba. Shipping agents never knew exactly when the Curaçao-bound schooner would arrive in the northeastern islands. In the absence of telephones or air travel, women followed word-of-mouth directions and set out in hopes of making boat connections on St. Kitts or St. Maarten. Many found themselves waiting as long as one or two weeks, on a new, strange island for the ship's erratic arrival, upon which the long-suffering migrant women would begin a six- or seven-hundred-mile, two-week journey to Curaçao.

In 1943, Janet arrived on St. Kitts by a small schooner from Montserrat. She had to wait two weeks for the arrival of the larger schooner, ominously named *Crawling Dyke*, to take her on the long sea voyage to Curaçao, via St. Maarten en route to Aruba. In the hectic war years at the Lago oil refinery, production rates climbed to an all-time high and Aruba's population peaked, as migrant workers labored tirelessly at the refinery to meet the Allied Forces' fuel demands.

Janet had seven male cousins, all migrant workers at the refinery. She knew little about living conditions on Aruba, but her cousins assured her they would beat the system by setting up a ghost employer to sponsor her. She was young, unmarried, childless, penniless, and ready to take her chances, horrific travel and all. But Janet's journey was particularly grueling:

> I can't even remember if there were any other women on board. I would never forget that trip. Me, with my face always in a basin, the ship rocking and rolling. I was sick for almost the whole journey. I could hardly raise my head. They would bring me a little bowl of fresh water to use to bathe. I ate nothing for two weeks, and the heat, and darkness down inside that ship was something. I can remember how everybody had to get off in Curaçao. We had to get into another boat the "Ruby," to make the journey to Aruba. I was feeling better. We left about ten o'clock one night and got to the bay outside San Nicolas about four o'clock next morning. I can remember all the lights in San Nicolas as we waited for daybreak.

Ann recalled how she left her home in Nevis, journeyed by boat to St. Kitts, and then changed for a larger boat that took her to St. Maarten. This woman had several reasons to be excited about her impending journey. She was traveling to Aruba ostensibly on a vacation, but privately determined to leave her old life as a married woman behind. Besides, the invitation to travel had come from her father, whom she did not know but longed to meet at last. She would take her chances; she had always been a brave, outspoken woman. She set out, determined to find a work sponsor on Aruba, no matter how long it took. Very harsh living conditions, especially poor housing facilities, awaited the intrepid migrant domestics who arrived on the island.

Ann recalled disembarking in St. Maarten on a wooden jetty when she learned to her dismay that the schooner on which she would travel to Curaçao was delayed. She knew no one there, and dared not spend the little money she had:

What I going do? I don't know anybody on St. Maarten. I remember standing there at the end of the jetty where it touched the land, my big suitcase near my legs. I stand there for hours. People passing up and down, staring at me, teasing me, inviting me to go home with them. I don't know what to do. Then, a woman came up and start to talk to me. I was in luck. She used to work on Aruba. She know my father well. She invite me to stay at her house. It was a full three weeks living with those strangers before the Curaçao boat arrive.

Janet, the woman who traveled on the schooner *Crawling Dyke* to Curaçao and embarked on another, the *Ruby*, out of Curaçao, was met by her many cousins who took her to their house on the outskirts of San Nicolas; she recalled,

I remember when night time come, my place to sleep was on a cot. I would roll it out across the entrance—the only door to the building. Many a night, when one of the men come in late, and I already roll down my cot, they would disturb me. I would have to get up to let them pass. I didn't like living with relatives very much. That whole house full of people from Montserrat. Besides, because I new to the island, everybody know what best for me.

Relations with her cousins became more strained when they found her a job. Her employers, an Aruban man married to a Venezuelan woman, lived far away from San Nicolas in the distant, dusty village of Dakota. Bright lights, signs of U.S. materialism, paved roads, good wages, chances for making connections to better labor migrations—all her glorious expectations about Aruba had come to naught. Except for weekends, she labored as a live-in maid to people she considered low-status employers. She felt isolated in the island's backwoods.

Nothing of the wealth and glamour that she had expected in an oil-rich country was evident where she worked. Even water was at a premium throughout Aruba in 1943, and according to Janet, it was particularly scarce in the poor neighborhood where she was employed.[3] Besides, she lived in virtual silence; she neither spoke nor understood Papiamento, the lingua franca in the household, and in the village of Dakota. In her new job, she felt a long way away from poor Montserrat and the lucrative employment she had hoped to find on Aruba.

An employers' race and socioeconomic status assumed crucial importance in the women's job searches. Janet well understood the linkages between race and socioeconomic status. She felt that she had suffered grave disappointment in her first job, convinced that her employers' obvious low status augured ill for her chances of bettering herself. She had expected to land a job with a white, American, or Dutch family living in Lago's housing estate, "the Colony," reserved for the refinery's best-paid workers. She vowed to herself to find a better position, without the help of her meddling relatives. After seven frustrating months, she landed a job at the Colony. To her great delight she could again enjoy the bright lights of San Nicolas:

> No matter if a woman had a job already, she was never satisfied until she got a job in the Colony. There was security in a job there. Once you find work there, even if you left one job you were sure to find another. Besides, every woman had to get a good medical work-up before she get a job, and every year as long as she was employed in the home of the white refinery employees. Every morning at seven o'clock sharp the company old bus would be waiting right against the refinery wall over there and the maids would pile into it and it would rattle and roll us up to work up in the Colony. Every evening at five-thirty it would set off down the hill and unload all the women right out there again.

Stepping-Stone Migration

Women arrived as migrant domestics on Aruba through unlikely and circuitous methods. Edna, who was eighty-one years old in 1989 and the oldest woman included in the study, had arrived on Aruba in 1943 by the stepping-stone migration method. She had worked as a maid in her homeland, Grenada. From there she journeyed to Trinidad, where she worked as a maid for seven years. But she knew many brave women setting out for the foreign oil lands of Venezuela, Curaçao, and Aruba. When one of these women (whom she had known in Trinidad) wrote from Aruba offering her a job sponsor, Edna left Trinidad for the unknown.

She recalled how she landed at a dusty little airport near Oranjestad, Aruba, was met and then whisked off to live and work with an Antillean family. To her surprise, the family resided not in the larger town of San Nicolas, but in dusty, almost rural Oranjestad. The family overworked her. Whereas she wanted a job with a family from Holland or the United States, she had landed one with an Antillean civil servant. She imagined that a Dutch or American family would be richer, housed in better quarters, and perhaps living in a neighborhood where she would be in touch with other Caribbean people. At this household, she was a Jane-of-all-trades. Overworked, completely isolated, and underpaid, Edna went for long periods without hearing a word of spoken English.[4]

She quickly learned Papiamento and soon became fluent. She hardly ever visited the bright lights of the English-speaking town, San Nicolas, and could not boast about having been a part of the teeming black, migrant community which resided there. Nor could Oranjestad boast then of the wealth displayed among expatriate families employed by the Lago refinery in San Nicolas.

Women left their sending islands with great hopes of doing well on Aruba. But the refinery's operations encouraged ancilliary occupations that offered chances of social mobility, especially for low-level civil servants, merchants and other enterprising men who had Dutch Rights. The women experienced complete shock when they realized that some families on Aruba dissembled middle-class status, but lacked the substance to pull it off. Veronica found this out, to her chagrin.

She had arrived from Grenada in the mid-1950s, near the end of the Lago refinery's glory days as the economic backbone of the island. Aruba was her second choice; in 1955 she had been all packed to go to England. However, when that arrangement fell through, by sheer coincidence her teenage son met a tourist one day on the streets of St. George's, Grenada's main town. The man seemed very interested in finding a woman to work in his home on Aruba. Veronica's son gladly offered his mother as a likely person. She mused, "Is my son that find the work for me. I say, If he so helpful, I'd better try it."

Veronica set off for Aruba determined to make some money working hard for the family who had sponsored her by proxy. However, it was not to be; she had been in the household only one week when she concluded she could not stay. The tiny house had no living quarters for the new live-in maid, and food was inadequate. At the end of the first month of very hard work, her employers could not come up with the agreed-upon wages. A visit to the immigration authorities soon relieved her of the contract and helped her find excellent employment with a family where she remained for the next twenty-five years.

Aruba is not the apex of some women's migration aspirations, but many women never find a way of fulfilling their most cherished migration goals. Migrant domestics get stuck on Aruba; mired down in the pseudosecurity of regularly received wages, exchanged for grinding, menial, domestic labor. Some women can neither move on, nor manage to go back home. The years of separation from relatives in the sending countries erode connections, take their toll on relationships, and eventually make returning to the sending country an unattractive retirement option for many women.

In 1989 Edna had retired to daily puttering around in the crowded little house she had been renting for the past twenty-five years in the heart of Oranjestad. She had resolved the issue of never returning, as many women must eventually do:

I am an old woman of eighty-one, I have no one back in Grenada now. My mother and sister are both dead. I have a brother who was in Venezuela he must be dead now too. I don't know. I does get my little pension, I have the sisters from the church who look me up and I go to church as I'm able. My boss allow me twenty-five guilders in groceries each month from his family's supermarket. Aruba is home now for me.

Downsizing and Repatriation

Britain had been the colonial power in the women's sending islands when the first cohort set out from their sending societies. These women would have known by heart and often had occasion to sing, "Rule Britannia, Brittania rules the waves." However, migrant domestics in the younger age cohort were introduced to different power rituals marking the withdrawal of the strong British political presence in the Caribbean.

All during the first half of the twentieth century, the United States made steady encroachments into the Caribbean region: first through multinational corporations and their business incursions in agriculture and oil, then through the defense operations created to safeguard U.S. oil interests during World War II. All these established and normalized U.S. economic and political interests, intervention, and hegemony. These macrolevel changes altered and redirected the political allegiances of eastern Caribbean societies, and affected the economic and social lives of the people of the area.

The major western powers—the United States and Great Britain—had done some geopolitical repositioning. The result was the political and economic realignment of the Caribbean. Since the 1930s, Caribbean societies found themselves under the subtle but always relentless influence of the giant to the north. The new relationship destabilized the area and intensified out-migration flows with the United States as target country, the ultimate migration apex. Britain's former colonies in the Caribbean became willing or reluctant political vassals of the United States.

Boldly, the United States put in place political and economic strategies that treated the Caribbean area as a peripheral sector of its economy. In U.S. foreign policy jargon, the Caribbean region (including all the islands, Central America, Mexico, and some countries of South America) was designated "the Caribbean Basin." The Caribbean Basin would be a ready source of labor for U.S. "investments in primary products, import-substitution industries, tourism, and export-oriented manufacturing" (Paget Henry 1985, 100).

New and unstructured social spaces were opening up in job and labor migration opportunities for the ambitious and daring in the region. Caribbean women, in their search for hard cash, filled the spaces quickly by increasing their intraregional and extraregional labor migration and trading activities.

By the mid-1950s, the oil refineries on Aruba and Curaçao had almost completely mechanized their operations and also nearly completed a process of assiduously repatriating its thousands of migrant workers, who until then had helped run its myriad operations. The repatriated eastern Caribbean workers included trained nurses hired to operate the refinery's medical facility. White North American and European expatriates were also repatriated in the general down-sizing of refinery operations and its changeover from personnel to machinery. Any migrant domestics who could not find new employers when their expatriate employers were laid off from the refinery were also repatriated.[5]

Native Arubans were the beneficiaries of these drastic changes. They had received special training locally and abroad in refinery-sponsored educational programs during the late 1940s and early 1950s. The word went out that Arubans had first place in all hirings. From the 1950s until the early 1990s, Caribbean domestics on Aruba expected to have Aruban employers. The unexpressed travel ambitions held by many arriving women of finding a North American or European employer who would open up new emigration horizons to a beloved and trusted domestic had to be put into new perspective.

Labor migration to the enclave altered the marital behavior of migrant workers (Abraham-Van der Mark 1983). Migrants in the enclave defied mating and marital traditions in their sending societies. The marriage rate among eastern Caribbean men in the Dutch countries of the enclave climbed. Many male migrants had been job liaisons for their girl friends. However, migrant labor laws prohibited cohabitation and repatriated any pregnant, unmarried women once the pregnancy was disclosed. This impasse forced men to marry their migrant domestic mates, despite the hardships of finding suitable housing as stipulated by the law.

The marriage rate rose among returning migrants too, for many men married immediately upon returning home. Other eastern Caribbean men immediately hurried off to England to find work, but once there, wrote home to village women proposing marriage and begging them to come and help them pass the loneliness in the new strange country (Rubenstein 1987). Armed with tidy sums of money they had stashed away, men experienced the economic viability that their societies associated with the state of marriage. The new house-building business soared with the migrants' return and from the influx of their foreign-earned money.

Thousands of Caribbean men and women had been exposed to Yankee entrepreneurship and high wages, in the oil enclave and at U.S. Army bases in the Caribbean. These returned labor migrants claimed their raised social status in their sending societies. Some men entered politics, others opened businesses, and families sent their children to the best schools. Most of all, returned labor migrants displayed much restlessness. Luckily for them, Britain needed service workers and laborers. No sooner had many repatriated migrant workers landed in their sending countries than they began to make plans to leave again. Some left to offer their job experiences to newly opened oil refineries in Antigua and the U.S. Virgin Islands (Paget Henry 1981). From the mid-1950s to the early 1960s, however, England became the migration apex for many of these former male and female migrant workers.

The eastern Caribbean nurses who operated the Lago oil refinery medical facilities returned to their sending countries armed with letters of recommendation from their U.S.-based medical supervisors. No sooner were they home than they, too, were on their way again. These ambitious women immediately began finding work opportunities in British and U.S. hospitals. Just as nurses were being welcomed in the United States and England, and male and female service workers were also finding jobs in Britain, Canada and the United States opened up domestic worker schemes. Hospitals and households in the United States and Britain received more applications from young Caribbean women who desired sponsorship by North American employers than there were open positions (Frances Henry 1987).

World War II (1939–1949) had taken a manpower and financial toll on Britain, no longer the most powerful western industrialized nation. And the once-great power seemed willing, if not anxious, to allow its former colonies to go their own ways (Paget Henry 1985, 92). Britain began granting full independence, or a preindependence political status called "statehood," to its former Caribbean colonies; and allowed its longtime wards to retain only tangential connections with their "Mother Country."

The fading colonial power had taken limited but substantive measures to unite the region. Two well-equipped passenger and cargo ships, "federal boats," and two airline companies introduced with British financial help, connected the countries of the now-failed Commonwealth Caribbean Federation; as nothing had ever done before.

Since the extensive repatriations ended in the mid-1950s, each new generation of poor eastern Caribbean men has experienced high levels of unemployment. The most recent large-scale, intra-Caribbean male labor projects to pull in eastern Caribbean men began in the early 1960s. Massive hotel construction projects in the tourist economies of the U.S. and British Virgin Islands lasted for that decade and petered out in the early 1970s. A smaller and more predictable work scheme—the U.S.-sponsored H-2 worker program—has continued into the 1990s. It transported a few thousand men yearly, especially from Barbados and St. Vincent, to the U.S. eastern seaboard for six-month stints in agricultural labor.

Employment opportunities in the United States have tended to be in the service sector, and therefore female-gendered jobs; yet thousands of Caribbean male labor migrants have entered the country since 1965. Many of them used stepping-stone migration from the U.S. Virgin Islands to get into the mainland. Others gained entry through wives or children who found employment, then brought their menfolk under the family reunification clauses of U.S. immigration laws. A significant minority are in the United States as undocumented workers. Promises of fortuitous political change did not affect the poverty of most people's lives. And all during the 1960s, eastern Caribbean women tried myriad ways to obtain cash.

THE SECOND COHORT (1960s–1980s)

> I don't know what happen to the young girls in the islands today. A woman barely thirty years old come here to work and she tell you that she leave five children behind. What's wrong with them they like they out of control![6]

This is part of the musings of one of the retired migrant domestics. In 1989, Ivy, a seventy-year-old woman tried to express what she observed as drastic differences in childbearing behavior between the women of her age cohort, who arrived from the eastern Caribbean in the 1940s and 1950s, and that of the younger women who came later. Since the 1960s, most arriving eastern Caribbean migrant domestics were already mothers of several children. Ivy stated emphatically that the majority of her age cohort who arrived on Aruba during the 1940s and 1950s were childless or, at most, had left only one child behind with relatives. Maybe she was onto something.

In the 1960s, women setting out for Aruba to find work as domestics, did so during heady political times in the eastern Caribbean. Hopeful tales of impending economic prosperity were in the air. Politicians held before the Caribbean people visions of independent territories in which new citizens of postcolonial states would experience political "self-determination" in a federation. Initially, the words of the Caribbean Federation anthem promised a quick end to social and economic hardships experienced through a long, harsh colonial past. When the Federation failed, the same themes re-echoed in each independent country's statehood and national anthems.

The pioneering labor exploits of women to the foreign oil countries during the 1930s–1950s had not gone unnoticed by women of the area. Female labor migrants to the oil lands returned with interesting travel and work stories. These women displayed modest, yet ostentatious, evidence of wealth. They had bettered themselves.

The examples of foreign travel by ordinary women, and their exposure to international influences, stimulated the travel and wage-earning ambitions of other women, helping prepare the way for increased female labor migration to more distant and foreign countries. Eastern Caribbean women have intensified local cash-raising methods, and expanded traditional and established systems of inter-island trade. The island of Trinidad continued to be the main trade and labor migration apex for poor Caribbean women from the smaller southeastern islands.

Female Labor Migration and Trade Routes

The creation of the oil enclave in the southern Caribbean and the intensification of the U.S. military presence during World War II gave impetus to female petty trade. Eastern Caribbean women have not had a long history of large-scale trade as have the "higglers" of Jamaica or the market women of Haiti. However, eastern Caribbean domestics' labor migrations to Aruba must be viewed within the context of the age-old custom in which Caribbean women engage in a multiplicity of occupations to raise cash. Since the 1930s, labor migration treks have taken women on short, or long and circuitous journeys to English-speaking and foreign countries within the region.

During the 1960s, the regional female labor flow followed three major trade and labor migration routes. In the 1940s and 1950s, women who had only been to Trinidad or never traveled intraregionally, began to do so alone, breaking ground as petty entrepreneurs. As they journeyed to new labor and migration points, basic trade patterns developed. The women island-hopped or set out to specific destinations to buy fruit, vegetables, clothing, jewelry, and to trade in general; or if the opportunity arose, to find wage work (Pulsipher 1993; Carnegie 1987; Richardson 1983).

Since the 1960s, Puerto Rico and the Virgin Islands became trade and labor hubs, especially for women from the northeastern Caribbean. Puerto Rico became the shopping destination: a place of giant shopping malls where eastern Caribbean women exchanged their hard-earned U.S. dollars for fashionable goods. This U.S. protectorate became the "little New York" for women from the northeasternmost islands of Antigua, Montserrat, St. Kitts, Nevis, Tortola, Virgin Gorda, St. Maarten, Anguilla, and St. Eustatius.

Women from the island of Dominica became experts in trading agricultural products. Beginning in the 1960s, Dominican women inaugurated an island-hopping trade. They rented spaces on inter-island schooners, and loaded on bags and crates of accumulated produce to trade during the schooners' northeasterly island-hopping routes. Exposed to beatings from the elements, these women would spend a month at a time selling their produce on the northeastern Caribbean islands: Montserrat, Guadeloupe, St. Kitts, Nevis, St. Eustatius, St. Maarten, and the Virgin Islands. St. Maarten became the shopping hub for the Dominican women traders, where they would load on manufactured goods for trading on their homeward journeys.

Women in the southern islands also expanded their labor migration and trading initiatives begun in the 1940s. In the late 1980s, Trinidad, Venezuela, and St. Maarten were important shopping hubs for women in the southern Caribbean. Numbers of women traders from St. Vincent and Grenada made weekly treks on island schooners only to Trinidad, to sell their fruit and vegetables, and returned with manufactured goods to sell in the local markets of their islands.[7] In the 1980s, enterprising women traders from Grenada, St. Vincent, Trinidad, and Barbados frequently flew to Caracas, Venezuela, and the Venezuelan island of Margarita for free-port shopping in manufactured goods.

Once back home on their islands, the women could be seen displaying their goods at roadside kiosks or walking from door to door, plying their wares. These women traders, regularly exposed tiny, isolated islands to the most modern forms of U.S. materialism. Dresses and panty hose, men's suits, jewelry, shoes, makeup kits, cameras, candy bars, and toys became publicly available, on reasonable terms of credit, to increasing numbers of rural people in the eastern Caribbean who had no relatives abroad to remit these modern manufactured goods to them.[8]

In the 1970s, Curaçao and Aruba experienced serious downturns in their economies. Experiments with tourism felt the pinch of each downturn in North American and European economies. Unrest broke out again on several islands (Sunshine 1994; Abraham-Van der Mark 1983). As Caribbean unemployment figures remained high, especially among males, women assumed greater financial responsibility for their children. Intraregional migration remained an important wage-earning source.

Labor migrants have been going back and forth to Aruba and the other oil lands for decades. And although labor ties between the eastern Caribbean and the foreign former oil lands weakened, labor connections remained in the form of a female migrant worker community. In the 1980s, Aruba was still an attractive work destination to poor women.

Structural and Demographic Changes

The very locus of labor migration, from which migrant domestic treks had emanated in the anglophone eastern Caribbean for nearly thirty years, has changed. Young women arriving on Aruba in the 1970s and 1980s increasingly came from the southernmost eastern Caribbean islands, and especially from Grenada and St. Vincent. Perhaps poor women from the more northerly islands have lost their employment liaisons with Aruba, found new wage-producing sources, or are finding migration destinations nearer home, in more economically promising northeastern tourist islands (Olwig 1993).[9]

By the 1970s and 1980s, the immigrant assimilation apparatus (a welcoming immigrant community) was almost nonexistent for eastern Caribbean women. Age had taken its toll on the first cohort, and that community was dwindling fast. Newly arrived women had to depend on acclimatization lessons from their own "green" community of harassed migrant domestics, or members of the two or three black, English-speaking church communities. The congregations of these churches are still comprised of now stern and matronly former domestics.

Aruba's second and younger age cohort of migrant domestics noticed that tourism had replaced oil refining as the chief industry. Each new arrival was sure to meet and converse with retired or employed older domestics who had remained on Aruba. They corroborated important sociohistorical information about the significant social and economic changes that had taken place since they began arriving during the island's economic heyday in the late 1930s to the mid-1950s. The older women delighted in describing the wonders of San Nicolas, the town that welcomed them and the Lago oil refinery.

Since then, San Nicolas, the former oil town, had steadily declined in importance. The oil economy had been superseded by tourism and banking that had pulled resources to the island's capital, Oranjestad, leaving San Nicolas dilapidated and neglected until the late 1980s. Middle-class house-holders who sponsored eastern Caribbean domestics lived in and around the busy island capital. The Colony, exclusive residential housing for expa-triates, and the huge Lago refinery medical complex were no more. The latter had been imploded when the Americans left, and the company houses had been sold at fairly low prices.

Oranjestad was the epitome of foreignness to newly arrived, English-speaking women. Holed up in silence all day as live-in maids, the lively sounds of Papiamento, Spanish, and Dutch swirled around them. How would this continuous stream of women fare on Aruba? Within what seemed like a common thread of poverty, African phenotype, and equally small English-speaking sending islands, could be found various points of differentiation among the migrant domestics.

The younger women in the study differed in family and household composition. Six of the domestics—five childless—and one who had six children, had been living at time of migration in extended families that included both their parents. Ten had come out of extended, female-headed households comprised of one of their parents—their mothers—and their children. Two had been living in consensual cohabitation arrangements at the time of their departure for Aruba, and two were head of their household, residing as the only adult with their children.

Social and political changes in the eastern Caribbean since the 1930s had resulted in some limited stylistic, but not broad-based financially substan-tive forms of social mobility. For example, two women from the older cohort who had glowing reports when they left elementary school, later picked cotton as field hands and worked as domestics to gain some cash prior to leaving for Aruba. Not so with the similarly educated women of the younger age cohort, who refused to work as domestics in their sending islands, even though they could find little else to do. They quickly grasped the opportunity to gain access to consistent wage sources as domestics on Aruba.

Eight women of the second age cohort had finished all their years of elementary school, equivalent to about two years of high school under the British system of education. Of these eight "more educated" women, five had been shop clerks, one had been a seamstress, and two had been nursery school assistants. These women had never worked as maids before arriving on Aruba. It was the women who had not completed elementary school who had supplemented various wage-earning strategies with working almost steadily as maids before arriving on Aruba.

The poor women's response to work calls, as documented in this study of eastern Caribbean migrant domestics, belies the culture of poverty models of the poor, and replicates the findings of other social scientists who have studied poor communities. Rather than rolling around in laziness and debauchery, it always seems that more people make inordinate sacrifices to find wage work than there are job openings to offer them.

THE "CALL"

The "call" is a term that the migrant domestics used to describe what they interpreted as the urgent, serious overture made to them by a prospective employer on Aruba. Sometimes a call came directly from a sponsor or potential employer by telephone or letter. However, it was much more common that a woman on St. Vincent or Grenada, for example, would be contacted by a friend or relative already working on Aruba.

A variety of situations triggered the call. Maybe a maid on Aruba intended to leave her job for a more lucrative one, but realized she could only break her contract if she had a replacement. Or she was planning to move on to North America or return home, but did not want to leave her employer in the lurch. Perhaps she wanted to be able to use her return ticket, which her mistress and the immigration authorities had in their control. Hence, an unexpected or long-awaited call is received by an unemployed woman in the eastern Caribbean. It is an urgent call, asking her to venture forth to Aruba and into wage labor.

For the women who took the offer to become migrant workers, the call was always a heady, mind-boggling event. There was something special about being chosen by name from a throng of other poor women and offered wage work. Women were prepared to forsake everything—children, gardens, elderly mothers, fathers of their children—and respond with all alacrity to a call from an unknown sponsor. For a short period, as she made hurried plans for the journey, a woman's mundane life would be caught up in a flurry of bustling, almost happy excitement. The decision to leave represented a tremendous leap of faith and daring for the women; and although Aruba is within the Caribbean, they felt they were taking off to a very foreign country.

Louise, a mother of six, recounted the day that a letter postmarked Aruba arrived, addressed to her:

> I say to myself, Aruba? I ain't know anybody in Aruba. I open it and read it. It was from my godmother. She left my village to go to St. Maarten, and she did promise to look for something for me. Me never know she had gone on to Aruba! The letter say that she was coming home with plans to go to the States, and she want me to go take her job in Aruba. Ah frighten. What I know about Aruba? What I go do with with all my children?

But she did leave everything and hurry to Aruba.

The job liaison on Aruba often used the fact that a woman had several children or the news that she had recently given birth as the rationale for finding her employment. As one of the women who found a job for a niece who had recently given birth put it: "I say to myself, 'let her get a chance. She ain't doing nothing back home but making children.' "

The knowledge of their own labor insecurity was a probable explanation for some of the women's haste to answer work calls. The prospective sponsors on Aruba, as well as the eastern Caribbean women awaiting their calls, were well aware that migrant domestics were easily replaceable. Because they were seen as cheap labor which could be bought by proxy, and held low social status both in their sending countries and on Aruba, the women were exposed to great personal inconvenience, and sometimes bizarre and unusual call situations.

In June 1989, Marjorie, a woman from rural Grenada, related how she responded to a dramatic call seven months before and had hurried to Aruba. She was called one day to the house of a well-off local woman who owned a small grocery in her neighborhood. The shop owner told her that she had great news—a job awaited her on Aruba. This meant that she should set out almost immediately.

The shop owner told Marjorie that at least a year earlier her phone had been used by a woman employed as a maid on Aruba, who had been vacationing at home on Grenada. This maid called her mistress on Aruba and gave her employer the shop's phone number as the place where she could be contacted. The maid eventually returned to Aruba, but subsequently left there for the United States, thus placing her Aruban mistress in the lurch. In urgent need of a maid, the Aruban mistress made a long-distance call to the number in Grenada, and put in her short-notice request for a maid. According to Marjorie, the shop owner promised to find her a decent, hard-working woman.

Marjorie had exactly seven days to renew her expired passport. Her three teenaged children were away at boarding school in another village, so before setting out, she wrote each of them and apologized for leaving without saying good-bye. She begged them to be good, and said that she was going in order "to make better for them." But seven months of hard work and isolation on Aruba had taken their toll and given her time to assess her situation. In July 1989, Marjorie bemoaned her hurried departure, and wished that she had taken more time to think calmly about the call, and what turned out to be a major change in her life:

> I didn't have time to even tell my children goodbye. The woman sent to say that she want me immediately, and I drop everything and run. My boyfriend is vexed with me still. He says "Well, I don't count for anything. You make your plans. You didn't even have the manners to tell me. The same time you tell me is when you taking up yourself to leave."

Not all calls were genuine. It was a buyer's market that operated in favor of the women's employers. This upper hand in the negotiation process allowed prospective sponsors of domestics to renege on promises with impunity. Sometimes, once women arrived on Aruba, their mistresses immediately changed their minds about wages previously offered, or reworked the terms and conditions outlined and agreed to in letters or phone calls. As irksome as this was, at least the women could argue face-to-face and resolve their differences. However, migrant domestics experienced worse.

Christine, a woman from the island of Dominica, recalled that her mistress pestered her for a long time, requesting that she find a good worker from the eastern Caribbean islands for one of her friends, a wealthy Aruban woman. She requested that such a maid be found from among those women Christine had left behind in her village.

After some reluctance, Christine notified one of her cousins who was working illegally as a maid on one of the U.S. Virgin Islands. The call to legal employment on Aruba was sufficiently attractive to make the woman quit her job on St. Croix and travel back to her home island of Dominica, where she procured the necessary travel and employment documents required by the Aruban immigration authorities. Anxious to set out, the prospective maid offered to purchase the travel ticket herself, as long as she was assured reimbursement upon arrival on Aruba. Agreement reached, Christine notified her mistress about the date of her cousin's arrival:

> Imagine my shock when she say that her friend find somebody who was already here on the island. Why she bother me? My cousin put herself to expense and got all her papers, just waiting for the call. I ask her how I could ever face my cousin again, and if she would pay her expenses? The woman tell me that that is not her business.

But it could have been worse. A prospective sponsor, having brought in a woman, could take an instant dislike to her face or demeanor and decide that she could not employ her after all. Immigration and labor laws concerning migrant labor allowed the sponsor to rescind all arrangements and send the woman back immediately.

Travel Requirements

Women who received urgent calls to Aruba became overwhelmed by pretravel arrangements, and later by the travel experience itself. If the requirements for international travel faze sophisticated travelers, the bureaucratic stipulations utterly confused the migrant domestics. The list of required documents was formidable, but standard (Philipps 1988, 34–37):

1. valid passport,
2. four photographs of good likeness,

3. a certificate of good conduct, not older than one year, issued by the local police,

4. a smallpox vaccination certificate,

5. a medical certificate, issued immediately before commencement of voyage, stating that applicant is not suffering from any contagious disease,

6. a statement issued by competent authorities of her domicile, stating that she is not known to have belonged to or supported political parties or factions which could be considered hostile or opposed to the interests of the government,

7. an official certificate proving that applicant is not married.

Most of the women have no cash flow. However, they must find at least two hundred fifty dollars eastern Caribbean currency (about one hundred U.S. dollars) to procure their travel documents.[10] Besides, on average, an airplane ticket from the eastern Caribbean to Aruba costs about one thousand dollars in eastern Caribbean currency, or about four hundred U.S. dollars. Each migrant domestic must be prepared to make arrangements for the downpayment on a one-way plane ticket back to her sending country as security, in case of the woman's premature departure, or eventual and final exit from Aruba.

Sponsors sensitive to the womens' impoverished plight may speed up the travel arrangements and relieve the women of some financial worries by employing a kind of "go now, pay later plan." The traveling women would simply collect two tickets and some pocket money, via the airline office. An agreement is made between employers and domestics that the cost of travel be deducted from their monthly wages. This magnanimous method is hardly followed, but could simplify matters for all. Some women are directed by their job sponsors to pay their own way to Aruba, on the promise that their arrival fare will be reimbursed. If a woman has the means to comply, she may later discover to her chagrin that she is employed by an unscrupulous mistress, and that reimbursement might not come easily.

Many of the women in this study lived in rural areas, and none had ready means of transportation or communication with employers or travel agencies. Nor did they have any practice in working the bureaucratic system that processed their emigration. Trips to passport and travel offices in the sending islands presented much difficulty, and frustrating bottlenecks awaited the women's travel preparation efforts. Marjorie, the woman who hurriedly left Grenada to take up employment after one week's notice, recounted:

See me like a crazy woman running up and down. My passport expired. I don't have no phone and the woman in Aruba promise to send me the ticket through the airline. I make three trips from my home in the country on the bus, to St. George's.

However, most women have other, more pressing, travel concerns than the procurement of their documents. Who would take care of their dependents? Travel money is a necessity because journeys sometimes involve stopovers or overnighting on at least one neighboring island. How would the women put their hands on ready cash so that some could be left with their children's "other mothers" (Collins 1990)?

By the time a woman made her frantic and tearful rush to the waiting airplane for takeoff to Aruba, she might have incurred what she considered to be serious debt. In reality, though, the debt might constitute no more than a few hundred dollars owed the village shopkeeper or a few relatives in her community. However, this is a huge amount for women without access to regular cash, and whose credit worthiness was so negative that no one dared lend them more than a few dollars.[11]

The women spend most of their first two years' earnings repaying the mountain of migration debt and remitting nearly all the rest of their wages to their dependents. Even when a woman has firm intentions to remain only a year or two on Aruba, her financial situation may force her to stay longer. The women undertook their debt stoically, and viewed it as an investment: albeit an insecure one, totally dependent on each woman's physical and emotional endurance, and the relative stability of the precarious household arrangements she left behind.

The women told of lying in their lonely rooms within their mistress' households during the first months on Aruba. They tried to carefully plot out their lives in Aruba, in ways to make the migration effort and sacrifice worthwhile. Their most pressing personal constraints and concerns involved implementing wise strategies to keep themselves in reasonably good health. They needed foolproof methods to control their reproductive organs so they could fulfill the financial expectations of their dependents. They made personal resolutions to avoid being repatriated before earning some well-needed cash, at least to repay their debts.

The Journey and Arrival

Any well-informed woman about to set off in the 1980s from the eastern Caribbean for work in Aruba knew that there were few through flights to their destination. In 1989 migrant domestics from the islands of Grenada and St. Vincent (who intended to get to Aruba in one day) had to take the first flight of the day by the only airline, LIAT, early on any Thursday morning and change planes in Trinidad for the flight to Aruba. Marjorie, the Grenadian woman already mentioned, was not well-informed when she set off for Aruba on an early Monday morning flight in January 1989. It was a trip that she would never forget.

Flustered and frantic, she boarded the plane in Grenada believing that by late evening she would be safely ensconced in the household of her unknown mistress on Aruba. She was shocked to discover that the connecting flight she boarded in Trinidad went via the island of Curaçao. When she finally arrived on Curaçao at 4 P.M. that day, she was mortified to hear that everyone should disembark. The flight terminated on Curaçao. Overnighting was not part of her planned itinerary.

> I've never been frighten so in all my life. See me at the airport. I can't understand one word anybody saying. Is only papiamento or Dutch. Then they tell me that I have to put up at the airport hotel. All day traveling and I can't get to Aruba. I don't sleep one wink in that hotel. I sit up all night in a chair. Me, let my back touch the bed? What if somebody come in the night and kill me? I don't know the place. Next morning mid-day we land in Aruba.

Arriving migrant domestics are in luck if they hear their names being announced over the public address system as they walk off the airline and into the airport terminal in Oranjestad, Aruba. That means someone is there to meet and take them through the maze of immigration.

Marjorie had traveled to Aruba without all the necessary documents. There had been no time to procure them before setting off from Grenada. Her mistress, according to the maid, was a "powerful woman" on Aruba. She had promised to meet Marjorie at the immigration booth upon her arrival in Aruba, presenting her with a job contract and the return ticket mandated by the immigration authorities. This, according to Marjorie, was one of the few promises that her mistress kept.

The young woman from Dominica, who left her five children and newborn baby to take the job for which her godmother had been liaison, was not as lucky. No one was there to meet her when she arrived on Aruba. Immigration officials at the terminal noticed that she seemed lost, and asked if she was expecting to be met by someone. She replied that she hoped so, and waited some more, but there was no one. After hanging around the customs area, she was beginning to feel conspicuous and frantic, when an officer asked her to show him the address of where she was going, and he called her a taxi.

> I was very frightened. Me sitting in the back of a taxi driving through this strange country. It don't look anything or like anywhere I ever been before— dry and ugly. The taxi driver took me to the address, and it was a good thing that I had some money because my mistress wasn't even there. There was a handy-man and a housemaid there and they were Venezuelan. They could only speak Spanish. When she did come she made some excuse or other and the next day I understand that she plan for me to work at her house and look after her husband's old mother who lived in a house about a half mile away. Soon she dismiss the two Venezuelans and I had to do everything.

The Aruban people are separated from the women not only by ethnic traits such as language, but also by political rights barriers and other formidable privileges and differences created by class and race. Differences in cultural customs became apparent at the women's entry to the country at the Princess Beatrix Airport immigration booths in Oranjestad. Myrtle, a domestic from Grenada who was born to unmarried parents (as most poor eastern Caribbean children are), explained:

> I almost get in trouble as soon as I land on Aruba. The letter from my sponsor was addressed to me in my father's last name because that is the name I does go by because he claimed me. But in my passport my name was different. They put down my mother's last name. So the immigration officer asked me if I was one and the same person because my mistress letter sponsoring me give one name and the passport have another. I had to think fast. I tell him that I was married and had since divorce.[12]

The households in which the migrant domestics lived and worked erected their own class, racial, and cultural barriers. The new mistress greeted Marjorie at the airport and inquired about her travel. Marjorie mistook her inquiry for genuine interest in her comfort; she was mistaken. According to her:

> The woman meet me at the airport. She ask me how I doing? I tell her how tired I feel. I spend time telling the woman about my troubles and how I was two days in travel. The woman listen to me and as we enter the house the woman lead me to the kitchen and put me to work. I tell you, these people heartless.

Her mistress's urgent concern was to establish immediate social distance. The maid, by law a resident in her home but certainly not her social equal, needed to know her place quickly. Hierarchical class and gender relations that foster and maintain inequality constantly overlapped as mistresses and maids tried to negotiate workable relationships. The migrant domestics, in day-to-day interaction, often mistakenly resorted to the logic of a common gender and shared humanity. Their mistresses focused firmly on the domestics' use value, and treated their work as a commodity.

Every householder who sponsored a migrant domestic insisted on secondary relationships between worker and the adult residents of the household. Capitalist, racialized rhetoric that promotes efficiency and productivity in the work place also masks active stratification strategies. The following statement made by a woman from Montserrat, employed by a family in Canada, encapsulates the perennial workers' complaint felt especially in the maid/mistress relationship. She aptly expresses emotions shared by the domestics on Aruba and felt cogently by domestics cross-culturally: "You expect to have a personal relationship with the employer, woman-to-woman, but here they don't want to get close" (Turrittin 1976, 312).

Prospective employers expect their maids to show deference in their demeanors. An unpleasant welcome awaits the migrant women once they arrive at the place of employment, if their body language denies their low-class position. Rollins (1985, 162) recalls how, as a participant/observer, she had posed as a domestic to research firsthand the labor relationship between employer and employee. According to Rollins, she almost lost a job because she forgot to fulfill an important social interaction require-ment—she failed to act the part of a subservient, obsequious maid.

Christine, who prior to migrant labor, had been a cashier at a large supermarket in her island of Dominica, had an experience on Aruba that matched Rollins'. A tall, attractive woman, Christine carried herself with assurance. She was one of the women having at least the equivalent of two years of high school, and the only younger woman in the study to marry (a former migrant worker, twenty years her senior) while working in Aruba.

According to her, she had found her mistress quarrelsome and disagree-able from the first day she arrived, so it did not surprise her when one day, during the first month of her contract, her mistress screamed, "I took one look at your picture (mug shot) and knew that I wouldn't get on with you. I didn't like the look on your face." When she asked her mistress what was wrong with her face, the woman replied that Christine's face in the photo-graph told her that she would be too proud to do servant work.

Mistresses sought to enforce customs of class differences early and repeat-edly in the women's work place so they would quickly know their places of subservience in the household and society. The women soon learned to perform what Rollins described as "playing the part," in order to keep their jobs and be treated kindly by their employers. One of the women in the study, Eliza, complained about another maid, Catherine, whom she felt was quar-relsome and difficult. Catherine had just boasted emphatically that she never had problems with any mistress, and that she found all of them to be easygoing and kind. Once she was out of ear-shot, Eliza commented:

Catherine is a different person when she is in front of her madame. You see how disagreeable and miserable she is with us, I was shocked to see how she was talking in front of her mistress. The other day I passed by her work place. I nearly faint she was "Yes, Madame this, No Madame that." Catherine was all smiles, gentle and a different person. I could not believe it was the same miserable woman I know. If you hear her in that house in front of her mistress. You would have think she nice.

Class and cultural differences between the domestics, their new house-holds, and society manifested themselves interestingly in a change in the women's diets. They bitterly complained about the food employers pro-vided them. In reply to the question, "What are some of the difficulties you met when you first arrived," Marjorie promptly replied:

The food. What they call food I don't call food. They working you hard, hard, and every day is white rice or they invite you to make a sandwich. Look at me, I turn skin and bones in the woman's house. I miss the good Grenadian food. You yourself know the kind of vegetables we eat there. I miss the little pumpkin, and cabbage, and potatoes that I used to plant and get to cook from my own garden.

Inevitably, the women work out an arrangement whereby the employer includes a food subsidy in their monthly wages, so they can purchase food that pleases them. Dissatisfaction over food might seem a petty complaint, but it is the tip of the iceberg of acculturation discomforts that the women experience. The women's complaints hint at genuine loneliness and drastic readjustments which must be overcome if they hope to quickly settle into their new lives as migrant domestics.

Upon arrival in Aruba, the women experience utter isolation, a common and effective technique used by employers to break in the newly arrived women and keep them in their place. Several women found themselves in households where other maids were employed; however, when the other maids were from South America, communication was nearly impossible, and the newly arrived women were plunged into a world of silence. Besides, the live-in foreign domestic and her potential maid community encounter similar constricted circumstances, most of them virtually housebound and working long days. One of the women bemoaned: "Before I came to Aruba I was my own big woman, coming and going as I want. Once I arrive in Aruba, I suddenly become a little girl, having to ask permission to leave the house."

Their inability to speak either the mother tongue, Papiamento, or the other widely spoken languages—Spanish and Dutch—exacerbated the women's isolation. Besides, one of these languages dominated all household conversations. This effective isolation caused women to alternate between behaviors that seemed childlike, subservient, and reticent before employers; and quarrelsome, competitive, and clannish, especially in relations within the migrant domestic community.

The women's inability to understand or communicate with the people around often worked as a practical disadvantage; an everyday impediment to social discourse. Only one woman in the study, Edna, who had lived all her years in Oranjestad when few English-speaking maids lived there, could speak Papiamento fluently. Ann, the retired domestic also from the older cohort who arrived on Aruba already married and conned the authorities, remarried many years later, this time to an elderly Aruban. By the time of her second marriage, she was already middle-aged and had worked on Aruba for twenty-two years, but had not learned Papiamento, and her husband could speak no English. Ann mused wistfully about what must have been a peculiar marital situation:

I might have learn Papiamento, you know. In fact, I know I could have learn it because when I arrived in Aruba, my father had two young children with his wife and that was the only language they could speak. So two of them keep talking it all the time. It used to make me mad, because I feel they were talking about me. It cause so much confusion that my father ban them from talking Papiamento in the house.

Eventually, newly arrived women must venture into the streets and public places. They negotiated their difficulties by deliberately choosing a few "safe" public spaces, such as the immigration office, post office, bank, bargain basement shop, and sometimes an English-speaking church. The women's limited public interaction kept them effectively on the edges of the society.

Their sense of social exclusion, however, came from more than language. Much about the domestics' general appearance clearly disclosed their foreignness to observers. The women's skin color, general phenotype, and simple dress, compounded with their linguistic inadequacies singled them out. They soon discovered too, that the society had no intention of including or welcoming them warmly, no matter how long they remained. Even after women spent most of their working years on the island, became elderly, and retired, they still remained outsiders: "Britishers," "island women," or "the English," as the native Arubans called them.

Chapter 6

Migration and Motherhood

On a warm, moonlit June night in 1989 I began walking the streets of Oranjestad, engaged in my usual activity of scouting for migrant domestics. My eyes searched out the configurations of each approaching female figure to see if they fit those of a migrant maid from the eastern Caribbean. I had chosen the hour carefully, for I discovered that the time between 6:30 and 8:00 P.M. offered the best opportunities to encounter migrant domestics. During this period, *free-signing* women sauntered home from a long day's work or cooled out on the secluded, tree-lined curbs.

I was in luck that evening. In the shadow of Oranjestad's main public library, sitting on the pavement were five black women, all migrant domestics from the eastern Caribbean. It was a typical moonlit-night scene, common to many villages and towns in the eastern Caribbean, but these women were far away from their sending communities. Together the women comprised a tiny part of an international labor category sometimes labeled "foreign temporary guest workers."

Before me that evening was a fairly unusual group. A family, comprised of a forty-five-year-old mother and her two daughters, twenty and twenty-two years old respectively, formed part of the group. The woman explained as her daughters smiled:

I was here in Aruba working hard minding them, and all they doing is making children back home. So I send for them to keep them busy. I don't know how long they will stay. As you see, they still young. I old now, but for now, they here.

The older woman surveyed her daughters with an air of satisfaction. She had managed to beat the immigration authorities on two counts. She legally pulled off family reunification with her daughters (usually debarred migrant workers) and had used her daughters' labor migration as an effective contraception method on their own behalf—she hoped.

Few eastern Caribbean migrant domestics get pregnant or bring pregnancies to term while employed on Aruba. The womens' long work hours as live-in maids, their sense of purpose, Aruba's strict labor migration laws regarding pregnancy, and the social disgrace that a woman's repatriation due to pregnancy caused in sending communities, combined to operate as strong deterrents against the prevalence of pregnancy in the eastern Caribbean maid community on Aruba.[1]

The women before me that evening and others scattered throughout the Dutch Antilles were sacrificing much. The younger women had given up social (and perhaps sexual) lives. Gone for at least a while, if not forever, were the complicated personal and social pleasures of childbearing and rearing, carried out among peers in a community. Migrant domestics exchanged all these for isolation and drudgery in a life among strangers, except for the occasional comradery of other, mostly middle-aged domestics.

Just as their mother had found female kin willing to care for them during their childhood, so had the two younger women found "other mothers" with whom to leave their young children. Their mother had left them with the female kin before either girl was ten years old. For twelve years she was the sole breadwinner and good provider for her distant, extended family/household.

Three women—mother and daughters—were locked into a supportive partnership, geared to provide for young children and other dependent kin in their sending society. This kind of concerted survival effort made by poor wage-earning women on behalf of the family unit or household in many ways exerts a stranglehold on individual workers.[2] The women's combined remittances sent to one or more women—maternal kin—would keep the family/household back in the sending island well-stocked with food, and the children well dressed in ready-to-wear clothes from Aruba. Such families are the envy of their neighborhoods.

EXTENDED FAMILIES AND FEMALE-HEADED HOUSEHOLDS

In the United States, policymakers increasingly associate extended families and female-headed households with deviance, immoral mating behavior, and a high probability of family and household poverty. An increase of more than 20 percent in the incidence of "women-headed homes in the United States, Canada, and northwestern Europe has occurred since the 1960s" (Blumberg 1994, 23).

Nonnuclear family arrangements have always comprised a large sector of family and household arrangements in New World black communities.

It is noteworthy that marriage rates have dropped or remained very low in black communities in the United States and the Caribbean, but so too have overall birthrates, even among teens. There does seem to be a close correlation between low household income and single parenthood, especially when the single parent is a woman.[3]

Disorganization theories of society, and especially the culture of poverty model, have been particularly popular in analyses of eastern Caribbean societies (Dirks 1972; M. G. Smith 1962). Social biological or Darwinist models of society operate within a linear paradigm. In it, institutions such as family supposedly reflect a society's level of "progress" and "development." Social Darwinist models of society declare the innate worth and potential of people and families from core industrialized societies. Societies in which nuclear families predominate therefore fall high on the evolutionary scale.

This model of social development indicts countries such as the Caribbean. Endemic poverty and strange institutions there, supposedly indicate the people's natural inadequacies. The indictment suggests that poor people in poor (or rich) countries have made little progress because of personal and group deficiencies that cause backwardness. Poverty reflects people's inability to contribute and create better conditions of life for themselves. According to this logic, poor women and their nonnuclear family arrangements have been unable to conform to the cultural advances practiced by people in more developed societies.

How then can increases in the incidence of poverty and female-headed families, even among white women and their children in industrialized countries, be explained? A heated debate on the topic continues. Some blame the irresponsibility of parents, and especially of working women. Working mothers, according to one argument, deliberately or inadvertently inculcate nontraditional family values in their children. Working women have tainted entire societies with independent attitudes. These arguments foist many of society's ills on the increasing incidence of woman-headed households.

Some social scientists conclude that variety in family and household forms reflects structural changes in late-twentieth century capitalist societies. The wage economy, arranged to advantage white males, now benefits smaller numbers of them inordinately. Shrinking leftovers of the economic pie get shunted to greater numbers of people (Brower 1992). Some argue that in the face of increased incidence of divorce, separation, widowhood, and high levels of male unemployment, social policy has not made the wage economy provide adequate social and economic safety nets for women and children (Blumberg 1994; Glenn 1994; Mencher and Okongwu 1993).[4]

In many eastern Caribbean islands, the majority of families are poor, and well over 70 percent of children are born into other than nuclear conjugal arrangements. Mother/child ties traditionally strong, remain prominent.

Tradition in Caribbean societies allows women relative freedom to be breadwinners and good providers. Women depend more on other women, and less on men, to assist them in the day-to-day care and overall support of their children (Senior 1991; Reddock 1988).

However, women, mothers of young children, and daughters of aging mothers leave their dependents in extended family arrangements, break off relations with mating partners for indefinite periods, and become labor migrants. This ability of women to travel is held up as proof of Caribbean female independence. Such independence is earned at a great cost.

Origins of the relative female independence have been linked to African cultural survivals (Herskovits 1947). Maybe inherited cultural arrangements evident among New World blacks of the African Diaspora developed during the centuries of enslavement experienced by their African ancestors (Collins 1990; Reddock 1988). Perhaps conditions of recurring economic need in postemancipation Caribbean societies caused people to organize their family relations to address these needs (Senior 1991; Reddock 1988; Edith Clarke 1966).

STRUCTURAL FACTORS

Gender and Wage Work

Cross-cultural research strongly indicates that capitalist incursions into preindustrial economies superimpose new gender and work relations, and cultural values on both the host and sending societies (Fernandez-Kelly and Sassen 1995; Repak 1994; Hansen 1992; Boserup 1970). Institutions experience disruption and rearrangement evidenced especially in families and households that organize daily life in workers' societies.

Experiments and innovations in production usually demand that new models and images of manhood, womanhood, motherhood, parenting, and family emerge to fit the new forms and relations of labor generated by the socioeconomic changes (Fernandez-Kelly and Sassen 1995; Joan Smith, Wallerstein, and Evers 1984; Bernard 1981; Swidler 1986).

All during the twentieth century, a distinct cross-cultural pattern of economic and labor relations emerged, as the industrialized world co-opted the cheap labor of economically peripheral countries such as the Caribbean. Workers from poor countries found low-waged jobs at production sites in urban industrial centers. In the Caribbean and other parts of the world, heightened participation of poor women in the informal economy has been a clear, identifiable response (Tinker 1994).

A work place feature of modern industrial capitalism is its calculated gendered labor demand. Initially, large numbers of males find work at urban and industrial work sites (Boserup 1970). For decades, since the 1850s, Caribbean men chased wage labor wherever they could find it—intraregionally, and later extraregionally. But by the 1950s, anglophone Caribbean women had established themselves as regional labor migrants. They next ventured farther afield, in response to demand for female service workers from urban centers in North America and Britain (Layton-Henry 1992; Foner 1979).

Employers manipulate gender norms. They employ myriad strategies, such as alternating between strictly gender-specific and gender-neutral job expectations. In the eastern Caribbean and North America since the 1960s, semiskilled and unskilled males have experienced high levels of unemployment. However, during this same period, the demand for low-wage female workers increased (Dill 1995, 154; Olwig 1993).

Women maneuver the barriers of gender, too. Poverty and lack of economic opportunities also encourage women to disregard structured gender divisions in the work place, and take on male-type wage work at lower levels of the economy. Increasingly, poor women find low-wage employment as launderers, hospital cleaners and orderlies, and guards of public buildings—the former work domains of poor men—and intersperse these with traditional female-gendered occupations.

It suits employers to have poor men and women in competition for the same jobs. Yet, a wage differential in favor of men remains in the eastern Caribbean work place; even when men and women find employment in identical or similar jobs. Besides, even as large numbers of women find low-wage employment at the lowest levels of the labor bureaucracies, small numbers of males still retain major supervisory positions over them (Berheide and Chow 1994). In boom or bust times so prevalent in unstable Caribbean economies, men always seem more able to get their hands on larger amounts of cash to invest in small businesses, and infiltrate predominantly female trade domains in the informal economy (Abraham-Van der Mark 1983; Senior 1991, 118). This, despite the fact that women are often the main family providers.[5]

Employers maximize their bargaining power through promoting the work ideal of "flexible production" (Fernandez-Kelly and Sassen 1995, 118). The labor market shows much versatility in job categorization, such as: part-time, half-time, homework, self-employment, and contract work. All these, implemented by employers "to maintain industry's competitive edge in domestic and international markets" at the poor workers' expense (Fernandez-Kelly and Sassen 1995, 118).

Race and the Economy

Few English-speaking Caribbean countries enlist the use of foreign guest workers. Caribbean women "looking for work" drift into neighboring islands, ostensibly on vacation and remain illegally; finding wage work "under-the-table." The U.S. Virgin Islands and the Dutch Antilles—two sets of eastern Caribbean islands that have had strong infusions of multinational investments—retain restrictive labor migrant policies. The degree and type of racialization that organizes life in receiving societies determine the rigidity of labor migration policy.

All of the Netherland Antilles inherit and share the same unfree labor migration policies. Since the mid-1970s until now, St. Maarten's tourist economy, stimulated by European and U.S.-based investments, pulled in thousands of workers from the entire Caribbean; particularly from Haiti, the Dominican Republic, and Jamaica. Thousands of others poured in from neighboring islands. However, labor migration laws on predominantly black St. Maarten are less strictly applied than they are on Aruba and Curaçao. Migrant workers on St. Maarten find fairly easy ways to participate and experience inclusion and assimilation in the society and in its informal economy.

Female-Headed Household Formation

A variety of structural factors seem conducive to female-headed household formation (Blumberg 1994, 15). Widespread and recurring unemployment seems to be an important factor. Structural changes in the economy must occur, forcing men to relinquish their traditional first rights to jobs and headship of households. These changes undermine social norms that support strictly gendered divisions of work.

The labor market must sideline its male workers, and businesses shut down or relocate. The weak economy then neutralizes gendered employment. It decategorizes former "male jobs," and offers them to females at lower wages. Once women's composite earnings from all sources compares well with those of the men of their class, the process of female-headed household formation begins (Blumberg 1994, 15).

High male unemployment rates and heavy male out-migration provide reasons and excuses for menfolk and fathers to be transient (Olwig 1993, 160). Poor women who are main wage earners bear children. In time, a gender tradition develops that allows men to be mainly impregnators, but frees them up from assuming roles as stable providers. To fill the support gap opened up by men's unpredictable contributions, wage-earning women incorporate female fictive and blood kin as resources.[6]

GOOD PROVIDERS IN EASTERN CARIBBEAN FAMILIES

The economic and labor history of western capitalism discloses that select groups of males in core industrial societies were recipients of preferential treatment. Economic and labor policies based on gender, class, race, ethnicity, and citizenship stipulations ensured socioeconomic stability for some men and their families (Fernandez-Kelly and Sassen 1995, 116). As social and economic strategies in the core industrial countries molded male citizen workers into good providers, the same economic system excluded other lower-status workers (Miles 1993).

Large numbers of men in industrialized societies experienced deliberate exclusion from economic opportunities. They did not possess the right attributes for good-provider status. Stratified industrialized nation-states used the good-provider status as reward and social marker. Low-status men could not start "legitimate" families. Even when they defied the odds and married, they could not easily confer on their wives and children the appropriate social status meant to engender feelings of well-being and social inclusion allowed legitimate breadwinners and their families.

Core economies create low-status workers in economically peripheral regions. In poor countries, a low-status reserve army of male and female workers wait to respond to the beck and call of the international economy. Even when they become labor migrants in core countries and industrial sites, poor workers' allocation in the labor economy remains firmly ascribed (Glenn 1994; Wong 1994; Satzewich 1991; Bonacich 1972).

The nuclear family model that portrays the breadwinner father at the center of his family's economic survival cannot be applied to the socioeconomic realities of Caribbean life (Safa 1995). Economic policies that developed "the family wage" around the dependable male wage earner, good-providing husband/father, and citizen are not part of Caribbean family and economic history. The nuclear conjugal family never gained widespread popularity as practice for the majority of people in eastern Caribbean societies. Eastern Caribbean men have never been able to consistently "accumulate the income, benefits, or property necessary to facilitate 'stable,' economically viable households with dependent subordinate wives" (Reddock 1988, 131). Despite its long history and extensive connections with the Caribbean, the industrialized world effectively excluded the majority of Caribbean men from the respect, protection, and long-term rewards of the capitalist economic system.[7]

Women as Good Providers

Migrant workers and their families evoke pity when compared with good providers: admirable, stable married men with disciplined and tractable lives (Bernard 1981, 134; Swidler 1986). The stereotypical image of migrant workers remains as shiftless men who voluntarily drop out of normal society; migrant workers, rootless laborers of the world, who cannot or will not commit to normal life in society. From the traditional nuclear family perspective, labor migration continues to be viewed as desertion, a form of voluntary exile, a lack of social commitment, and the occupation of social misfits (Bernard 1981; Swidler 1986).

Intermittent wage labor performed under harsh conditions in foreign countries, offered the only job opportunities to ambitious Caribbean people. Migrant labor was the main method through which emancipated Caribbean men and their descendants purchased land and businesses and gained some measure of respectability. For many Caribbean men, migrant labor became a relatively lucrative wage-labor category in which they (and later women) accumulated cash. This form of labor offered a socioeconomic niche through which many men, and now women, wormed their way into the landed peasantry of their sending societies.

Wage earning, the working man's master status, has societal approval. Social customs generally allowed male good providers to pursue occupations minus the encumbrance of family. Men have been given freedom to claim both the public sphere of work and leisure. Would the same obtain for female migrant worker good providers? "The good provider was a 'family man.' He set a good table, provided a decent home, paid the mortgage, bought the shoes, and kept the children warmly clothed" (Bernard 1981, 129).

Bernard's male good provider was no homebody. In the image of Parson's instrumental husband/father (Parsons 1955), Bernard's good provider launched headlong into the nitty-gritty of work away from the problems and comforts of home. His hard work undergirded the household with financial stability and security.

What did it mean for women, thrust out into the wage-earning market to assume the attributes of migrant worker? What about women's ascribed traditional gender attributes as nurturers, and maternal expressive caregivers?

Female eastern Caribbean labor migrants performed an almost identical role as that of the good provider. The migrant domestic in foreign countries seriously assumed the "instrumental" persona of worker, in just as concerted and deliberate ways as her celebrated male good provider ideological counterpart. Female labor migrants took over what was essentially a male wage-worker status, superseded and augmented it, albeit in the informal economy. Both Parsons (1955) and Bernard (1981) include a wife/mother, good housekeeper in the family arrangement. She freed up the husband/father so he could set out daily and involve himself in instrumental activities, while she undertook the nurturing and service activities of the household. Poor eastern Caribbean domestics engaged in wage labor in order to provide for their households, but many of them were mothers of dependent children. Labor migration finally fulfilled poor women's long-held dreams of gaining access to consistent wages. As instrumental wage earners, the women negotiated between the harsh work lives in foreign environments and their households back in the sending societies. The women became very efficient regular remitters of hard cash and manufactured goods. They streamlined and expanded their instrumental roles as chief providers for their families. Throughout the twentieth century, poor women left their communities and combed neighboring and foreign Caribbean islands alone, in search of wage labor.

Labor migration laws showed a preference for women at the peak of their childbearing years. Thus, mothers of young children, the eldest daughters, or the most capable female wage earners in households often became labor migrants. But social services and economic opportunity in the islands have not kept up with the needs and rising expectations of the very youthful and elderly populations created by female labor migrations. Female Caribbean labor migrants needed help to run their households once setting off on their wage-earning treks, so they left their nurturing and care taking roles in the care of other women.

New forms of mothering had to be practiced, and new concepts of the good mother developed so that women could be allowed to leave. Female labor migration reworked and extended existing arrangements and relations in female-headed families. The malleable eastern Caribbean family form makes labor migration of family members possible.

A long tradition of child-minding behavior in eastern Caribbean societies shouldered the shock caused by women departing from their young children. Women formed social and economic ties with other women. Through these blood and fictive female kin, migrant women extended their family relations and household arrangements.

Childhood is a short-lived period in poor Caribbean families. Because many poor women make their living in the informal economy, various kin and non-kin assume hands-on care for infants. Young children, and especially the youngest in poor Caribbean households, become the center of attention. The infant is usually breast-fed for at least a few months, and is constantly held and cuddled by everyone in its household.

Not much importance is given to infant bonding with biological parents. Children raised in a neolocal residence interact with members of that household and family. Children raised in poor households are cared for and interact with as many or few women and others incorporated into cooperative care giving. Once children are past infancy, practical instrumental activities replace pampered attempts at parent/child bonding and exaggerated expressive behaviors, such as hugging, touching, and overt shows of emotion in child nurturing, which are so common in middle-class families.[8] Therefore, a migrant domestic's mothering care and concern could be written, spoken over the phone, rehearsed, and performed by other mothers.

Mothering and Work

The domestics became very focused on work productivity. In fact, women vowed privately to impress employers through hard work. They put their lives, mates, social persons, and public individuals on hold, undertaking selfless activities as workers and wage earners intent on "making life better," especially for their dependents. In order to fulfill this mission, the women denied themselves normal, everyday comforts. They regularly remitted barrels of food and clothing, and most of their hard-earned wages to eastern Caribbean households.[9]

Eliza was the picture of thrift as she recounted her shrewd saving methods:

I begin saving after I was here only five months. The extra twenty guilders [$12 U.S.] the mistress give me as Christmas gift, I opened a savings account with that. I begin working for sixty guilders [$42 U.S.] per month. As I get the money I would bank ten. I keep twenty, and send home the rest for the children, so they could bank a little and spend the rest.

Back in the sending countries, families of migrant workers display consumer goods and other material signs of wealth that belie the hardships experienced by the women who work tirelessly to get them. For example, after saving for fifteen years, Eliza had a brand new house built for her children back in St. Vincent.

The women engaged in small-scale, dyadic cooperative activities in order to provide for dependents. Rubenstein (1987, 161) notes that few people engage in large-scale cooperative economic ventures. According to him, people aware of their susceptibility to the vagaries of luck and chance, prefer to put faith in ad hoc work efforts. People prefer to engage in individualist, even competitive, economic strategies, not joint endeavors.

Images of women engaged in small-scale, seemingly noneconomic activities mask the intricacies of cooperation and coordination used by the migrant women to mobilize scarce resources. True, their entire existence is precarious; a veritable house of cards that must be handled carefully and boldly at the same time. Take the case of two women, fictive kin who shared an apartment in downtown Oranjestad, and cooperated precisely around the care of the younger woman's toddler daughter. The younger woman was constrained by child-care responsibilities to take only day work in the immediate neighborhood, while the older woman took care of the toddler. Promptly at 5:00 P.M. daily, the mother returned to relieve the older woman of her child-care duties so she could attend to church activities. It worked.

This is the level of barter, cooperation and exchange that permeates female family and household relations in the eastern Caribbean. Economic activities in the informal economy of their sending societies depended on face-to-face relations. Finely tuned, businesslike cooperation between two or more women predominated too, in their long-distance household strategizing. Daily, in poor eastern Caribbean families, one or more wage earners engage in the instrumental role while other mothers complement the wage earners' activities. Distance complicated the arrangement for migrant domestics, but did not cancel out the possibilities for parenting. Remittances, letters, phone calls, and kin liaisons made up for hands-on nurturing activities.

Simulating Motherhood

Aruba's labor and immigration laws do not allow migrant workers to practice family reunification, but many women left infants and very young children behind when they found jobs there. The women divulged intimations of their nurturing abilities and perhaps private longings for their own children in tales about the children entrusted to their care in their places of employment.[10] They were particularly fond of children they helped raise from infancy and a common saying was, "That one born in my hand," meaning, "I nurtured that one from birth." Ann, who illegally had two babies in quick succession, had to dispense of each baby almost immediately after birth. She recounted a touching incident involving an infant when she went seeking employment.

Determined to find employment, she set out for the prestigious Colony in the mid-1940s, responding to a job advertisement. Families who requested domestics often had need of child-care givers. The mistress of the house was out that morning when Ann knocked at the door. According to her, the mistress's husband came to the door clutching a baby of a few months in his arms. He was followed by two older children:

> I will never forget how before he could even start to interview me I took the baby's little bare foot and kiss it. Then I stretched out my arms and said, Come, give me a kiss." The child came straight to me. The man say, "The job is yours."

During the summer of 1989, Eliza, the woman who had saved for fifteen years and built a house for her children, was very unhappy in her new employment. She had taken a job with a couple who had an eighteen-month-old daughter with physical disabilities. Eliza complained about the untidiness of the house, the fact that the big pet dogs were allowed to wreck the house daily, and that no one but herself ever held the baby. After having heard the tales of woe on several occasions, I broached the question, "Eliza, why don't you leave and find another job?" She gave me a sickly smile as her reply came without hesitation: "The therapist say that the child is much improved since I start taking care of her, and doing the exercises with her. How I go leave now? Is my child that."

Bernice had been with the same family for twelve of the fifteen years since her arrival on Aruba. She was perhaps the highest paid of all the women in the study, making about 550 guilder or $320 U.S. per month. The mother in the family lived for most of the year in the United States to be near the older girl and boy who went to prestigious schools in Massachusetts.[11] Bernice was housekeeper/mother in the family and everyone knew it. She began working for them when the third child was an infant, and she considered this boy (who was twelve years old in 1989) to be her child.

Bernice constantly conversed with the boy in English, the only language she spoke and understood. The designated languages in the household were Papiamento and Dutch, and the boy's parents had admonished her often about hindering the boy's facility in these languages. But he was her companion, her chief interpreter and liaison with the outside foreign world. He had taught her the little Papiamento and Spanish she knew. In 1989 she was already beginning to grieve about his impending departure to boarding school in the United States: "What I go do when my boy leave? I may be out of a job because my boss will be able to manage somehow on his own. One thing I know is that old age is very lonely in Aruba."

I walked across Oranjestad with another maid, Evadne, in order to make funeral plans for one of the domestics who had died. My companion was delighted to recount with me the sights and cities of the northeastern United States. She was aware that I knew Boston particularly well. She had worked for eighteen years with the same wealthy family on Aruba, and had helped to raise their children. The youngest daughter, Melissa, had gone to school in the United States and had a Boston wedding:

> Melissa write me to say that I had to come to she wedding. She send me the ticket, and she call me on the phone to beg me to come for the wedding. She say that my face there that day would make her very happy. So I went, and I had a great time.

MATING, MOTHERING, AND POOR FAMILIES IN THE EASTERN CARIBBEAN

Mating behavior and family/household arrangements practiced in poor eastern Caribbean societies have fascinated and confused social scientists for a long time. Some of the confusion arises from the fact that there are obvious patterns in the Caribbean mating relations and family arrangements, yet there is much variety and instability of form and structure within these poor family and household patterns (Dirks 1972; M. G. Smith 1962). A team of researchers doing a survey of family/households in Grenada, for example, displayed obvious frustration in its efforts at analysis of families and households after follow-up visits: "There can be cases where it is difficult to define which is the same family as before or if there is one at all" (Burpee, Morgan and Dragon 1986, 2).

Marriage and Mating

Although Caribbean people are socialized into social and religious values regarding the importance of marriage, not more than half of the adult population of eastern Caribbean societies ever marries. And those who marry usually do so between age thirty and middle age, after many are already parents. Those who marry before starting families and middle age are usually members of the small, well-off middle-class groups (Aymer, forthcoming).

A three-option mating pattern is clearly discernable in eastern Caribbean society (M. G. Smith 1962). Marriage is the legally recognized form in which children's paternity is officially recognized and inheritance rights are outlined in the law. Marriage is expected of members of the small local middle-class. Among this particular socioeconomic grouping, there is close adherence to much the same patterns of engagement and marriage before age thirty that are practiced by the large majority who marry in most western industrialized countries.[12] For West Africans and their descendants, enslaved by Europeans and put to work on estates and plantations in the Caribbean from the seventeenth to the nineteenth century, marriage was clearly the right and privilege of the master class only (Reddock 1988, 121). At the end of the twentieth century, for the eastern Caribbean lower class, marriage still holds connotations of socio-economic stability, commitment to the status quo, intimations of up-pityness, and of Christian religiosity.[13]

Two parallel normative systems seem to guide mating in eastern Caribbean society (R. T. Smith 1987). Social class, a person's actual access to wealth and social status, assumes much importance. The society looks keenly for signs of ambitious behavior, and judges whether people "have ambition," or "bad mind," as stated in local parlance. Marriage is used as an indicator of ambition; remaining a significant but unclear social marker that suggests actual or attainable socioeconomic class or the presumptuous ambitions of eastern Caribbean couples. At the same time, another norma-tive standard pervades poor societies. The social facts reveal widespread practice of extraresidential mating and cohabitation relationships. Eastern Caribbean societies do not exert strong social pressures such as condemna-tion or ostracism on poor couples who do not marry early.

M. G. Smith (1962) postulated a pluralist model of eastern Caribbean society, presenting evidence of three clearly separate societies living side by side. Each society closely correlated with socioeconomics and phenotype. According to Smith, each society followed distinct normative systems. Others have argued that in complex stratified societies, social arrange-ments—such as mating and marriage—may be normative without being ideal (Rubenstein 1987, 265–66), and institutionalized without being legal-ized (Aymer 1997).

Marriage is not viewed by the lower class as a practical, problem-solving activity that helps mitigate socioeconomic problems. Poor people, and especially poor mothers who have, as they put it, "sucked salt to raise their children," do not encourage their male or female children to marry early (Stack 1974; Moses 1977). Ann, who had been married upon entry to Aruba in 1945 and defied the authorities by refusing to return to her husband in Nevis, became pregnant and bore a son a year after her arrival. She had used various strategies to take care of her son under very harsh conditions. Ann disapproved of his marriage:

> He could have wait to marry. He don't consult me. He don't ask me a question. Me and he go through too much hard time together for him to treat me so. When we had our hard time there was no wife or nobody else. I have nothing against the wife, but I keeping to myself. I won't ever visit them in Holland, not me; because they know that I didn't approve of the wedding.

In fact, the culture encourages men to financially support their mothers, and a son's marriage is often seen as a selfish act of ingratitude toward the mother who has sacrificed much for her children.

Poor people in Caribbean communities depend on malleable norms that operate within some fairly firm social and ideological guidelines to direct their lives, and especially their family arrangements. In lower-class eastern Caribbean culture, childbearing is a social obligation (Senior 1991, 66); marriage is a social practice. Though often mutually exclusive, the two may sometimes coalesce.

Men, the fathers of the young women's children, are considered to be by nature irresponsible and undependable in most matters, but especially in consistently providing for their offspring. Caribbean society has long historical proof that women's hopes of their menfolk's consistent economic self-sufficiency may be wasted. Male employment, often precarious and short-lived, is seen as being regulated by factors outside of women's control. So females are taught by example and precept that smart women must always be on guard against men's careless insensitivity or unforeseen bad luck. Boys and men should not be given complete control in crucial matters concerning the upkeep of the household.

The recurring, predictably high levels of male unemployment which prevent men from being dependable economic contributors to their families and households, has also worked to safeguard poor men from being pestered by "unreasonable" female expectations and requests of early marriage. Mothers of dependent children know they must subsist on their own smarts.

Extraresidential Mating and Cohabitation

For Caribbean women, childbearing is a rite of passage, a sign of maturity, a tentative step into the world of women. Poor women feel they have a right and duty "to make their children while they are still young." Older women speak to childless younger women, prefacing sentences with "When you make your children," without mention or thought of marriage as part of the child-making equation. The large majority of Caribbean populations begin mating in the mid- to late teens with extraresidential activities. This resembles the dating customs of North Americans that have become widespread, especially in the United States since the 1960s. In the eastern Caribbean, age (especially that of the female partner) is one of several factors that tends to determine the openness of coupling. The older the mating couple, the less likely sexual extraresidential encounters are to be furtive and clandestine. However, no matter the age of the mating pair, pregnancy is an anticipated outcome of sexual relations (Aymer, forthcoming).

New births strain the women's scarce resources and act as rude awakenings that force women to become economically independent of men (Gussler 1980). Young mothers usually lean heavily on an older woman or women in the family/household. The trade-off for the older women is that a new mother, having now entered full adulthood by giving birth, is expected to undertake more responsibility in the household. Often completely under the thumb of the older women, the young mother takes on adult chores of child care, doing loads of laundry, cooking, and the full variety of tedious service chores and skills performed by women. She is constantly reminded that she "turn woman now," or, in other words, through her own volition she has entered the world of adult women.

The older women in families deliberately intensify efforts at teaching young mothers strictly female-gendered skills. These have a survival payoff; they enable younger women to cooperate with other women at "turning their hands" to earn small amounts of cash in the underground economy. Female-gendered skills prepare young women to become capable service workers, ready to set off as labor migrants. Consensual cohabitation, (M. G. Smith 1962) locally called "friending" or "keeping" is a mating relationship that may simulate marriage. Long-term cohabitation, in which couples raise children, achieve economic stability, and gain the respect of their community, has been well documented (R. T. Smith 1987; M. G. Smith 1962). Sometimes, a middle-class married man may have both a nuclear family household and also keep another household in which the mating relationship, complete with children, is one of consensual cohabitation.

Cohabitation may be a sign of a couple's relative socioeconomic stability; an indicator that at least one of the partners is able to provide the basics, such as housing (Senior 1991; Rubenstein 1987). But consensual cohabitation can be a short-lived, unstable mating arrangement too. Social censure effectively prevents women from entering extraresidential cohabitation arrangements, frequently or indiscreetly. However, very poor women may use frequent changes of partners as a strategy for finding a dependable man to help them raise children born in earlier relationships (R. T. Smith 1987).[14]

A poor woman who begins to cohabit or gets married, makes a fairly strong and maybe foolhardy statement about a significant shift in her resource base. In choosing to move in with a man, either through marriage or cohabitation, a woman may unwisely signal rejection of her former, largely female, resource pool and network. She has "hedged her bets" and placed them all on one person; the man with whom she has chosen to live.

The only woman from the younger cohort of migrant domestics who had found a husband on Aruba married a domineering divorced man, twenty years her senior. The other migrant domestics, especially the younger maids, treated her and her unusual status with distance and coldness, mixed with respect and some jealousy. Once she married and moved into her husband's large house just outside Oranjestad, she could no longer fraternize with the other women. She missed their company and the comradery she had known in the loosely knit maid community. She complained:

I made a big mistake to marry him. Everybody think that I have this big house but they don't know that I like a jumbie [ghost] or prisoner in it. I can't bring my friends in it because it's his house and he says that he don't want any gossiping maids in it. But he brings his women friends to visit and I can say nothing about it.

She continued working as a maid because it gave her some financial independence. Her fellow domestics whispered about her being battered, and her husband's alleged infidelity. They giggled over the fact that she was having to act the part of a married woman, and had to give up much personal freedom in exchange. No doubt the women envied their former friend's increased financial stability and secure resident status, which were no small gains.

One of these women, who now viewed her from a distance, vowed never to be as foolish as her married friend. According to this woman, she had given birth to five beautiful daughters on St. Vincent, and left them with her mother there ten years before, so she could work on Aruba. In 1989 this woman, Myra, was in an explosive and complex relationship with a black Aruban man of eastern Caribbean parentage. According to her, this man was several years younger than she was, and his parents resented their relationship. She asked rhetorically,

What they 'fraid of? I don't want to marry their son. I don't want to marry nobody. I never live in a house with a man in charge yet. My mother had me and my brother and I never see any man in the house. My mother never marry and I going be just like she.

MIGRANT DOMESTICS AND CHILDBEARING

Migrant eastern Caribbean women on Aruba grew up in poor families and in societies where the majority of women had their first children in their late teens. Unlike their counterparts in the United States (Garfinkel and McLanahan 1986, 85) and other industrialized countries (Spensky 1992; Trost 1975), unmarried teenaged (and older) Caribbean mothers generally have no publicly provided resources or social programs to help them set up house and live on their own as single mothers and heads of households.[15] Louise from Dominica had a babe in arms, her fifth child, when she received the call to work on Aruba. She mused:

I would be making children still if I was back home in Dominica. Making children is what women do. I didn't know anything about contraceptives then, and even if I did know, I wouldn't have money to buy it, and I would have been ashamed to go and ask for it in the drug store. Here, you have your money, you buy what you want and nobody know you.

Swidler (1986) analyzes the dynamics of intimate heterosexual relations in the United States by interpreting old and current love myths which she attests support mating and marriage behavior. According to her, in the old love myth that formerly guided courtship and marriage in the United States (white middle-class) men committed to social life. They took on the stability of consistent wage labor, and later marriage and family life, after eventually reining in their wild sexual rovings and penchant for exhilarating masculine adventure. How does this imagery of the decent family man and citizen compare with that of the breadwinner, female migrant worker?

Women like Louise had given up the titillations of mating, its intense rivalries, and the uncertainties of childbearing in a familiar community. They exchanged them for the boring and lonely, but stable regimen of wage labor as good providers on Aruba. In the old love myth, steady work for the breadwinner husband marked the beginnings of stable family life and the comforts of home. Steady employment for many eastern Caribbean women meant exile from home. In fact, the lives of migrant domestics on Aruba simulated (maybe caricatured) those of independent, focused, child-free, career women of the industrialized world. Both kinds of female workers followed wage earning wherever it took them, leaving community and family connections behind.[16]

Attempts by employers and the state to control the women's lives makes them vulnerable and conspicuous sexual targets. Every migrant woman knows that getting pregnant while on contract is breaking the law. The women's health insurance gives them reasonably good access to medical care and contraceptive devices, which they utilize. Although abortions were officially illegal, domestics on Aruba did have abortions safely performed by doctors, at the prohibitive cost of a woman's entire monthly wage. Eighteen of the twenty-six women in the study had hysterectomies—the ultimate contraceptive.[17]

Any woman who became pregnant had to be very careful about her enemies in the maid community. Such pregnant women were prime targets for secret reports made to the immigration office by other maids. Immediate medical examinations of the reported women thus ensued. If found pregnant, they were deported almost immediately (Philipps 1988).

Women who were already mothers upon arrival to Aruba usually had no more children while on contract. Young, childless migrant domestics who intended to bear children experienced much conflict between leaving jobs on Aruba to follow the maternal mandate, or remaining in assured employment with economic independence but relative sexual isolation. In fact, migrant domestics left Aruba precisely because they hoped to have children, and feared that their biological clocks might run out. Three of the women in the older age cohort chose to remain. They never married and, in fact, had hysterectomies while still in their thirties. They knew that the choice to remain longer on Aruba automatically cancelled out their childbearing chances. A few brave or careless women did find tiny niches in which to defy the law, become pregnant and bear children while on contract.

Anytime our discussions centered on pregnancy and mothering, the migrant domestics in Oranjestad recounted a sad tale with great solemnity. According to the tale, a plump, young migrant domestic got pregnant while on the job as a live-in maid in Oranjestad. The young woman told no one about the pregnancy and gave birth one night in her room. She placed the baby in one of the drawers of her dressing table.

The cries of the newborn infant finally drew the mistress's attention. The immigration authorities were contacted, but because the child was already born, the mother and child escaped deportation. Besides, the child's father, a young man who had Dutch Rights, lived with his parents in San Nicolas. According to the women, the story had a happy ending in that the man had his parents take the baby. The woman was put on probation and her live-in time, if she remained on Aruba, was extended by two extra years.

Some domestics married on Aruba and bore children while employed. These wage-earning foreign domestics and mothers experienced unique child care problems. Two of the women from the older cohort bore children on Aruba. One of them married her migrant-worker boyfriend, and as husband and wife they continued to live precariously on Aruba. Ivy, the same woman who found work in the 1940s for her boyfriend on the pretext that he was her "brother," became pregnant sometime after his arrival on Aruba. She managed to hide the pregnancy and gave birth before the immigration authorities discovered her condition. When she got pregnant with a second child, her boyfriend married her.

She told of enlisting Aruban women who could not understand her English, nor she their Papiamento, to baby-sit her two small children. She would rush off at dawn to her job as a maid in the Colony, and try to get back before dark. She told how she would drag herself home to two children and a husband. From her long days as a maid, she tried to find an opening for "half-day work." According to her, she took a succession of half-day jobs in the hope that she would be released early and have some energy left to take care of her babies. However, she discovered to her chagrin that half-day employment was a misnomer that hid the intent of mistresses for a full-day's work at half-day's pay. In 1989 she divulged how, back then, she often envied the freedom of unmarried maids who did not have to go home from tedious jobs to begin a second shift of labor.

According to the law, the family's residence in the host country rested on the husband/father's employment. Migrant workers could remain only if employed, and if he could not find work (even after the immigration authorities' two-week grace period), he had to leave. It mattered little that the migrant worker's wife had a job.

Ivy's husband worked with contractors. The absence of stable employment put the entire family in constant fear of imminent deportation every time a job ended. Ivy stated matter-of-factly that she and her husband always had five packed suitcases under their beds, so they could move swiftly if handed repatriation papers.

In the late 1950s, her children were getting near to high school age, forcing their worried parents to make decisions about their education. The perennial questions that face foreign labor migrants in host states such as the United States, Germany, Britain, or France, confronted this family. What were the rights to education of children born to foreign guest workers? How long would generous labor and immigration law allow the father to find employment? What kind of education would be best for the children of migrant workers? The real possibility existed that after being tutored in Dutch and having been exposed to Dutch-styled pedagogy, parents would be repatriated to their British island colony.

The decision was made. Ivy would return to Montserrat with the children, then ages nine and eleven. She was to try being the traditional housewife, while her husband would become the sole breadwinner and remit the family's financial and material allowances to Montserrat. She reported how with great sadness they bid the husband/father good-bye and traveled home to Montserrat, to try to give her children an "English education." It did not work. After nine months, in Ivy's words:

> Nothing was working out. I thought the man would be able to support us with his job. But the money he send was not enough. I could find nothing to do in Montserrat. I decide to go back to Aruba with my daughter and leave the boy behind. He was admitted to the grammar school in the town. I ask my mother to leave her house in the country and come to stay with the boy and keep house for him. Well, the arrangement last only a short time. My old mother miss her house in the country. So she leave him and go back home to her house.

The couple's daughter returned to Aruba with her mother, and regretfully, according to Ivy, was educated in the Dutch system. She never mastered the various languages spoken on Aruba.

Ann, the woman who arrived on Aruba already married but childless, had been intent on remaining there as a migrant domestic. However, a year after her arrival on Aruba she became pregnant. She concealed the birth of her son as long as she could; however, when he was still a toddler and she became pregnant again, she sent him back home to her sister in Nevis.

The arrangement Ann made for the care of her young son lasted for several years, then fell through, and her son was returned to her.

> When my sister send to say she can't look after him anymore, I had to take my chances and bring him back here, and he lived with me. He went to high school and everything. He get married and all. We had some hard times together.

The only woman in the study's younger age cohort who became pregnant on Aruba and brought the pregnancy to term was from Grenada. She had left a seven-year-old daughter in Grenada with her mother, and traveled to Aruba to find work. She had always wanted to find a way to have at least one more child while employed on Aruba, but she could only do so legally if the man was Aruban or had Dutch Rights and married her.

She had been there for six years when she became pregnant in 1988 by a black Aruban. Although threatened with deportation she and the father of her unborn child cleverly informed the immigration authorities of their intention to marry; he did not keep his promise. Although he was still interested in the child's welfare, nearly two years after the child's birth, in 1989, they continued an extraresidential mating relationship. Life was inordinately difficult for this young mother. Her status as black, English-speaking, migrant domestic in Oranjestad (the center of mestizo native Aruba) isolated her, yet made her conspicuous. She lacked a supportive community, but had managed to enlist the aid of a retired former maid. Both women hailed from the same island and set up house together.

EXTENDED FAMILY ARRANGEMENTS

Experience has taught poor Caribbean people about harsh socioeconomic conditions and they have developed coping strategies to help manage pervasive and persistent impoverishment. Some of these are routinized responses to predictable forms of impoverishment (Liebow 1967). Others are innovative, ad hoc methods used to address new situations. The extended family, as malleable in meaning as the arrangements it defines, includes non-parents and immediate family members in child-care, nurturing and support services. A family may form without a resident heterosexual couple being its nucleus. In fact, one woman and her children or two generations of women and children may form the nucleus of the family.

The form of the family and household arrangements supported by migrant domestics varies over time. The domestics' extended families take form from the resource base each woman had available upon her departure. The household arrangements women put together from a distance reflect changes of the microlevel order; changes in the lives of family members and in the domestics' work situations. Macrolevel sociopolitical and economic changes in both the sending and host societies also determined what happened to the women's household and family arrangements.

Extended family arrangements in their broadest definitions mean arrangements that include blood and fictive kin that cooperate in household activities, nurturing, and child care, as well as the pooling of wages among several adult residents who live together and share limited living quarters. The blurring of household and family demarcations marks the arrangement. For example, food cooked each day in one residence might be shared with others—fictive kin who are "as family," but live several streets away.

The incorporation of neighbors and friends into family activities is common in extended families.

Who Minds the Children?

There is a mythical, maternal figure who is central to models of poor black extended families, both in the Caribbean and the United States. She is sometimes presented as an elderly, caring woman who lives in the same dwelling as the family she cares for, or somewhere in the immediate neighborhood. For young women stressed out over the care of young children, she is a maternal resource and lovingly beckons, "Girl, bring a child for me to mind. Meh frock open wide" (St. Victor 1986, 86). This maternal figure may or may not have had any of her own biological children, but she is well known in black mythology for having taken care of and nurtured countless children.

Care giving and nurturing are female-gendered activities inculcated into young girls. This mythical other mother is the keeper of the culture at its most moral and altruistic. Her teasings about the importance of motherhood are strongly tinged with seriousness as she encourages young women to "make their children while they still young."

She operates outside of and despite destructive structural factors that weaken family arrangements. The absence of this mother figure is deeply regretted in a sad tale told by St. Victor (1986), in which a distraught woman takes her children to the marketplace in Trinidad and tries to sell them. The account does not cite social structural deficiencies, the state's obligations to poor mothers, or the absence of the children's father. But it does search in vain for the mythical other mother who, in the family mythology, ought to have emerged from the unfortunate mother's extended family:

> For some reason, this woman's support system had broken down. There was no relative to extend a helping hand: no one to defray the tension of coping with a difficult situation. . . . Ordinarily, a female relative (or close friend) would have intervened at a much earlier stage to relieve the tension of caring for the children. (St. Victor 1986, 85).

I could find no consistent pattern of typical "other mothers" among the care givers left in charge of the migrant women's children, except that the care-giving other mother was most likely to be a maternal kin member: mother's mother, sister, or aunt (Soto 1987).

Every woman in the study who had left young children behind was asked the question, "Who is taking care of your children while you are here in Aruba?" The answers were as varied as the socioeconomic conditions existing in the womens' sending societies and their families and households. Ivy, the woman who had returned to Montserrat to give her two children a British education, was disappointed when her elderly mother could not conform to being an other mother and had returned to her home in the country. I questioned Ivy, "Who took care of your son, then?" She giggled embarrassedly and replied,

> He take care of heself. I keep sending money and food and he just keep going to school. I did ask a neighbor to cast an eye on him at first and help him with washing his clothes, and so. But as he get older, nobody look after him. Of course I was writing him often and warning him to behave himself. The boy did very good in school.

Elderly care givers became isolated and emotionally stressed out as they did a second round of child rearing at the same time that their own need for medical care and attention was increasing. The tropical climate of the eastern Caribbean islands allows much outdoor social interaction, and the street life and culture takes young people, especially males, outside of the direct ambit of elderly women/care givers. Family members who work the neighborhoods may be able to keep abreast about their neighbors and their own family members through gossip, observation, and general interaction. If the elderly care givers' physical activities were curtailed for whatever reason, however, they often found themselves cut off from the neighborhood grapevine and oblivious to what was happening in the lives of the children left in their care (Olwig 1993; Gussler 1980).

The migrant domestics expressed concern about the physical and biological changes occurring in their children and elderly mothers. The explanation for many women's worry or desire to return was often: "Well, my mother getting old and can't really manage; so the older children helping to take care of the younger ones."

But an other mother could also very likely be an overworked, barely teenaged girl, a sibling of the children in her care (Gussler 1980). Many a youngster became the ears and eyes, and the Jack or Jane-of-all-trades for an aging grandmother who is left the task of being the other mother (Olwig 1993).

Caretaking situations became problematic if the domestics still had young or elderly dependents to care for. Most women had prolonged absences from their sending countries. Young and elderly other mothers lived uncertain, unstable lives in the sending countries. During their long periods of absence, migrant domestics lost personal contacts, and became less apt at managing important crises in their sending communities.

Poverty, unemployment, and personal health problems can erode the care-giving resource pool in the sending society. From Aruba, it was sometimes impossible for the women to easily find dependable, capable, or willing other mother replacements to take care of their children when crises arose back in their home villages. Child-rearing conditions, very difficult for labor migrants in large nation-states such as the United States and Canada, present insurmountable problems for mothers in small, more unfree receiving host societies (Waters 1994; Chaney 1987; Soto 1987).

The migrant domestics used remittances as their best bargaining chip, but remittances could not guarantee stability in distant family/household arrangements. Ironically, the regular receipt of remittances may work against community support for an elderly care giver left in charge of children whose mother is a labor migrant. Sometimes the receiver of hard-earned remittances forfeits the comradery and trust of her neighborhood once she and her wards "turn rich on everbody." Receipt of regular remittances by the care giver and her wards may encourage ostentatious displays of material goods that put them a cut above their neighbors (Gmelch 1992, 81). When remittance recipients and their neighbors were poor together, they formed part of a cooperative support system.

Females—maternal kin—were the most likely other mothers chosen by the migrant women to be in charge of the children they left behind. But three of the women in the study had left men, their "keepers" (cohabiting mates) and a brother respectively, to take care of their children (Aymer 1997). There is widespread use of poor, elderly, and young, unemployed male family members as other mothers in black communities in the eastern Caribbean and the United States (Stack and Burton 1994; Jarret 1994; Gmelch 1992).

Child Lending

Child lending is practiced widely in the Caribbean and African American communities in the United States (Stack and Burton 1994; Pulsipher 1993; Soto 1987; St. Victor 1986). Poor women lend their children to well-off relatives or residents in the community in an arrangement that simulates an informal kind of adoption. The purpose is always to offer the child better living conditions in exchange for whatever help the child and mother can offer its benefactor. Children run errands, do light household chores, learn skills, and sometimes remain until adulthood with the person or family to whom they have been lent. Because the child's connections to its birth mother and her relatives are retained, many children do return relatively easily to the blood mother or her family (Soto 1987).

Often, a well-off relative or member of the community gets singled out to be an other mother. Stack and Burton (1994) state that poor families operate by "kinscripts: an unspoken agreement or understanding about the varying statuses, strengths, and abilities of respective family members." So that in time of need, particular family members are often selected willingly or coerced by other family members to assume kin work and mother work.

Poor women purposefully select women or men for special attention and favors. Later, acceptance of a request to be godparent or to take a child represents the return of favors received. Ann, the woman who had two babies in quick succession after arriving from Nevis in the mid-1940s, chose a sister to care for her first child, a son. Her second child, a mixed-race daughter, was born a year later, and in danger of deportation, Ann had to act quickly. She was friendly with a high-ranking civil servant who worked for the Dutch government and traveled between the three islands of Curaçao, Bonaire, and Aruba. Ann asked the woman to be the baby's godmother, and soon she offered the baby girl to the benefactor. The woman accepted. The high-status godparent, well known in Latin American countries, is the middle-class godmother or benefactor of the eastern Caribbean.

Mothering from a Distance

Few mothers set off to Aruba without finding in-house or specific neighborhood supervision for their childen. Whenever these tenuous arrangements fell through later, the migrant mothers did what they could from a distance to ensure provision of their children's basic material needs. Sometimes women resigned themselves to the fact that their children were without any in-house adult supervision.

Designated care givers ceased to provide care for any number of reasons. One of the women, Eliza from St. Vincent, had left her brother in charge of her four young children. Her mother was already dead and her youngest child only two years old when she set out for migrant labor on Aruba. Her brother also lived in the house and promised to help take care of the children. He and Eliza's eldest daughter, a teenager, were put in charge. As promised, Eliza faithfully sent home two-thirds of her wage every month, and huge barrels filled with foodstuff and other goods to her family each year. But the family situation changed when her brother married and his wife joined the household. According to Eliza, they absconded with the money they were supposed to have been banking. She was shocked to receive news that her brother had left the children to fend for themselves.

Eliza turned to non-kin, whom she declared were like real family to her in this predicament. She resorted to writing her children's neighbors, a couple whom she had charged to "cast an eye" on the children even when her brother had been in charge. This couple appraised her of her brother's dishonesty. Eliza immediately gave them the rights to oversee her children, as well as all her finances and legal affairs. According to her:

> The man [her brother] was no good. I had to ask the neighbors to put him in court and send the police to get my bank book from him. The neigbors was like family. That couple help me with the children. I write the children and tell them to behave themselves. I read the riot act to them.

A particular kind of nonresidential other mothering and community supervision of children emerged in the eastern Caribbean. Increased and widespread female labor migration helped create it. Children left behind by mothers—labor migrants—lived together without adult supervision in a common residence. Neighbors cooperated, and made regular checks on the children. Specific adults, or the teenager in the family, received the remittances and saw that the children's needs were met and that lives and limbs were held together.

Impoverished sending Caribbean societies have assumed charge of the social reproduction of children left behind by labor migrant mothers. These children must be raised and prepared for adulthood. Nurturing, bonding, and socialization become generalized—diffuse activities performed by a variety of persons and institutions in the community at large. The children of some migrant domestics were virtually the undeclared partial wards of the community.

Men feel threatened by women's labor migration (Grasmuck and Pessar 1991). In the study, women's care-giving problems increased if the key care giver in the sending country was their mate or the father of their children. Such men tended to exert inordinate pressure on the women to return. In fact, two women I interviewed on Grenada who had practiced return migration, said that the men in their lives constantly worried them to return.

The preciptating factor that caused Myrtle's return to Grenada occurred when her daughter suffered injuries in a car accident. The child's aunt requested that Myrtle return immediately. She did, and once home, the child's father grasped the opportunity to prevent her from returning to her job. In fact, he bought a house (using some of the monies she had remitted) and offered her marriage, which she accepted.

The women found themselves caught in several dilemmas whenever an emergence regarding their dependents arose. How could they fulfill their duties as good Caribbean mates, mothers, and daughters, while remaining bound to their work contract obligations in a foreign country far from home? Sometimes a woman went home on what she thought would be a vacation or asked her employer for a short leave to attend to what seemed to be a family crisis. Often, on return to their sending countries, women met care giving arrangements and households in such utter chaos that they decided not to return to Aruba. Hope, the second of the two returned women, told how her boyfriend, now her husband, wrote her often. Each time he complained about the hardship that their only son was experiencing without her care. He threatened that if she did not return immediately, she could consider their relationship ended, and he would claim that she had deserted her child.

Marjorie, who received a call to work on Aruba via the village shop-keeper's phone, was convinced that her rightful place was back home with her man, her old mother, and her children. In 1989 she was in constant distress:

Every letter I get from home, the man complaining about the way I treat him by leaving without telling him my plans. I ask him to cast an eye on the children. He have his own house, but it's not too far away from my mother's house. My old mother is there in our house with the children—they all teenagers—when they out from school. He more able to keep me inform. He sending all the time to tell me that I should come home and look after my children, especially my teen-age daughter who he say keeping bad company. I don't know what to do. But I make up my mind, I know he vex with me, but I going back home as soon as my year is up.

Most women were unable to leave their employment on the spur of the moment and be assured that employers would keep positions open for them until their return. Only women who had financial resources could respond quickly to emergencies. Free-signing women found it easier to leave for home when emergencies occurred; at least they could be sure their belongings would be secure when they returned. Sometimes emergencies occurred before women had fully repaid the cost of their return tickets through monthly installments, and they could only set out for home if the mistress received the money owed her.

The only woman in the study from the younger cohort in 1989 who had married while working on Aruba experienced two serious family emergencies in two consecutive years. With her husband's financial help, she was able to return to her sending island both times. She moaned regrets over the fact that her mother, the woman who for ten years had cared for her three children—two sons and an only daughter—had been ailing; and she was not there to help take care of her. She had arrived back in Dominica just in time, to be at her mother's deathbed. Nine months later, her nineteen-year-old only daughter took ill. By the time she got to St. Maarten, en route to Dominica, she received news that her daughter had died.

Most of the women on Aruba try to keep in contact with their dependents in the sending islands by working the phones and writing letters. The women tried hard at helping to manage their own households from a distance, by listening to and fulfilling their children's requests, refereeing family rows, and making long-distance decisions about crucial family situations and emergencies.

Catherine, a maid from St. Vincent, explained that she regularly phoned her seven children who lived together with her elderly mother. In 1989 her three youngest children were still in school. She explained that there were rows sometimes in her distant family/household, during which it was reported that the younger children refused to obey the elder siblings. Whenever she recieved a frantic collect call telling of unrest in the household, she spent time trying to handle the matter over the phone. When the phone call ended, she continued the discussion on paper, writing to each child individually. Generally, the women knew that they could only do so much from a distance.

Two women, fifty-year-old Eliza from St. Vincent, and forty-five-year-old Louise from Dominica, had been especially close friends. They engaged in a form of cooperative, long-distance mothering, both respectively corresponding with Louise's mother and children. During the summer of 1989, the womens' relationship became strained. The older woman tried to explain how a migrant woman needed a friend who became like family. But, she warned sadly, that friends often betrayed trust:

> I used to help her out a lot. I let her stay in my room when she had a half-day off. Whenever she come into Oranjestad and night catch her, and she too 'fraid to walk back alone six miles into the cunuku (deep country), is me walking back in the dark with her. I does even write all her children and her old mother.

My next questions were, "Do you know her mother and children?" and "Have you met them?" Her quick reply was,

> No, I never meet them. But you know she always worried about her children, they younger than mine. Besides, when they have any trouble and she want to calm her old mother, I would write and encourage the old lady to keep trying her best with the children.

Women whose work lives had turned them into distant wage earners and good providers were manipulating the specialized work role that had been imposed on them. They had interjected innovations into the breadwinner role that included aspects of the traditional maternal chores and obligations of women in families.[18] Among other innovations, the women have created a mothering and family form that allows long physical absences by migrant wage-earning mothers. Still expected to display maternal qualities, the wage earner depends heavily on at least one other female who acts as co-mother, supervisor, co-nurturer, and general overseer of the labor migrant's family.

In August 1989, Catherine, the woman who worked the phones in order to keep in touch with her seven children in St. Vincent, began announcing the impending visit of her twenty-four-year-old daughter, a teacher in the sending island. That Sunday during the first week of her daughter's visit, many maids and visitors attended the English-speaking church in Oranjestad. Catherine's daughter, a lay reader back in her home church, was invited to assist the pastor in conducting the worship. Catherine could hardly hide her joy. After the worship was over, she led the tall young woman to me by the hand and smiling with pride she presented her, asking rhetorically: "You see what me and my mother do?"

The women with dependents in the sending country exist emotionally in two worlds—that of the families to which they give some of the best years of their lives for a living wage, and their sending societies. They are very aware that as women, mothers, and daughters, they were socialized into behaviors and activities that emphasize hands-on caring—especially for their aging mothers and young children. But their hands-on care and physical presence at the life-cycle stages of their kin had been made impossible by the realities of race, class, ethnicity, national borders, immigration laws, distance, and the regimen of wage work.

Resisting Mothering

Not all women cherish their maternal mandates or live up to them. Inez, Eliza's niece, at first rejected the position that her aunt had found her on Aruba, and went back to St. Vincent after a very short work stint. But she eventually returned to Aruba to find work, leaving two young children behind. She seemed almost petulant about the harshness of her life and how much the support of her children demanded from her. She recounted how she resented the attitude of some employers who suggested that the maid was surrogate mother to the children they were being paid to care for: "I have my own children back in St. Vincent, and even them I don't want to see sometimes. My own children is enough, I don't want to take on anybody else children as my own."

In eastern Caribbean family ideology, a woman's children are a form of private insurance. In the absence of publicly organized programs such as social security, people envision grateful grown children as their chief safeguard from need; to ease them through their old age. Once women bear children, mothers must, on pain of public condemnation, look after their children well. Children, in return, should show eternal gratitude.

There was a socially shared opinion among the women and their sending societies about the obligations and responsibilities of women who leave their dependents and travel abroad to be migrant domestics. Several women told a sobering tale with a moralistic, mythical ring that supported the family-centered philosophy. It was a warning to any woman even slightly tempted to abrogate her obligations as a good woman/mother.

The women all knew about a former migrant domestic from Grenada who had grown old in Aruba. According to them, she often wandered the streets of Oranjestad, demented and dishevelled. The old woman had been diagnosed as mentally ill, and was hospitalized often, but she had escaped each time to continue her street wanderings. The maids stated that Aruba's immigration authorities had written to the woman's grown son, a Grenada resident, asking him to come and take his mother home. This is how one woman told of his response:

> He say not he. He ain't coming nowhere. He say when things were good and she was well and strong, she didn't remember he was alive. Her whole life was Aruba. Now she in need, let Aruba take care of her.

Sending societies will forgive female labor migrants for being unable to do their duty in administering hands-on care to their dependents, but they had better be altruistic, self-denying, instrumental providers.

Eastern Caribbean migrant domestics have inculcated and claimed the characteristics of the *good woman*. Whenever anyone raised the subjects of remittances, letter writing, and remembering their children in the sending countries, the women talked as if they were born with maternal mandates and nurturing instincts. Eliza's voice was vehement with emotion as she held forth on the topic:

> If any woman come here and forget those she leave back home or move to another country without letting them know where she is, she have bad mind; you may as well call such women "no-good."

A finite end to migrant women's ties to their sending countries did arrive. The umbilical cord severed especially when a woman's mother died, or when her children married or emigrated to countries outside of the Caribbean. Then it seemed that the purpose for the migrant domestics' hard life on Aruba was accomplished.

Chapter 7

Migrant Domestics on Aruba

Female temporary guest workers make labor and immigration authorities nervous. Accommodation, a top priority, fulfills strict immigration stipulations. More "unfree" female migrant worker schemes insist that female contract workers reside in well-supervised locations. For female migrant domestics, this usually means mandated live-in accommodations within employers' households or residential compounds. On Aruba, for the first two years of migrant domestics' contracts, employers must provide all of the women's boarding and lodging needs. At first sight, the residential arrangement seems to ensure the women's safety and comfort; and it can. But many of the eastern Caribbean migrant domestics on Aruba in 1989 had been heads of households prior to their arrival. Besides, the women came from sending societies in which the poor developed a lively culture of the streets and outdoors. To an unsophisticated rural woman, the house of her employer on Aruba becomes a virtual prison.

Marjorie complained that not only was she holed up in her employer's house, but she lacked privacy:

> I tired ask (I'm tired of asking) madame for a lock and key for my room-door. The door have no key. So she can come in on me without knocking, saying that she looking for something or other when I'm lying down. Besides, when I'm not there she can go into my room and search my things.

THE MAID COMMUNITY

The domestics on Aruba are a microcosm of ethnic minorities created cross-culturally through labor migrations (Repak 1994; Small 1994; Kasinitz

1992; Chaney 1987). Ethnic and racial differences emerge and become starkly significant in immigrant communities whenever social structures in receiving societies constrain social interaction within marked ethnic or racial boundaries. Sometimes ethnic boundaries might be the result of hard-fought struggles that finally achieved ethnic pluralism in a society. More often, ethnic demarcations dissemble rigid inequalities and socioeconomic exclusion of certain groups in racialized societies. Ethnic pluralism then becomes a euphemism for marginalized ethnic minorities, disadvantaged and dominated by one or more powerful groups.

The eastern Caribbean migrant domestics on Aruba form themselves into several distinct circles or knots of relationships. Together, these small groupings are enclosed within an overarching, broader circle known as the English-speaking maid community. Membership in small, close-knit groups often underscored a common country of origin. For example, women from Dominica tended to look out for each other, visited each other, and even included elderly, retired Dominican women in their socializing. The lack of facility with the three languages spoken by Arubans has been problematic. Women from the anglophone eastern Caribbean have not been able to fraternize with Spanish-speaking maids or Haitian maids and vice versa, even when they live in the same households.

One of the women, Myrtle, told how she and another woman from the same village in Grenada arrived to work at a household on Aruba. Her friend and cousin was the cook, while she was the laundress. It was late November when they got there, and by mid-December her employer's household packed up and journeyed to the United States to spend Christmas vacation with relatives. She recounted:

> They leave very little food in the house. So in a few days all was finished. They didn't leave any money and we had none. Even if we had money we don't know where to find the shops and we don't know anybody on Aruba. We had noticed an elderly maid working in the house next door. So one day we call out to her. She was an old Haitian woman and she couldn't speak one word of English. See us making signs to her and telling her we hungry. I will never forget that old Haitian woman, every day she sneak out bread, eggs, and milk for us from her mistress kitchen. That old woman save we life.

National origins in the English-speaking islands commanded allegiance if numbers were sufficient to jell relationships, or if other allegiances did not supersede. The women's residential situations often superseded national alliance. And women who worked together in the same household or neighborhood became attached to each other; despite disparate countries of origin. Women remained in fairly long-term, tenuous relationships until distance, gossip, or a more compelling relationship intervened and separated them. Some relationships resembled inseparable schoolgirl cliques. The same little band of friends could be seen together each Sunday in church, at the bargain basement stores on Thursdays, or the particular Oranjestad bank and post office frequented by the maids.

Maids from the anglophone eastern Caribbean formed a loose but important network. This "maid's grapevine" relayed gossip, translated the bureaucratic red tape that regulated the women's lives, introduced them to services, spelled out their rights, and warned them against aiding and abetting employers in exploitative behavior. The maid's grapevine also relayed the word whenever a new woman arrived. It was customary for one of the maids from the woman's sending country to go out of her way to contact the new arrival. Sometimes the new arrival made her first appearance decked out in her Sunday best at morning worship in the "English church" (the Oranjestad Methodist church).

The maids in the grapevine, long exposed to the tricks of their rich employers, warned Marjorie that her mistress, the wife of a wealthy surgeon, had no right to deduct the cost of her travel to Aruba from her first month's wages. Before Majorie left Grenada, her sponsor had agreed to stand the cost of her travel to Aruba. Nor should Marjorie have been paying for her own health insurance. Her fellow maids advised her that only the cost of a return ticket in the form of a down payment to the immigration office should have been deducted from her wages. She acted quickly on this advice:

> I hurry down to the immigration office and inform them how my mistress was taking out so much money from my wages. I hardly had any pay left over after she take out for two tickets and health insurance. The immigration phone her and threaten her. When I get back home she shocked that I had the sense to report her.

The members of the migrant domestics' community seemed tied together in an uncomfortable, love/hate relationship. Harsh combativeness intersected the women's closely knit comradery. Long work hours, live-in housing arrangements, competitiveness in an unfair labor market, size of the island, and loneliness: all tended to stimulate gossip and rivalry among the women. In fact, several women gave maid's gossip as the most unpleasant aspect of life on Aruba. Frequent attendance at the same church forced women to work together, but their cooperative participation created much friction. In reply to questions about friendships on Aruba, and whether each woman could identify a best friend to whom she would turn in a crisis, many women replied, "Nobody."

Eliza explained how she had gone out of her way for a friend but had only been handed ingratitude in return. She had all but given up on her friendships: "Me I don't want one more friend. Just me an God alone. You get too much disappointments from friends. I do too much for Louise for the bad treatment she hand me."

However, migrant domestics had limited recourse whenever they experienced exploitation and injustice in the work place. They did turn to each other for help. Like most minorities in racialized political economies cross-culturally, the domestics saw themselves as disadvantaged together because of their common group membership. Women found themselves in situations that demanded cooperation. In times of crisis and personal distress, these women who lived in constant stress and relative isolation, rallied around each other. All the women knew tales of how rows with mistresses ended with immediate deportation for migrant domestics. Only if an unemployed woman had lived more than two years on Aruba, was she allowed a grace period of at least two weeks to find another job. It was then that the maid's grapevine went into action, as the women tried to find job openings for women to prevent their repatriation.

Jennifer, one of the women I had known from my youth in Grenada, was on a hospital bed dying from ovarian cancer when I returned in 1989. She and her friends recounted a trying housing situation that occurred some years before, when Jennifer was still a live-in maid. The incident forced her to apply for "free-signing" and set up house with another maid.

The history of the eastern Caribbean migrant worker presence on Aruba has left strong cultural marks on a receiving society that often eschews its own African connections. Carnival celebrations and festivities, legacies of African survivals and Caribbean enslavement, occur yearly in most of the Caribbean. In the 1940s, Carnival began to be celebrated yearly on Aruba, as a series of local entertainment events organized by the black, male migrant workers living in San Nicolas. Aruba's government quickly envisioned the monitary benefits of the celebrations and claimed the carnival as an annual national celebration. For the past several decades, Carnival has been promoted vigorously to boost the country's tourist industry.

Jennifer left her mistress's house one Saturday night to attend Carnival celebrations in San Nicolas. The arrangement with her mistress was that she would return late Sunday night, but it was not until Monday at noon that she arrived home. She was just about to ring the doorbell, when she noticed all her earthly possessions stacked outside the garage at the side of the house. She knew that she had to try a more independent living arrangement; besides, she had met the law's stipulation as a live-in maid. She was able to find a friend willing to take her in. Her first priority, however, was to quickly find new employment or face certain repatriation. Her maid friends rallied around her and she soon found a new job.

Joyce, a woman who left Nevis at barely seventeen and had arrived on Aruba after maid stints in the Virgin Islands and Curaçao, respectively, explained how the maid's network enlisted her services. She said she received a call one day from another maid who had recently arrived from Nevis to work on Aruba. The employer had taken an almost instant dislike to the woman, and had subsequently thrown her out of her house and onto the streets of Oranjestad. Migrant labor law in such instances makes deportation immediate and inevitable. Joyce had never met the newly arrived maid:

The woman call me with her problem. I don't know her [the new maid] from Adam, but somebody give her my number. I ask my mistress if she could stay in my room with me. She agree, but say I must go down to tell the Immigration where she was because we all could get in trouble. Me and the woman went down to the Immigration Office. We ask them for an extension so that she could look for another work. They refuse. I ask them if she could leave for the airport from my room. They does usually make the mistress load the maid off as a bundle of old clothes that she dumping at the airport. The Immigration agreed. They say that my mistress had to call and confirm the arrangement, and when we get back from the airport somebody have to call to say she gone. So we do that. At least the mistress didn't have the pleasure to laugh at her.

This tiny victory was related with an air of triumph.[1]

Social Life on Aruba

Black ethnic coalitions organized within the exclusionary parameters of race, augmented the domestics' scarce social resources. Retired maids have wisdom about life in the society gathered over the decades. Some of the churchgoing younger women made friendships and spent much time with the older women. By their retirement, many of the older former maids had found reasonably comfortable housing in which to eke out their last days. Such elderly women posed no threat to the younger women, offering no competition in the rivalry over scarce men.

It was not uncommon to see older church women befriend younger ones and mentor them to find respectable positions in the church's organizations. If they originated from the same eastern Caribbean island, the bond was even tighter. Such an attachment between a younger woman who arrived in 1972 and an older woman (a resident black) was very noticeable. Although originally from St. Vincent, the older woman and her husband had settled on Aruba and become well-off residents. According to the maid, Myra:

The lady is my good friend. She take me anywhere I want to go and she picks me up to go to church and other meetings. I go in my spare time and help her with anything. She and me is from the same island.

Other black church-going Aruban residents—Dutch Antillians—also became the women's advisors. These black residents could be depended on to translate public documents from the Dutch, walk the women through bureaucratic red tape, give them inside information about accessing the best health care, and invite them on sight-seeing tours. An air of kind condescension pervaded the black residents' helping activities.

Much of the social life that the women experienced took place within the maid's community and in immigrant institutions, such as the English-speaking churches and benefit societies. Catherine, a woman from the younger age cohort, depended almost completely on the maid community to help entertain her daughter, who arrived on a vacation during the summer of 1989. Catherine beamed with pride as she announced that her daughter, a schoolteacher in the sending country, was to arrive soon on a visit. This was the same young woman who participated in the worship activities, whose proud mother could hardly restrain her joy as she showed off her daughter to the congregation.

I asked how they hoped to spend the vacation. The mother divulged that several of the elderly maids had invited her daughter out to meals, and another church member had promised to take her sight-seeing. Catherine stated that her daughter would accompany her to weeknight, church-related activities.

I observed the mother and daughter several times during the visit. Life continued as harsh and demanding as ever for the middle-aged mother all during her daughter's vacation. One day as I walked the main street in the shopping district of Oranjestad, there in full public view on a sidewalk stood Catherine poised on a short ladder, mop-in-hand, washing shop windows. Her moonlighting job brought in extra money. Besides, she later reported:

> I make a lot of friends with the Aruban women who work in the stores. They miss me when I don't go to work cleaning. Some of them make Aruban dishes and bring for me to taste, and they always inviting me to places. But I don't go. Look, one of them even invite my daughter, now that she is here, to visit them at their home.

I happened to get on a bus one mid-morning, a week or so after witnessing the window-washing episode. A few rows away from the entrance of the bus sat four sad-faced women—Catherine, her daughter, and two elderly, retired, former maids from the younger woman's island. Crowding the bus aisle, and jammed against the women's legs were two huge, out-of-place-suitcases. Catherine's daughter was leaving that day, and the solemn, strangely quiet women were en route to the airport via public transportation.

Few local people ever transported their luggage by bus to the airport; public transportation was not geared to accommodate airport travelers. For example, the bus runs along a highway that passes in full view of the airport. However, the nearest stop for anyone hoping to get off was a good thousand yards from the terminal. Besides, for bus riders the entrance to the terminal could only be accessed on foot by first crossing the busy highway, negotiating across a wide, often packed parking lot, and then across the road that runs in front of the terminal building. I waved them good-bye as they alighted at the roadside of the busy highway. Then, I craned to watch the women, each laden with a suitcase or package, as they trekked in line formation across the busy highway and into the airport precinct. The migrant network was operating at optimal efficiency, and the women were making the best of their situation.

Catherine's daughter had traveled to a foreign island, visited her mother, and according to her, had an enjoyable vacation. Many young women in the sending islands would be envious at the opportunities for travel and other benefits that seemed to accrue to children whose migrant domestic mothers worked in distant Aruba.

Two days after her daughter's departure, Catherine apologized for not visiting me as she had planned. She then related a tale that resembled Marjorie's unpleasant air travel from Grenada to Aruba. It underscored the maternal woes of migrant domestics, and the women's continuing image of distance and foreignness between countries in the region, even in the late twentieth century:

> I phone the airline counter twice before my daughter leave Aruba and before we went to the airport to make sure that she could get a direct flight to St. Vincent. The day when she was leaving I ask them again and they confirm it. Can you believe that my daughter was sleeping on airport bench the night she leave here? Then the plane take her to Trinidad and she was there for many hours again. I couldn't go to work I home bawling after she call me from Curaçao. I could not work or sleep until I get a call from home saying that she arrive there safe and sound. It take that child two days to get home.

Sexual Life on Aruba

It was difficult to uncover details about the migrant domestic's sexual lives on Aruba. Theoretically, sexual liaisons between maids and locals were frowned upon and considered almost illegal. Popular images of the black foreign domestics as asexual work automatons carried unreasonable expectations of the women. These suggested that foreign domestics work hard, live respectably in employers' households, then return to their sending islands.

Cross-culturally, women gain social respect through a few prescribed methods: marriage, childbearing, and visible economic contributions to their households. A migrant worker can experience none of these in the receiving society, where she would be employed for some or most of her life. The social situation created by immigration laws and community norms set the women up to be socially and sexually deviant or irresponsible. And young migrant domestics did have reputations of being women on the loose.[2] Married and older women in the black Aruban community spoke of the migrant domestics with some fear and much disdain.

It seemed that observers envied the women's freedom from traditional maternal activities. Outspoken members of the resident black community and members of the black churches often suggested that the sexual escapades of decent women should end once they became mothers, especially of several children. It mattered little whether the children lived with their mothers or not. The criticisms suggested that the migrant domestics had unfairly been given child-free work lives, leaving them with too much time on their hands. Foreign women—many mothers—answerable to no normative system or local community yet allowed clandestine sexual license, could be dangerous to themselves and the social order.

On Aruba, social customs and prejudices, fueled by racism and ethnic and class differences created new social and sexual dilemmas for the women. They told time and again about the scarcity of single and marriageable men. Two women explained the mating situation to me this way:

> Aruban men and women get married young. So by the time a woman get here and she meet an Aruban man he already married. Beside, they does marry their own Aruban people, or South American or Dominican. Very few if any marry black people and they won't marry a woman who have children already. They does pay a lot of attention to us in the night when nobody can see them.

If a young, heterosexual migrant domestic wanted male company and had ruled out getting the attention of young Aruban men, to whom would she turn? Veronica, the elderly woman who was chief baby-sitter and other mother to the toddler daughter of a young migrant domestic, voiced her displeasure about the sex lives of the younger migrant domestics:

> They all too greedy. They want too much. Those young girls would do well to make do with what they have. I don't know why they don't learn to behave themselves like decent women. If they spend less time down by the wharf chatting to the men who come in on the boats to sell fruits and craft work, I think they would be better off.

From this comment, I deduced that a possible source of black male mates for the women were the seamen and traders from Haiti, the Dominican Republic, and Venezuela, who arrived on Aruba to sell their wares and remained only for short periods. Gloria, a young woman, bemoaned the shortage of black men as long-term mates. She stated that black Caribbean men, especially from Jamaica, did arrive on short-term contracts as construction workers in Aruba's booming hotel construction business. But she said,

> You don't know anything about these men who here for a short time. Most of them must have women and wives and children back where they come from and a woman can't get too involve with them.

Women jumped at chance meetings with black men and made the best of such encounters. Sometimes such a man worked briefly as an artisan in their household, attended the women's church or benefit societies, visited the St. Maarten Club in San Nicolas, or worked at a downtown shop. Christine, the woman from the younger cohort who later married while still a maid, was attractive and seemed to have caught the attention of an immigration officer who gave her some good labor advice: "One day I was outside washing down my mistress car and one of the immigration who I know and who does pass and chat with me stop and tell me that washing my mistress car is not included in the work contract." This same woman told how she met her husband:

> My mistress was getting the roof of the house repair and he was in charge of the construction. He keep looking at me all the time and trying to talk to me. He tell me that he wasn't married and that he would like to get to know me. All the time the man was still married, but separated from his wife, amd I didn't know.

It must be remembered that in its constant gender gerrymandering of migrant worker cohorts, the labor market remains oblivious to the social and sexual needs of young women. This insensitivity to female workers gets exaggerated if they are foreign eastern Caribbean migrant domestics. There was no scarcity of men for migrant domestics who arrived on Aruba during the 1940s. The labor demand for male migrant workers from the anglophone eastern Caribbean at the time exceeded the demand for migrant domestics.

The authorities, having discouraged family reunification and cohabitation, recognized the social and sexual needs of male workers employed by the Lago refinery. The Dutch government legalized, regimented, and supervised prostitution in the Dutch Antilles, including Aruba. Aruba's local government and the refinery cooperated in sanctioning the operation of licensed, government-supervised brothels in the village where most of the male migrant workers lived. Female migrant workers were at the mercy of the sexual double standard.

When the women were asked what they did for relaxation and how they spent their free time, several mentioned San Nicolas as the place they traveled to for fun and recreation. It was at the St. Maarten Club in San Nicolas that the women fraternized with local black men. There, they attended dances and "let their hair down," as they mounted the podium to croon love songs on the microphones. These unsophisticated rural women, many of whom had never seen the bright lights before arriving on Aruba, went to the St. Maarten Club. There, they forgot their children, their harsh lives, and the drudgery that awaited them in the kitchens of Oranjestad, if only for a few hours.

Most of the women voiced no interest whatsoever in marriage. However, as some women aged, having given up hopes of getting to their migration apex, they began hankering for respectability and the material security and accoutrements associated with marriage. Ann, the woman who arrived on Aruba already married and tricked immigration about her intentions, later married an elderly Aruban almost on his deathbed. This act raised her status, and made her reasonably well-off so she could boast that she was "two hundred times better off" than the women of the poor eastern Caribbean village she had left some forty or more years before. As if this were not enough, she boasted:

> I could have married a third time you know. A year after my husband die the children of an elderly Aruban man who was my late husband's good friend approach me and ask me to marry him. They had notice the good care that I did take of my deceased husband. But I say, "No." I feel it was time for me to relax. I work hard all my life, then taking care of my sick husband. I had no need to go through that again.

Her mission had been accomplished. If Ann's popularity as a potential wife were true (and I had no reason to doubt it), how ironic that black, English-speaking domestics, unattractive as wives in youth, became very attractive as middle-aged nursemaid wives to bedridden Aruban men.

Eliza, the maid who seemed tied to the baby undergoing physical therapy, had a secret to share with me:

> Don't tell anybody, but I may be getting married. There is a man who worked downtown in a store who say that he interested in me. He say that he been looking at me a long time and he want my answer soon.

Why would a man in his right mind take on a poor, work-worn, middle-aged woman, whose heart was torn between making hard-earned wages on Aruba and being reunited with four grown children on St. Vincent? She divulged that the man was originally from her island, and perhaps like her had hopes of returning. Although it seemed like wishful thinking to me, I hid my skepticism.

Veronica, the elderly woman who told of the greedy younger maids in Oranjestad who frequented the wharf in search of male company, told a heart-breaking story of unfulfilled love and dashed hopes of nuptial bliss. She had been housekeeper for over twenty years in one household, and eventually, according to her, she and a less well-off brother of her employer became lovers. She was not sure that her employer knew they were seeing each other clandestinely, but she believed the family did suspect their relationship. When this middle-aged man took ill, he was moved to a bedroom within the house and was attended by a private nurse who had orders not to let Veronica see him. The domestic suspected race and class prejudices:

These are prejudiced people. They didn't want me for him and even on his deathbed they wouldn't let me even see him. He died there without me being able to get near to him. It was really sad.

The women were sitting ducks for the wandering eyes of men who attended their churches. By far the most prevalent tales of illicit sexual liaisons, told by resident blacks on Aruba, are those between the migrant domestics and husbands of church members. Rumor told that although wives often threatened to report the women to the immigration authorities, they had to contend with the wrath of their unfaithful husbands.

Marriage or further labor migration offered the women hope for change in status and a break in the monotony of maid work. Even the middle-aged women retained hopes of getting a final burst of migration luck. They still imagined encountering a kind employer or liaison who would offer them a chance to work in the United States or Europe. Younger women hoped to leave so they could get on with living.

The two women who left Aruba and moved to North America were the youngest from my own island who befriended me, and I them, in the mid-1970s. Both of them wanted children. Brenda had left a boyfriend in Grenada and intended to get married. The other young woman had no boyfriend. Because they knew that mating on Aruba involved casual, mostly illicit relationships with married men, they planned to leave. One of the women, now married and living in Maryland in the United States, explained how she employed the help of an older woman to ward off the aggressive attention of married men on Aruba:

I thought that I would have got a chance to work and further my education in Aruba but Aruba was just work and more work. I left a boyfriend in Grenada and we kept corresponding. When he left Grenada for Canada I knew that I had to keep far away from those nasty married men on Aruba and try to get to him. When I was in Aruba, I would travel everywhere especially to Benefit Society meetings in San Nicolas with Veronica, and introduce her as my mother. She would watch to see what was happening and she would rescue me from any man who was bothering me too much. Or if they started to annoy me and ask me for dates, I would tell them to talk to my mother and get her permission. That would make them leave me alone.

The other young woman who wanted to bear a child but not through an affair with a married man, used her wits to emigrate to Canada. How could she get out of Aruba and still make a living? Tired and frustrated, she first returned to her sending island, vowing never to return to Aruba; but she did return. Job scarcity on Grenada forced her to "eat her words" and return to her former mistress. Gladys eventually encountered her escape valve and her chance to have a child through a Canadian visitor, who sponsored her to be a migrant domestic in Canada. She has since had a daughter there.

ON THE JOB

Women who arrived on Aruba in hopes that domestic work would be a "step up" from the grinding "maid work" they knew so well in their home islands, were in for sudden shock. They quickly came to terms with the clear and subtle barriers to their social mobility. Labor migrants imagined that they would grasp opportunities for further education. Some arrived with hopes of finding go-betweens who would ease them through to better wage work in the United States. The women believed that their employers would be their best allies. They were mistaken.

They discovered very quickly that a migrant domestic had to perform as "Jack-of-all-trades." Employers expected women to be gardeners, dog minders, pet minders, caretakers of property, and butlers. But traditional women's work as caretaker of the elderly, cook, cleaner, child minder and laundress awaited the migrant domestics, too.

The immigration authorities' stipulations excluded certain jobs from the women's contract, but this changed their daily work realities very little. Evadne worked with a family who owned a chain of jewelry stores in the Netherlands and the Netherland Antilles. Her work place employed a permanent gardener to maintain the manicured grounds of their large bungalow on the outskirts of Oranjestad. However, she chipped in as gardener whenever he took leave or went on vacation. Louise, who arrived from Dominica, soon found out that she was hired to work at two houses. After cooking and cleaning all morning, she was expected to take lunch to her mistress's elderly mother-in-law who lived a half of a mile away. Then began her second tour of duty. Household chores and care of the elderly woman continued until late evening. This arrangement had not been explained to her before her arrival.

Sometimes women were employed in households run by single (young or elderly) men. Then, the domestics' responsibilities spanned a wide range. Louise's second employer was the manager of a large bank in Oranjestad. He was in his late thirties and had never been married. Louise, a six-foot-tall, striking black woman and mother of six, became her boss's "Man Friday," butler, and valet. She carried his briefcase and checkbook when they went shopping. He took her with him, seeking her advice and opinion, when he went to buy clothes. He asked her to be present whenever he interviewed clients and sensed the possibility of a threat to his person. She was an important asexual, work-related part of his life:

> If you see my boss you know that I was not far behind. I run his house for
> him and help him when he had to entertain guests. He would give me his

credit cards to buy stuff for the house. We got on really well. Then he took sick, and went to the States for treatment. When he come back to Aruba, his relatives took him over, fire me and won't even let me see him. He died soon after.

Maid and Employer Relations

There is a dynamic of exploitation which inevitably develops between people locked into intimate relations based on inequality. At its core, the maid and mistress relationship is built on dependence and cooperation, usually between two women and sometimes between a maid and a male employer. However, dependence and cooperation assume love at most, trust at least. These emotions are stunted and thwarted by traditional rights, behaviors, and privileges of authority and superiority, as well as expected responses of docility and subservience, built into the servant/employer relationship. A hierarchical work relationship between people of the same social class, "race," and culture that demanded menial labor on the part of the employee would be problematic. Here, other inequalities based on the domestics' gender and migrant worker status further complicated the women's relationship. Maids and their employers experienced intense and conflicting emotions toward each other.

Local stratification systems must be inserted into the global economic model. Class, race, and ethnicity may operate as unjustly at local levels in the peripheral countries as they do in the larger, core countries that generated them. The women became labor migrants intent on using their well-learned ways of niche-finding to generate personal socioeconomic progress. Migrant domestics hoped that their work places and their mistresses' kind initiatives would present them with initial breaks. To the shock of many women, their presence in the households freed up their mistresses and entire households to enter or perform well in the formal local and international economic systems. Domestics formed the invisible foundation of their employers' economic sphere. But their efforts remained unrecognized, deliberately disconnected from the formal economic system which they so adequately supported.

Class divisions exist within the large-majority black population of eastern Caribbean societies. Poor blacks in the eastern Caribbean must daily maneuver socioeconomic barriers placed between them and a small but growing black middle class. This class is so new, small, and tenuous, however, that poor blacks have relatives who are aspiring to be or are middle class, with whom they socialize on a regular basis. Some of the domestics on Aruba worked as maids in the households of middle-class blacks in the sending societies prior to travel. But class prejudices between middle-class blacks and poor blacks in the sending eastern Caribbean societies and the receiving society, Aruba, manifested themselves differently.

Racial taboos and boundaries exist between blacks, who make up about 80 percent of the population in most islands of the eastern Caribbean, and a small white planter/business class (Henry 1981). In the women's sending societies, especially since the 1950s, workers have negotiated racial prejudice through concerted community pressure. The power of gossip, the mobilization of trade unions, and pressure exerted by local politicians, inevitably reach the ears of erring white employers and mitigate some of the most crass offenses.

The migrant labor category depends on intersection of several systems of inequality. On Aruba, the women—mistresses and maids—shared no common history, race mythology, or culture. Power relations operated on Aruba, unmitigated by social sentiment, obligation, or kind condescension. Class divisions underscored the women's first encounters. The women of the house—mistress and maid—lived in intimate proximity, well aware of the clear and permanent socially constructed barriers between them. It suited employers to ensure that the rigid divides remained.

The illogicality of racism reveals itself in all racialized economies. Up until the 1980s, the preferred maid's phenotype—skin color—and ethnic origins remained strongly eastern Caribbean. Usually lighter-skinned maids from South America or the Dominican Republic who, like their mistresses, were fluent in Spanish (one of the languages widely spoken on Aruba), were constantly disparaged in the media and blamed for breaking up families. Therefore, all during the 1960s until the 1980s, the racial fad showed an upsurge in Haitian domestics and steady enlistment of women from the anglophone Eastern Caribbean. These fickle preferences lasted until early in the 1990s. Aruban employers, still playing the race game in domestics, have recently been pulling in South American and Filipino maids in great numbers.[3]

A black domestic from the eastern Caribbean fits perfectly into the household hierarchy. A virtual deaf mute in the presence of household members, she could hardly dream of usurping the position of her mistress. Janet told how in the 1940s she was employed by a Dutch family. She neither spoke nor understood Dutch. However, from the sound of their conversations, deliberately conducted in Dutch, she surmised that the mistress and her husband often engaged in heated arguments. One day, her mistress, dressed for traveling and about to leave for the airport, called out to her:

> The woman explain to me that she and her husband just get divorce. She was leaving him and the three children with me, and I should take care of them until he make up his mind about what he intend to do. Look at my trouble, I was in shock.

Employers enlisted a variety of methods to underscore the women's subservient positions in the households. Some mistresses insisted that maids wear uniforms around the house. Eliza told me with delight that many women did wear uniforms, but that a maid's dress size could present a daunting problem to the mistress's plans: "My mistress did bring four uniforms for me. But I couldn't get the dress over my head and she didn't bother to worry me with anymore."

Other power strategies proved more effective. One day I met a young woman standing at a street corner in downtown Oranjestad. It was not Thursday afternoon, the maid's half-day, when the women roam the streets freely. I approached her and struck up a conversation. I asked if she was waiting for someone. She replied:

> No, my mistress like to walk around the house naked, and whenever she want to, no matter if it is inconvenient to me, she does ask me to leave the house for a while. She don't want me there. So I just walk around for an hour or two. I getting tired of this.

Certain types of labor migration, and specifically the category defined as migrant labor, depend for their existence on deliberate focus being placed on differences in "race," ethnicity, and class attributes between employers and the employed. Racial and class demands overlap, irritate, and confuse migrant domestics (Rollins 1985; Turrittin 1976). The domestics' sense of their own humanness, and memories of their sending societies' culture that so easily co-opted fictive kin into extended family relations, caused the domestics to experience identity conflicts.

One day, Marjorie, painfully struck by the harsh contradictions in her work relationship in the household, screamed at her mistress: "All you know you don't like black people. You think black people have no feelings. Then why you send to call people from so far away to ill treat them?"

All the way across the Atlantic and in Toronto, Canada, Turrittin heard similar sentiments from migrant domestics from the island of Montserrat who were live-in maids in Canadian households: "but they have no feelings towards you whatever. They expect you to work without any feelings" (Turrittin 1976, 312).

The cultural differences, based on values defined by social class, strike the women as bizarre. Barely able to survive, the women who managed through employing strategies of cooperation, barter, exchange, and personal self-denial, were struck by their employers' crass materialism and stinginess of spirit. According to Marjorie:

> The woman would not let me touch one piece of food in the morning until I feed her birds and dogs. There were days when we had little to eat in the house because she forgot to buy food but there was lots of food for the animals. The woman consider her dogs before she consider me.

It was this same maid who told how every week she had the boring chore of shining every piece of her mistress's brass collection:

She would show off the brass things to visitors and boast how I was doing a good job at shining them. If she only know how I hate those brass things. What I know about brass things! I never touch one before I enter her house. She like the brass things better than me.

Whether the women knew it or not, perhaps they served their best purpose by displaying their inferior status as maids and for their use value, rather than as surrogate mothers or housekeepers. Myra, a free-signing maid, told how she worked for five years with a family as a short-order cook. They could not afford to pay her health insurance, and she was often underpaid or paid only partial wages. She did not leave because she felt like a family member, engaged in a common struggle to get their "takeout" restaurant started. They reassured her that she was part of the family and would one day be reimbursed for her hard work. She left without ever having received the backlog of unpaid wages owed to her. Soon after this, she became a free-signing, moonlighting maid and was hired to clean for a well-off man who lived alone:

He know that I was working all day at his house and that there were no shops in the area. But there was nothing in the fridge for me to eat. Besides, he handed me two potatoes and a steak to make his dinner. Exactly what he could eat and none for me, even though I been working hard, for hours. That was the last time he set his eyes on me.

The growing literature on maid and mistress household relationships exposes not only pervasive employer insensitivity and labor exploitation, but employer dishonesty. The migrant domestics soon discovered that wealth and high social status did not translate into generosity of spirit. In fact, the employer's seeming conviviality could be a deliberate ruse to disarm, and be detrimental to the maid's best interests. Women always needed to be on guard and exert vigilance on their own behalf, for even nice employers were prone to exploitation tactics.

Myra told how in the household where she worked when first arriving in Aruba, she noticed that the load of clothes to be ironed always seemed to exceed the load she had washed. Apparently, her mistress had announced to one of her friends that the new maid was good at ironing, and invited the friend to bring her own washing to be ironed. Myra announced to her mistress that she was willing, as long as she was paid more for the extra ironing that she was doing. The additional clothes ceased.

In the absence of any access to a union, ombudsman, or employment agency which could investigate and seek redress on behalf of an aggrieved migrant domestic, the immigration office was the place of first and last resort for domestics on Aruba. Sometimes women sought redress nearer home, and enlisted the help of the husband in the household in contentions that domestics had with their mistresses.

The women learned effective methods of maneuvering the hierarchy of power within the household without being too confrontational. However, when all else failed, women resorted to confrontation knowing well that it could backfire, and they could find themselves on the next plane to their sending countries. The migrant domestics used a well-known strategy—they got in cahoots with the man of the house. The domestic looked out for his welfare, cooked what he liked, ironed his shirts better than any laundry could do, and generally softened him up by working herself almost to death on his behalf.

Edna, the oldest woman in the study, told how her mistress kept her wages very low. It was her mistress's husband who announced one day that he was so pleased with the maid's work that he intended to raise her wages:

The husband, the man, he respect my worth. He see that I was a worker. He insist on raising my pay. Especially when he raised it to twenty-five guilders [about $15 U.S.] per month, the wife, she was mad. She was a stingy, disagreeable woman. If it wasn't for the man and the children I would have quit long ago.

In the final analysis, however, the migrant domestics' use value, the purpose of their hire, and their commodification as a cheap but high-return labor investment remained paramount. Veronica arrived in 1955 to be a migrant domestic. After an initial bad placement, she found an excellent position at the home of a wealthy family. Her employer's wife was pregnant with their third child at the time. A month after her arrival, the mother died in childbirth. In Veronica's mind, she had become mother and housekeeper to the family. The grieving husband hired two more maids to assist in the house, and Veronica became a powerful woman, "manning" a household and staff of servants. She hired, fired and ran a tight ship. She raised the children and was especially close to the last child, who was in her words, "born in my hand."

In 1988, then nearing seventy, she took ill and journeyed to the United States to be with her son and get needed medical care. She underwent major surgery and remained eight months in the United States, much longer than she had envisioned when she left Aruba. On her return, she had no job. Her former employer had hired two maids to replace her and refused to have any conversation about her firing or a pension, which might have been due her after twenty years of employment. Veronica commented on his ingratitude and heartlessness: "No matter how long a woman works with a family; a maid is a maid, there to work for the boss, nothing more."

Chapter 8

Conclusions

In the 1990s, a third generation of eastern Caribbean women continue to trek across the Caribbean to work as maids on Aruba. Many will remain for good, renewing their contracts and working until they become elderly. They will die there. After more than five decades of continuous work as domestics, how have the women done? Are they "in development?" Can migrant workers—foreign guest workers—be "in development?" If entry into wage labor through labor migration signifies development, then these women, along with millions of female labor migrants across the world, are in development.

WOMEN IN DEVELOPMENT

Blumberg and Pilas Garcia (1977) devised a measure of development for women. They suggest that each woman's development can be gauged by (a) her level of participation and equality in a society; (b) her ability to pursue life options, such as making her own decision about whom to marry, whether to marry at all, or when to dissolve a marriage; (c) her ability to regulate her reproduction and therefore make decisions about family size and timing of births; (d) her exercise of household authority; and (e) her ability to have access to educational opportunities. Using these standards, the migrant domestics on Aruba, along with most eastern Caribbean women and most poor women cross-culturally, are not in development.

However, development, like freedom, has different meanings for social scientists and policymakers than it does for the subjects being studied. Meanings are grounded in the socioeconomic and political life of real societies. I argued elsewhere in this book that *freedom* for the domestics on

Aruba meant consistent access to wages, the ability to provide for their dependents, and welcomed anonymity. But even such relative freedom that the women experienced was entangled with demanding family obligations, grinding work, social ostracism, and virtual exile.

I asked each woman in the study, "Are you better off than the women you left behind in your village? Their answers fell neatly into separate age cohorts. All the elderly women thought they had done remarkably well. The majority of them had become faithful church women, held offices in the women's organizations, or taught Sunday school. Ann had excelled, and became head of a migrant worker benefit society. She boasted:

> I am a leader in the church and Chief Grand Master [the most prestigious position] in the lodge. I am refusing re-election, but everyone begging me to take it. I represent the lodge and the church all over the Caribbean.

The younger women showed more dissatisfaction with their situation. Louise said that when she returned to Dominica on a visit, the young women there seemed to be doing well from remittances they received from relatives who had gone abroad. She wondered then if her hard life in Aruba was worth it. Apparently it was, for she did return to the drudgery and consistent paycheck as a domestic in Aruba.

Development, in its most limited meaning of access to predictable wage sources, had been attained. The women had formed a bridge between their dependents in the sending countries and access to more than basic resources for survival. Marjorie, one of the younger women, put it succinctly in a letter to her daughter, who was "playing the fool" and taking her mother's Herculean efforts for granted. "I'm prepared to take this hard life, so long as I know something good will come from it," she had warned.

Labor migration, the most difficult yet exhilarating in the mix of methods employed by tens of thousands of labor migrants, does assist poor women to ferret their way out of dire poverty. Of all their various risk-taking economic endeavors, labor migration promises and often delivers the best options and rewards to the region's people. People passionately desire the chance to travel and find work, for themselves and for their family members.

However, for the majority of women in this book, Aruba failed to deliver the grand prize. Further labor migration for themselves (perhaps to North America or Europe), or making labor migration connections for one of their daughters still unemployed in the sending islands, marked the proverbial jackpot. Ardent believers in a world without borders and in freedom to trade, the women saw the region—North America and beyond—as open to laboring possibilities.

Most of the cohort in 1989 had already entered middle age, yet many still retained hopes of a final lucky break to move them out of Aruba, to a better life. Bernice, just turned forty-five, almost made it into Canada. The woman, whose twelve-year-old ward was due to leave soon for high school in the

United States, felt sure that the boy's departure would mark the end of her long-term job as housekeeper and domestic. Her close friend and liaison was Daphne, the young woman who found a Canadian sponsor on Aruba, and absconded to Canada. In the mind of the migrant domestic community, Daphne had struck gold. Each domestic had this same fairy tale scenario engraved on her mind: the white sponsor who would whisk her away to better job opportunities.

Once in Canada, Daphne found Bernice a job sponsor. Surreptitiously, Bernice prepared for impending travel. Then the results of her medical examination arrived; she had breast cancer. Sad, and back at work after her operation, she murmured fatalistically: "I guess it was not my luck to go. What can I say?"

Gendered labor migration, valued as the best social mobility avenue for poor families, may be destructive in many of its repercussions. Women become work machines and value themselves by their ability to work hard and provide. The economic deal delivers some limited agency to the women: consistent renumeration for hard work, but inevitable exile, ostracism, and lack of community in the host country—take it or leave it. They take it.

The prevailing economic system specializes in gendered labor that increasingly includes mainly female labor migration. The system subtly but steadily makes men, and particularly young males, economically worthless. I asked each woman, if it were possible to find work for the father of her children whom she had to leave behind, would she invite him to join her. Without hesitation, the reply often was: "Where he going? What I going do with that useless man?" Gussler (1980), in her study of poor women on St. Kitts in the Caribbean, and Jarrett (1994), who looks at poor black mothers in the United States, record similar responses of poor women to the plight of the men in their lives, whose economic situation seemed hopeless.

TRANSNATIONALISM

Core industrial countries such as the United States consider national identity formation as crucial to the defense and strengthening of nation-states. National identity, a desired yet unclear, complicated mix of cultural and political traits remains especially elusive for Caribbean people. Claimed by Britain and called West Indians, the people of the region were never truly British subjects. Released by Britain to an uncertain geopolitical status, beginning in the 1960s, the United States gradually but firmly changed the region into *the Caribbean*, and its people into *Caribbean blacks*.

The tendency remains for these island people to hold firmly to the insular titles imposed on them long ago by Britain. However, in exile as labor migrants in North America and Europe, and while experiencing exclusion, labor migrants crave identities. Identity formation among Caribbean labor migrants takes place in resistance to racism and ostracism. An overarching West Indian/Caribbean or black solidarity results, and is often subsumed by or interchanged with ethnic, if not national, identity (Bryce-Laporte 1987). On Aruba the women are "the island women," "the black maids," "the English maids," first; race and a pan-ethnic mold, not national identity, regulate their relations with the citizens of the host country.

The eastern Caribbean people had nation-statehood thrust upon them. Over the past thirty years, politicians in each tiny island have tried to stimulate national pride by making use of nationalistic ideology and symbolism. The islands' geographic proximity to the United States, the most powerful nation-state in the world, has not helped the Caribbean in its elusive quest for nationhood. Besides, constant labor migration from the region complicates any nascent feelings of nationalism. Are migrant domestics on Aruba transnationals?

Transnationalism describes a situation of ambivalent citizenship allegiance. Labor migrants become transnationals when "migrants and their families have multiple home bases [but] have ongoing commitments and loyalties that straddle territorial boundaries" (Wiltshire 1992, 175).

By definition, temporary guest workers should not be able to experience transnationalism. However, migrant workers often have labor contracts renewed repeatedly over long periods, or may for various legal or illegal reasons remain in the host countries. The term "transnational" suggests that the receiving country, originally seen as a way station to work opportunities by the labor migrant, eventually rivals the sending country as home. At its most ideal, the transnational lives in two cultures—physically and emotionally—feeling a sense of belonging and inclusion for both, attachments and connections with both. Another definition of transnational suggests that "the offspring of wealthy families become the conduit for capital exports, and the points of family business expansion in the United States" (Ong 1992, 131).

The social class positions of the transnationals in the sending and receiving countries must first be known in order to examine the transnational phenomenon. So-called transnationals in the same country may have very different migration experiences. However, the most salient experience that transnationals share is the status of outsider, foreigner, and allocation to the ranked category of "other" in fragmented, racially and ethnically stratified host societies.

Receiving countries, reluctant to include labor migrants, institutionalize relations that prevent the workers from feeling accepted. In fact, Miles (1993) theorizes that national identity formation by citizens of host countries depends on the creation of migrant worker labor categories and continuous exclusionary strategies devised against those same foreign labor migrants—"the other."

One aspect of Caribbean transnationalism increasingly portrays continuous overt political and economic participation by labor migrants in their sending countries (Pessar 1995; Chaney 1987). Middle-class, largely male professional labor migrants in industrialized host countries display a vibrant form of transnationalism. As U.S. political and economic involvement in their sending countries increased, so did the transnationals' interest in local politics and economic development (Pessar 1995; Ong 1992; Chaney 1987).

Female eastern Caribbean labor migrants form a less financially secure category of labor migrants than that represented by the Caribbean middle-class transnationals. The domestics on Aruba comprise a sector of low-status Caribbean women who travel and work intraregionally and in North America. These women, visible at regional and international airports, hassled, harried, and lugging mountains of bags and boxes, are most unlikely international traders, traffickers, and workers. They work hard in host countries, remaining in exile for as long as the situation in their sending countries demands. These workers, who negotiate money, goods, and labor between two or more countries, are increasingly more female than male. These women's remittances provide more than one-third of the Gross Domestic Product (GDP) of many of the sending islands of the eastern Caribbean (Olwig 1993; Rubenstein 1987).

The migrant domestics on Aruba displayed little interest in the broad political or economic development of their sending islands. The women's keen concerns included immediate and extended families, and the neighborhoods and religious denominations to which they belonged in their sending islands. This focus perhaps reflects their own lower-class roots and their own socioeconomic constraints.

On Aruba, the women's interest in their sending islands dissipated as the demands on them to be good providers weakened. However, the insecurities of not belonging anywhere persisted. Only one of the six older women still regularly visited her sending island intermittently. Inez, the only elderly, non-retired domestic, had her own demons which kept her working. She had no children. I first met her on the street, returning from her moonlighting cleaning job. At seventy-one, and still active, she had recently returned from visiting her elderly sister in the mountains of rural Grenada. She had kept her Grenada passport and declined becoming Aruban, even though her forty years on Aruba made her eligible to apply:

> I don't want to give up being a Grenadian. I don't know how I would feel if when I go back home to visit my sister the immigration stamp two or three weeks stay on my passport. And I born in the place. I had plan to go back there for good. But now I don't know. When I was there last month the little family house where my sister living, way up on this hill, far away from the grocery store, and from the doctor, and from everything. Here I have my own house, I could find a little job whenever I want it, I could get to the doctor quick. Life seem so hard this time when I was there that now I don't know what to do.

Raised expectations often set returned "transnationals" at cross-purposes with their sending societies upon their return. Travel and long stays in the host country raised the women's comfort levels. There was consensus among them that the islands they left forty or so years before had changed, and they could no longer live comfortably there. Janet, originally from Montserrat who had traveled to Aruba on the *Ruby*, returned to her home island for the first time in 1971, twenty-eight years after she had left. That visit made up her mind.

> I was not comfortable on Montserrat. I don't ever want to go back. Most of the people I left there were dead or had gone abroad. My own mother was dead. But worse than that nothing was right. Even the electric lights were not as bright as Aruba, everything was different. Either the place itself change or I change.

These "work horses" had fulfilled their mission for their sending societies, but were still deprived of the comforts and pleasures of social acceptance in the wider Aruban society. The "English Church," the haunt of a dwindling number of elderly retired women, stimulated whatever ethnic and pan-eastern Caribbean nationalism the labor migrants needed to help them maintain their identities.

Ivy, who in 1945 had sent for her boyfriend and married him soon after, was other mothering two of her grandchildren in 1989. The childrens' parents had emigrated to the United States, and left them with her until they had "their legal papers." She was seventy years old, and seemed glad to have the company of the young people. After forty-four years on Aruba, and living in a predominantly Aruban neighborhood, she still had not settled. One day as we chatted, her neighbors who could speak no English, passed by outside her door, waved and shouted greetings in Papiamento. The neighbors' children came to play on a tree in her backyard and she admonished them in English about raking up the fallen leaves, while they replied in Papiamento.

To her hosts and to herself, she was still the migrant domestic, a foreigner on Aruba. She talked about her plans for the future:

> When the grandchildren leave I may go to visit their parents but I don't want to live in the United States. I decide not to take out citizen papers for Aruba either. I want to keep my Montserrat passport. In Aruba, I can get eye-glasses free. I also get free dentures and I don't pay to see the doctor, and medicine is free too, because I reach the age. But I won't give up my Montserrat passport. What if they make me leave Aruba? I could always go back to Montserrat or better still I might go to England because Montserrat is a crown colony of Britain.

Notes

CHAPTER 1

1. The U.S. Virgin Islands and St. Maarten have become the destinations of choice for poor women from the Leewards or northeastern Caribbean islands.

2. Sassen (1992) links the migration flow of workers to urban work sites to the economic, industrial, and political incursions and forays by industrialized societies into nonindustrialized countries. According to her, it is this exposure to the industrialized world which provides the greatest lure for poor and non-poor of the nonindustrial world to flock to metropoles and urban work centers.

3. Two women had gone on to England, some moved to North America, and a few died, while others had returned to their home islands. I later located two of the women in North America, and on a visit to Grenada in 1988, I met with two women who had returned there.

4. I had entertained hopes of observing maids within their households as they worked, or even substituting for them at their work places. This proved almost impossible, as households were very closed and private units. I managed to daily observe the interactions between my landlady and her young Haitian maid; however, they always conversed in Papiamento. I spent about four hours one day on the veranda of a house in a wealthy neighborhood where one of the women included in my study worked. As the maid worked in the kitchen, she chatted with me through a window and door which opened onto the veranda about another maid, known to both of us, who had died the day before. We were always within full view of her mistress, who sat at an ornate mahogany table playing solitaire. The mistress also knew the deceased woman, and occasionally interjected into our conversation.

5. The women who requested it got two hours off each Sunday, as long as employers did not need their services. They were expected to help with Sunday breakfast and be back in time to help make and serve a late lunch. Sunday was always a very social time for churchgoing migrant women; they dressed immaculately, and several would take part in the church service.

6. The poorest and most distressed of these women were those who left several young and dependent children behind. Other stressed-out women were those who had no female kin, such as mothers or sisters, to help them with their children.

7. This woman had one child, a grown son whom she had put through school before leaving for Aruba. In fact, it was this nineteen-year-old son who, as a clerk in a downtown store in St. George's, Grenada, had offered his mother's services to a tourist seeking to sponsor a migrant domestic for his household in Aruba.

8. Papiamento was introduced to Aruba, Curaçao, and Bonaire early in the nineteenth century by Portugese Jewish traders from the Azores. The language has a strong Portugese base, with other linguistic elements from Spanish, Dutch, English, and West African languages.

9. During the 1940s, white expatriates (mostly Netherlanders on Curaçao and U.S. citizens in Aruba) comprised a large part of all workers employed at the oil refineries in the enclave (Brereton 1981, 204; Hartog 1968, 361, 375).

10. Skilled, higher-ranked Caribbean men on Aruba could marry and start families or send for their wives (no children), as long as they had intact work contracts and could fulfill a strict housing stipulation.

CHAPTER 2

1. A transitional period of between four and ten years preceded what was supposed to be full freedom.

2. At the end of the twentieth century, Trinidad continues to be an eastern Caribbean migration apex, especially for women from St. Vincent and the Grenadines, Grenada, and Carriacou (less so for those from Barbados), who travel to trade in fruit and vegetables and to shop for wholesale goods.

3. British colonial governments in the sending countries found it necessary to provide official terms of engagement with labor scouts and migrant workers. Labor scouts were asked to pay a deposit to the treasuries of their respective sending islands, in case indigent migrant workers had to be repatriated from the foreign country (Brizan 1984, 217).

4. A 1938 labor commission formed by the colonial powers advised employers on Grenada to monetize the worker/employer relationship, and change it from the feudal system of obligations and privileges which existed at the time, to an exchange of "straight cash wages for labor rendered" (Sunshine et al. 1985, 31). The commission was formed to investigate labor disturbances throughout the British Caribbean in the late 1930s and early 1940s (Immanuel 1978).

5. According to Marshall, "between 1906 and 1923 more than 20,000 British West Indians died in Panama" (Marshall 1982, 8).

6. High technological input, higher cash flows, the presence of scientists and engineers in the area, and the oil enclave's physical plants and labor arrangements reworked the slave plantation model used until then to arrange life and work relations at labor camps in the Caribbean. The slave plantation model, with some modifications, still continues on farms in the United States and Dominican Republic, which employ Caribbean male migrant labor.

7. Oil was struck in 1902 at Guayagyayare on the southeastern tip of the island of Trinidad. By 1910 twenty-five mainly British and U.S. oil companies were already prospecting (C. G. Clarke 1986). In 1917 the first large oil field in Venezuela (the

Mene Grande field) was developed by a subsidiary of Royal Dutch Shell (Zuloaga 1950, 50).

8. The Dutch Antilles, or the Netherland Antilles, are the Dutch Caribbean colonies. Saba, St. Eustatius, and St. Maarten are known as the Dutch Windward Islands. Aruba, Bonaire, and Curaçao are the Dutch Leeward Islands. Surinam, on the Atlantic coast of South America, was considered to be the other Dutch Caribbean colony before it gained independence in 1975.

9. In the 1930s, some twelve affiliates of British Petroleum were operating in Trinidad under the title of the Petroleum Association of Trinidad. Most of Trinidad's oil was exported as crude, and a small quantity refined in two small, local refineries.

10. The United States had gained favor with Venezuela and prospecting access to its oil-rich lands by siding against Britain in a dispute about offshore boundaries between the neighboring countries of Venezuela and British Guyana. Early in the twentieth century, American oil assets in Mexico were lost through Mexican nationalization, and the abundant deposits of oil in Venezuela were just what U.S. oil interests had longed for.

11. Interestingly, Trinidad's petroleum economy peaked in the 1970s and 1980s as a result of intensive "offshore drilling, the installation of local oil refineries, and the discovery of new natural gas reserves . . . and (the) Trinidadian oil-refining industry which processed crude oil from Africa and the Middle East" (Richardson 1992, 117)

12. Curaçao's population is predominantly black, but has a small number of white (Jewish), old Dutch, and mulatto families.

13. The category of "migrant worker" was used to bring three levels of foreign female workers into Aruba. In the early 1930s, trained nurses began to arrive from the British colonies in the Caribbean and the United States to work at the Lago refinery's medical complex. In the early 1940s, women were brought in from Venezuela, Colombia, and the Dominican Republic and given licenses to become prostitutes in brothels managed by Aruba's local government. At the same time, migrant domestics began arriving from the eastern Caribbean.

14. The productive oil enclave was made crucial to the war effort by the demand for vast quantities of aviation fuel coming from the Allied Forces' war effort in Europe and brand new technology invented at MIT labs which made its production possible, the location of the Venezuelan oil fields to Aruba, and the direct routes of tankers from Aruba to Europe.

15. After the Japanese attack on Pearl Harbor in 1941, "the region was brought . . . under United States control, forming what was called the Caribbean Sea Frontier" (Hartog 1968, 358).

16. Wall (1988, 404), a historian for Standard Oil New Jersey, reports that "it was the first company to employ large numbers of women . . . and by 1949, the company employed some 1,500 women." This is probably a reference to its Venezuelan operation.

CHAPTER 3

1. Modifications have been made to the classical economic theory. The centrality of the free market system in capitalist economies remains. However, the neoclassical

economic theory has conceded limited proactive roles to governments in economic systems.

2. The project "Operation Bootstrap" had three goals: (1) to expand economic development and growth through the introduction of light manufacturing industries at a safe site in a U.S. territory; (2) to control the Puerto Rican immigration to the U.S. mainland, and keep Puerto Ricans gainfully employed on the island; and (3) to have the economic development project be a model to Third World countries, especially the rest of the Caribbean.

3. British Caribbean colonies began receiving their independence from Britain in the 1960s.

4. This indictment, despite the fact that various attempts at unity have been tried, ranging from the defunct Caribbean federation, to existing economic alliances in regional organizations such as the Organization of Eastern Caribbean States (OECS).

5. A recent 592-page Caribbean publication, *Time for Action—The Report of the West Indian Commission*, drawn up by Caribbean academic and professional elite— thirteen men and two women—examined the socioeconomic conditions of eastern Caribbean societies. The male-centered regional economy was the unit of analysis, and the report included only a ten-page section on *Gender*. A sub-section entitled, "Employment," reported that although women received relatively similar access to education as men, "this has not translated into high levels of economic activity among women" (West Indian Commission 1992, 338). The Commission warned that poor women needed to be protected from the antisocial activities of the informal economic sector (West Indian Commission 1992, 341).

6. William Demas, president of the Caribbean Development Bank and guest speaker at the inauguration of the National Advisory Committee of St. Vincent and the Grenadines on "Political Unity in the Eastern Caribbean States" (July 20, 1987), engaged in macro-structural images of economic cooperation and development for the region in his well-received speech. He referred to banking, shipping, currency, defense, nationalism, business, and investment, as if gender did not matter. Either all business happened in a male milieu, or women did business easily and enjoyed a comfortable place in the formal economy.

7. Massiah (1989) reported at length on the findings of the *Women in the Caribbean Project* (WICP), which studied the working lives of eastern Caribbean women between 1979 and 1982, on the islands of St. Vincent, Antigua, and Barbados.

8. Reddock (1988, 120) notes that as Caribbean slave economies declined, so did the subsistence provisions allotted to slaves. Slave women became very innovative petty entrepreneurs.

9. My argument is somewhat different from Boserup's (1970) in that many poor women learn and inherit entrepreneurial creative skills over generations of hardship. I modify Marx's idea of the industrial workers' alienation from their labor, simply to state that women have often created their own money-earning "businesses," and had fulfillment from them. The women in my study must make a choice between the unpredictability of cash gained from vending their craft, and the drudgery of assigned tasks for which predictable and consistent wages are assured.

10. During the 1980s, labor migrants particularly from the Dominican Republic, poured into St. Maarten, one of the Dutch Antilles. The women work initially as migrant domestics. Later, many manage to open beauty parlors, while still others work the streets selling food.

11. Barriteau (1996, 145–48) wrestles with the traditional Marxist concepts of classes in the Caribbean context. She suggests that middle-class status for many Caribbean people is a cooperative effort between upwardly mobile, wage-earning persons and kin engaged in exchange relations.

12. Gussler (1980) noted lone women in St. Kitts, sitting on rocky hillsides, breaking stones to be sold for local road-building purposes.

13. In 1951 male laborers made ninety-four cents per day while women made seventy-six cents (Sunshine et al. 1985, 37). Whenever there were increases, they were done on the basis that men should be paid higher wages, even though women are usually heads of households among the Caribbean poor.

14. In times of economic recession, men automatically become the preferred workers in supposedly non-gendered wage labor (Brizan 1984). So, in research done in the 1980s, Brierley (1993) could find no female farmhands hoeing or weeding in Grenada.

15. Women who work legally or illegally as maids on Trinidad, Venezuela, Curaçao, Aruba, the Virgin Islands, St. Maarten, or New York, also buy manufactured goods—clothing, jewelry, and electronics. They ply these wares on return visits, or engage "middlemen," usually relatives chosen to act as salespeople for the "traffickers," as the women call themselves.

16. For example, the official labor record does indicate numbers of women in manufacturing, but lumps together domestics and seamstresses, of which there were literally thousands. However, launderers were recorded as a distinct category (Reddock 1994, 81–84).

17. Domestics proliferate at times of change in the economy. Middle-class women on Trinidad, Aruba, and Curaçao became housewives and employed poor women to do the housework from the 1930s to the 1960s. Repak tells how, from the late 1960s, white women in the United States and particularly Washington, D.C., began "entering the wage labor force and demanding adequate child care" (Repak 1994, 512). Central American women arrived at Washington in droves to fill those job openings.

18. Hansen (1992) makes an interesting case for the construction of gender and sexuality by colonial whites and expatriates in Africa. She argues that so-called gendered labor that relegates native women to work in white households is not necessarily the norm. Native male resistance to having their womenfolk leave home to be domestics, and the interpretations of native peoples' gender and sexuality by whites, affect who are preferred as domestics. She states that native men, not women, have been the popular domestic workers in white households in parts of Africa.

19. Richardson (1983) calls this kind of labor migration "speculating." According to him, most poor Caribbean labor migrants make quick forays to nearby destinations because they have few resources to take them farther and many obligations awaiting their attention back at home.

CHAPTER 4

1. Stress on the voluntariness of indentured labor and foreign labor migrations minimizes the structural and other factors that uproot people and send them into

foreign countries in search of work. For many, their wage-earning options are few if they leave, but fewer if they remain in the sending countries.

2. Dark-skinned immigrants from former British colonies flocked into Britain all during the 1950s, until Britain put an end to their arrival and created strict immigration laws. The Immigration Act (1962) delineated the rights of immigrants and their offspring from those of the "true" British (Layton-Henry 1992, 75). Germany has always prevented migrant workers and their offspring from German citizenship (Castles 1986).

3. In 1936 the Lago refinery employed 2,810 foreign workers. Of these, 790 were skilled and semiskilled laborers from outside of the Caribbean. These white non-executive foreign workers filled "more than a third of the 138 supervisory positions" (Larson 1971, 379).

4. Venezuela, the only independent country in the enclave, showed much concern about depletion of its vast oil resources with little returns to show for it. The multinationals, backed by their respective nation-states, were able to wrest the best deals in their own interests through oil agreements with Venezuela.

5. White high-status workers from as far away as South Africa found employment in Trinidad at refineries operated by British Petroleum. There were endless complaints about their management style with the local black employees (Brereton 1981).

6. But even there, the republic was almost helpless to stay a constant legal and illegal influx of migrant workers from neighboring Colombia and the eastern Caribbean. Trinidad had more than enough labor migrants, who poured in from neighboring small islands. The Dutch colonial authorities welcomed workers with Dutch Rights from the islands of St. Maarten, Saba, and St. Eustatius into Aruba and Curaçao (Crane 1971). However, of all the countries in the enclave, it was sparsely populated Aruba that experienced the largest wholesale importation, proportionately, of foreign workers (Phalen 1977; Larson 1971, 379).

7. European nations transported refugees, convicts, and labor migrants to Australia, New Zealand, South Africa, and even Canada as "voluntary" (Miles 1993) or "unfree" (Satzewich 1991) labor from the nineteenth to the first half of the twentieth century.

8. Britain and the Dutch cooperated with U.S. oil companies to devise migrant worker schemes to the Caribbean oil countries. In 1941, despite the protest of Trinidadians, Britain signed a ninety-nine year lease with the U.S. government for hundreds of acres of Trinidad's prime real estate to build a U.S. naval base. For nearly thirty-five years, foreign companies had complete cooperation from Venezuela's President Gomez.

9. There is disagreement about whether there is more than one form of "racism." Balibar takes the line that racism has "a singular history, though admittedly not a linear one" (Balibar 1991, 40). Miles, however, seems poised to accept that there may be several types of racism. He argues that, at least, there is "racism of the interior," describing racialization within a nation-state. "Racism of the exterior" describes colonialism and neocolonialism.

10. Colonial domination separated neighboring island colonies from each other. For decades, Caribbean migrant workers from most colonies worked together at sites in Panama, Costa Rica, Cuba, and the Dominican Republic. Once in the enclave, U.S. hegemony of the area racialized the region further, and created a new kind of insularity. Local hierarchies based on skin color received a boost. The Caribbean

countries that gained special sporadic economic preference from the United States tended to see themselves as better than the rest of the region.

11. All these new connections with the industrialized nations did not happen as matters of course. My argument is that colonial labor migration demands, migrant labor schemes, and international trade and migration negotiations concerning the Caribbean, became possible because a new political space had opened up. I connect this new space to the presence of the industrialized nations in the enclave.

12. Satzewich (1991) makes important distinctions between labor immigrants and labor migrants. He gives labor migrants subcategories of "free migrant labour," and "unfree migrant labour." Temporary foreign workers, of the type that Satzewich would deem "unfree," feature in this book. These workers "are not granted the right of permanent settlement by the state in which they sell their labour power" (Satzewich 1991, 39).

13. Philipps (1988, 54) concluded in her study of migrant domestics on Curaçao that women entered the island under very harsh contractual labor and immigration agreements. The conditions of these agreements completely obliterated any hopes for social mobility.

14. Sometimes it takes social and political movements, such as the 1960s' Civil Rights Movement or the political upheaval and overthrow of apartheid in South Africa, to enforce the rights of citizens formerly treated as foreign migrant workers in their own country by a powerful status quo.

15. In Zambia, South Africa (Hansen 1992), and many other countries, including parts of the Caribbean, young men work as yard boys in middle-class homes and perform much of the outdoor work and care of household pets.

16. Migrant workers sometimes are used by governments in host countries to break troublesome trade unions and make citizens feel that their labor is dispensable. More often, however, the migrant worker is a sign of economic transition—often boom times in the host country's economy and periods of socioeconomic mobility for citizens.

17. Maids in South Africa, Lima, and the Caribbean, among other countries, tend to be housed in "out-rooms," attached or standing free at the back of the main dwellings in which they are employed. Aruba's arrangement is meant to provide full oversight of the migrant women's movements.

18. In 1969 there were twenty eastern Caribbean women who were listed in the census as married to Aruban men. In 1991 that number had dropped to eleven. In 1969 there were twenty-three eastern Caribbean men married to Aruban women, and by 1991 there were none (Eelens 1993).

19. In the 1990s, migrant domestics from the Philippines, the Dominican Republic, Venezuela, and Colombia, just like western European and Irish women who arrived in the United States at the turn of the century, are finding spouses and socioeconomic inclusion on Aruba.

20. An elderly woman on Grenada, and former nurse at the Lago hospital during the 1940s and 1950s, divulged with great sadness how only two years before she became eligible for her pension, her husband, also a migrant worker at Lago, was laid off. She had to leave the island with him.

CHAPTER 5

1. Mary Proudfoot was commissioned by the Colonial Office in Britain to conduct independent research to advise the Caribbean Commission on the readiness of the Commonwealth Caribbean for self-government.

2. Marriages occurred regularly among migrant workers in the oil enclave (Abraham-Van der Mark 1983; Philipps 1988). Besides, returned migrant workers sought out girlfriends and former mates for marriage (Rubenstein 1987).

3. Increased population in the dry oil-refining islands of Curaçao and Aruba caused a water crisis. Water for drinking purposes was shipped by barge from Venezuela; the nondrinking supply arrived from the Thames in the empty holds of tankers returning from delivering oil in Europe. Residents on the islands had to await the weekly arrival of water trucks for their water supply.

4. Edna was one of the few migrant domestics still alive in 1989 whose employer had worked at the first oil refinery—Eagle Refinery—on the coast just west of present-day Oranjestad. It was owned by Royal Dutch Shell, a Dutch conglomerate.

5. Any married migrant domestic whose husband was being repatriated also had to leave with him.

6. Could it be that women of childbearing age in her time did have just as many children, but infant mortality rates were higher; that the oil enclave in the southern Caribbean allowed many employed men to financially support their children, so that unmarried women with children did not have to leave them to become migrant domestics; or that the mandated higher upper age limit for arriving women attracted older women who no longer had dependent children, or older, childless women who wanted to be "career" migrant domestics? Besides, of the twenty younger women in the study, only four had more than four children and six of these had no children at all.

7. This perennial trade with Trinidad by people from the "small islands" increased during the late 1960s, and for the next two decades outgrew the inter-island transportation. The women bought cargo spaces on airplanes to transport their goods both ways.

8. These women traders also may have inadvertently decimated the home-sewing trades with their importation of ready-made clothing, and helped change Caribbean tastes in food and for fashionable U.S. goods.

9. Gussler (1980) notes that poor women on St. Kitts were flocking to the British and U.S. Virgin Islands. Gerber, Whitman and Greg (1971) record that migration from the northernmost islands of the eastern Caribbean such as St. Kitts, Nevis, and Dominica, was at its peak in the late 1960s. Koot (1981) writes that St. Maarten had become an important job-producing destination for the region, and even for Aruba, since the late 1970s. Aruba's immigration and labor authorities have also renewed their interests in Spanish-speaking domestics.

10. The Aruban guilder fluctuates in its exchange rate with the U.S. dollar, but in 1989 its value was usually between 1.80 or 2.00 guilders to one U.S. dollar.

11. Nearly all the women of the younger age cohort reported that their indebtedness to their sponsors (to the tune of one thousand dollars eastern Caribbean currency) caused them much worry during their first year on Aruba.

12. Children born to unmarried parents in the eastern Caribbean may often have at least two last names (surnames): that of their mother and of their father, and use them interchangeably. However, if the child's father has declared paternity, then his

child's official birth certificate will include his name, which she must legally carry. If this woman's father had "claimed" her, as she put it, her official document still carried her mother's last name.

CHAPTER 6

1. The women told me that Haitian maids did get pregnant on Aruba, but they usually went back to Haiti to give birth and later returned to their jobs on Aruba. There is a vibrant Haitian community in neighboring Venezuela. Boats arrived weekly on Aruba carrying Haitian art, fruit, and vegetables from the Dominican Republic. Perhaps Haitian maids were able to find Haitian mates through these avenues.

2. One of the weaknesses of extended family arrangements is the fact that pooled resources are usually spread thin among a variety of kin. Theoretically, nuclear families or single wage earners are more able to plan and use resources more efficiently.

3. However, cross-cultural research shows that female-headed households are not necessarily associated with poverty (Blumberg 1994, 26).

4. In the United States, social programs that house, feed, and generally provide for the poor have been blamed for causing poverty, keeping people poor, and encouraging poor women to bear children. In 1996 U.S. federal law allowed states to put a two-year cap on welfare receipts to each participant.

5. In January of 1996, I engaged in conversation a middle-age female beach vendor who was selling T-shirts on Grand Anse Beach in Grenada. When I inquired about her business and if it was doing well, she replied that all the women I saw selling shirts along the beach were employed by the same man; each woman made a commission on her daily sales.

6. The eastern Caribbean, with its absence of publicly run social services, negates the popular argument in the United States, that liberal welfare benefits cause poverty, dependence, and out-of-wedlock births.

7. Rodman (1971) and Rubenstein (1987) theorize in the case of Caribbean societies, as does Liebow (1967) in his study of poor African American inner-city males, that people often use routinized behavior rather than logical responses to situations that repeatedly confront them. So that female-headed households or extended family arrangements may continue as custom (at least for some time), even after the original structural conditions that spawned them no longer exist.

8. This resembles certain theories of working-class child rearing, or Cancian's "masculine styles of love" that provide protection and practical help in lieu of expressions of tender feelings (Cancian 1987).

9. Women tend to be more dependable in remitting money and goods, and in spending their earnings on their dependents than men are.

10. Rollins (1985) notes that black maids in wealthy white households often saw themselves as surrogate mothers and were viewed similarly by the children in their care.

11. I tried not to show my surprise as the maid named the prestigious university and the boys' boarding school that the daughter and son attended, respectively. She could tell details about their grades and U.S. tests for entering college. I had to ask

her how she knew all this. She said that she was always present as the parents made plans for the children.

12. Senior (1991) notes that the Caribbean middle class also liberally participates in the lower-class custom of having children out of wedlock and cohabiting before marriage.

13. In the eastern Caribbean, marriage is only one of three widely interwoven options of mating, childbearing, and household arrangement. However, the census and research analysis of any mating sample is able to capture only a snippet, a frame, of what is for the majority of individuals a series of alternating mating behaviors over their lifetimes. See Rubenstein (1987) for a clear treatise on the topic.

14. See Aymer (1997); Senior (1991, 84–86a); and Rubenstein (1987).

15. In 1996 the U.S. Congress passed new laws giving states the power to withhold substantial government-provided monetary aid from teen mothers under age eighteen. Much more responsibility for young, unmarried mothers has been placed on their parents.

16. Pessar (1995) writes about other Caribbean labor migration in which the entire family moves. Since the 1960s, entire families have left the Dominican Republic for the United States. Whether to find work regionally or in the United States, eastern Caribbean women tend to venture out alone; later, family reunification might follow.

17. Each woman was asked about her hysterectomy. The women seemed satisfied about the necessity of this major surgical procedure and acted as if they had gotten rid of an annoyance.

18. Soto (1987) tells how two Caribbean labor migrants in New York—the legal but separated wife and the girlfriend—forsook their rivalry over the man who had fathered their children. In order to earn and provide, the women shared in child care responsibilities for the children.

CHAPTER 7

1. I became part of the maid network when Jennifer died during my fieldwork in 1989. First, I received several calls about her illness and hospitalization, then about her death. Together, two maids and I made arrangements for her burial.

2. The migrant domestics' social and sexual lives have been a social issue for a long time. During particular periods, Colombian and Venezuelan women, and more recently women from the Dominican Republic and Jamaica, have been declared persona non grata because of their alleged ability to become mistresses and wives in the households where they found employment.

3. Between the end of 1989 and the end of 1992, Aruba's population increased by more than 10,000 persons. Out of a total labor force of 31,111, no less than 26 percent were foreign-born. About forty percent of all foreign workers are in the service industry and are mostly foreign-born women, the majority of whom originate from the Dominican Republic, Colombia, Venezuela, Haiti, Grenada, Jamaica, and Asia (Eelens, 1993; 49–54).

Bibliography

Abraham-Van der Mark, Eva. 1993. "Marriage and Concubinage among the Shep-phardic Merchant Elite of Curaçao." In *Women & Change in the Caribbean*, edited by Janet H. Momsen (Bloomington: Indiana University Press).

———. 1983. "The Impact of Industrialization on Women. A Caribbean Case." In *Women, Men and the International Division of Labor*, edited by June Nash, Helen Safa, and Maria Patricia Fernandez-Kelly (Albany: State University of New York Press).

Acosta-Belen, Edna and Christine E. Bose. 1995. "Colonialism, Structural Subordi-nation, and Empowerment: Women in the Development Process in Latin America and the Caribbean." In *Women in the Latin American Development Process*, edited by Christine E. Bose and Edna Acosta-Belen (Philadelphia: Temple University Press).

Augelli, John P. 1962. "The Rimland-Mainland Concept of Culture Areas in Middle America." *Annals of the Association of American Geographers* 52: 119–29.

Aymer, Paula. 1997. "Caribbean Cohabitation: Gender Antagonism or Gender Negotiation?" Unpublished.

———. 1990. *Capitalist Incursions and Intra-Caribbean Migration: A case Study of Eastern Caribbean Migrant Domestics in Aruba*. Ph.D. Diss. Dept. of Sociology and Anthropology, Northeastern University, Boston, MA.

———. Forthcoming. "The Resistance Theme Revisited: Intra-Caribbean Female Mi-grant Workers and Their Families." In *Marriage and Family Review*, edited by Barbara Settles and Marvin Sussman (New York: Haworth Press).

Balibar, Etienne. 1991. "Racism and Nationalism." In *Race, Nation, Class: Ambiguous Identities*, edited by Etienne Balibar and Immanuel Wallerstein (London: Verso).

Baptiste, F. A. 1973. "The Seizure of the Dutch Authorities in Willemsted, Curaçao by Venezuelan Political Exiles in June 1929." *Caribbean Studies* 13 (1): 36–60.

Barriteau, Eudine V. 1996. "Structural Adjustment Policies in the Caribbean: A Feminist Perspective." *Journal of the National Women's Studies Association (NWSA)* 8 (1): 142–56.

Barrow, Christine. 1993. "Small Farm Food Production & Gender in Barbados." In *Women & Change in the Caribbean*, edited by Janet H. Momsen (Bloomington: Indiana University Press).

Berheide, Catherine White and Esther Ngan-Ling Chow. 1994. "Perpetuating Gender Inequality: The Role of Families, Economies, and States." In *Women, the Family and Policy: A Global Perspective*, edited by Esther Ngan-Ling Chow and Catherine White Berheide (New York: State University of New York Press).

Bernard, Jessie. 1981. "The Good Provider Role: Its Rise and Fall." *American Psychologist* 36 (1): 1–12.

Best, Lloyd. 1968. "Outlines of a Model of Pure Plantation Economy." *Social & Economic Studies* 17 (3): 283–326.

Betancourt, Romulo. 1979. *Venezuela: Oil and Politics*, translated by Everett Bauman (Boston: Houghton Mifflin).

Blumberg, Rae Lesser. 1994. "Women's Work, Wealth, and Family Survival Strategy: The Impact of Guatemala's ALCOSA Agribusiness Project." In *Women, the Family, and Policy*, edited by Esther Ngan-Ling Chow and Catherine White Berhide (Albany: State University of New York Press).

Blumberg, Rae Lesser and Maria Pilas Garcia. 1977. "The Political Economy of the Mother-Child Family: A Cross-Cultural View." In *Beyond the Nuclear Family Model*, edited by Luis Lenero-Otero (London: Sage).

Bolland, Nigel O. 1992. "The Politics of Freedom in the British Caribbean." In *The Meaning of Freedom, Economics, Politics, and Culture After Slavery*, edited by Frank McGlynn and Seymour Drescher (Pittsburgh: University of Pittsburgh Press).

Bonacich, Edna. 1972. "A Theory of Ethnic Antagonism. The Split-Labor Market." *American Sociological Review* 37: 547–59.

Boserup, Ester. 1970. *Women's Role in Economic Development* (New York: St. Martin's Press).

Boue, Juan Carlos. 1993. *Venezuela: The Political Economy of Oil* (London: Oxford University Press).

Brereton, Bridget. 1981. *History of Modern Trinidad 1783–1962.* (Exeter, NH: Heinemann).

———. 1979. *Race Relations in Colonial Trinidad* (London: Cambridge University Press).

Brewer, Rose. 1988. "Black Women in Poverty: Some Comments on Female-Headed Families." *Signs* 13 (2): 331–39.

Brewster, H. and C. Thomas. 1967. *The Dynamics of West Indian Economic Integration* (Mona, Jamaica: Institute of Social and Economic Research).

Brierley, John S. 1993. "A Profile of Grenadian Women Small Farmers." In *Women & Change in the Caribbean*, edited by Janet H. Momsen (Bloomington: Indiana University Press).

Briggs, Vernon, Jr. 1986. "The 'Albatross' of Immigration Reform: Temporary Worker Policy in the United States." *International Migration Review* 20 (Winter): 995–1019.

Brizan, George. 1984. *Grenada Island of Conflict* (London: Zed Books).

Brower, Steve. 1992. *Sharing the Pie: A Disturbing Picture of the U.S. Economy* (Carlisle, PA: Big Picture Books).

Bryce-Laporte, Roy Simon. 1987. "New York City and the New Caribbean Immigration: A Contextual Statement." In *Caribbean Life in New York City: Sociological Dimensions*, edited by Constance R. Sutton and Elsa M. Chaney (New York: Center for Migration Studies).

Bunster, Ximena and Elsa M. Chaney. 1985. *Sellers and Servants: Working Women in Lima, Peru* (Westport, CT: Praeger).

Burpee, C. Gaye, James N. Morgan, and Alan Dragon. 1986. *Household Survey of Grenada* (Ann Arbor: University of Michigan Press).

Cancian, Francesca M. 1987. *Love in America* (New York: Cambridge University Press).

Carnegie, Charles V. 1987. "A Social Psychology of Caribbean Migration: A Strategic Flexibility in the West Indies." In *The Caribbean Exodus*, edited by Barry Levine (New York: Praeger).

Castles, Stephen. 1989. "Introduction." In *Migrant Workers and the Transformation of Western Societies* (Ithaca, NY: Cornell University Press).

———. 1986. "The Guests Who Stayed." *International Migration Review* 19 (3): 517–34.

Caulfield, Mina Davis. 1974. "Imperialism, the Family and Cultures of Resistance." *Socialist Revolution* (20): 67–85.

Chaney, Elsa M. 1987. "The Context of Caribbean Migration." In *Caribbean Life in New York City: Sociological Dimensions*, edited by Constance R. Sutton and Elsa M. Chaney (New York: Center for Migration Studies).

Chaney, Elsa M. and Mary Garcia Castro. 1989. *Muchachas No More: Household Workers in Latin America and the Caribbean* (Philadelphia: Temple University Press).

Clarke, Colin G. 1986. *East Indians in a West Indian Town: San Fernando, Trinidad, 1930–70* (Boston: Allen & Unwin).

Clarke, Edith. 1966. *The Mother Who Fathered Me: A Study of the Family in Three Selected Communities in Jamaica* (London: George Allen & Unwin).

Claypole, William and John Robottom. 1981. *Caribbean Story: The Inheritors* (London: Longman Group).

Collins, Patricia Hill. 1994. "Shifting the Center: Race, Class, and Feminist Theorizing about Motherhood." In *Mothering: Ideology, Experience, and Agency*, edited by Evelyn Nakano Glenn, Grace Chang, and Linda Rennie Forcey (New York: Routledge).

———. 1990. *Black Feminist Thought: Knowledge, Consciousness, and the Politics of Empowerment* (New York: Routledge).

Comitas, Lambros. 1964. "Occupational Multiplicity in Rural Jamaica." Proceedings of the Annual Meeting of the American Ethnological Society, 41–50 (Seattle: University of Washington Press).

Crane, Julia G. 1971. *Educated to Emigrate: The Social Organization of Saba* (Assen, Netherlands: Van Gorcum).

Cudjoe, Selwyn R. 1988. *V.S. Naipaul: A Materialist Reading* (Amherst, MA: University of Massachusetts Press).

Davis, Angela. 1981. *Women, Race, and Class* (New York: Random House).

Dill, Bonnie Thorton. 1995. "Our Mothers' Grief: Racial Ethnic Women and the Maintenance of Families." In *Race, Class, and Gender*, edited by Margaret L. Andersen and Patricia Hill Collins (Belmont, CA: Wadsworth Publishing).

Dirks, Robert. 1972. "Networks, Groups and Adaptation in an Afro-Caribbean Community." *Man* 7 (4): 565–85.

Eelens, Frank C. H. 1993. *The Population and Housing Census: Aruba—October 6, 1991* (Oranjestad, Aruba: Central Bureau of Statistics).

Ellis, Patricia, ed. 1986. *Women of the Caribbean* (London: Zed Books).

Enloe, Cynthia. 1990. *Bananas, Beaches, & Bases: Making Feminist Sense of International Politics* (Berkeley: University of California Press).

Fanning, Leonard M., ed. 1950. *Our Oil Resources* (New York: McGraw-Hill).

Fanon, Franz. 1965. *Wretched of the Earth* (New York: Grove Press).

Fernandez, Ronald. 1994. *Cruising the Caribbean. U.S. Influence and Intervention in the Twentieth Century* (Monroe, ME: Common Courage Press).

Fernandez-Kelly, M. Patricia and Saskia Sassen. 1995. "Recasting Women in the Global Economy: Internationalization and Changing Definitions of Gender. In *Women in the Latin American Development Process*, edited by Christine E. Bose and Edna Acosta-Belen (Philadelphia: Temple University Press).

Foner, Nancy. 1987. *New Immigrants in New York.* (New York: Columbia University Press).

———. 1979. "West Indians in New York City and London: A Comparative Analysis." In *International Migration Review* 13: 284–97.

Garcia Castro, Mary. 1989. "What is Bought and Sold in Domestic Service? The Case of Bogata: A Critical Review." In *Muchachas No More: Household Workers in Latin America and the Caribbean*, edited by Elsa M. Chaney and Mary Garcia Castro (Philadelphia: Temple University Press).

Garfinkel, Irwin and Sara S. McLanahan. 1986. *Single Mothers and Their Children: A New American Dilemma* (Washington, DC: Urban Institute Press).

Gerber, Stanford, N. Whitman, and E. Greg. 1971. "Notes on Recent Immigrant to the United States Virgin Islands." *International Migration Review* 5: 357–62.

Girvan, Norman. 1970. "Multinational Corporations and Dependent Underdevelopment in Mineral-Export Economies." In *Social Economic Research*. Jamaica Institute of Social and Economic Research, University of the West Indies.

Glenn, Evelyn Nakano. 1994. "Social Constructions of Mothering: A Thematic Overview." In *Mothering: Ideology, Experience, and Agency*, edited by Evelyn Nakano Glenn, Grace Chang, and Linda Rennie Forcey (New York: Routledge).

———. 1992. "From Servitude to Service Work: Historical Continuities in the Racial Division of Paid Reproductive Labor." *Signs* 18 (1): 1–43.

Glick Schiller, Nina, Linda Basch, and Cristina Blanc-Szanton. 1995. "The Nation-State Question: The Politics of Transnational Studies." Unpublished Paper prepared for Conference on Caribbean Circuits: Transnational Approaches to Migration. Dept. of Anthropology, Yale University, New Haven, Connecticut.

———. 1992. "A New Analytical Framework for Understanding Migration." In *Towards a Transnational Perspective on Migration*, edited by Nina Glick Schiller, Linda Basch, and Christina Blanc-Szanton (New York: New York Academy of Sciences).

Glissant, Edouard. 1989. *Caribbean Discourse* (Charlottesville, VA: Caraf Books, University Press of Virginia).

Gmelch, George. 1992. *Double Passage: The Lives of Caribbean Migrants Abroad and Back Home* (Ann Arbor: University of Michigan Press).

Grasmuck, Sherri. 1982. "Migration within the Periphery: Haitian Labor in the Dominican Sugar and Coffee Industries." *International Migration Review* 16 (2): 365–78.

Grasmuck, Sherri and Patricia R. Pessar. 1991. *Between Two Islands: Dominican International Migration* (Berkeley: University of California Press).

Green, Vera. 1974. *Migrants in Aruba: Interethnic Integration* (Assen, Netherlands: Van Gorcum).

Griffith, David. 1986. "Peasants in Reserve: Temporary West Indian Labor in the U.S. Farm Labor Market." *International Migration Review* 20 (4): 875–98.

Gussler, Judith. 1980. "Adaptive Strategies and Social Networks of Women in St. Kitts." In *A World of Women*, edited by Erika Bourguignon (New York: Praeger Publishers).

Hansen, Karen Tranberg. 1992. "Body Politics: Sexuality, Gender, and Domestic Service in Zambia." In *Expanding the Boundaries of Women's History: Essays on Women in the Third World*, edited by Cheryl Johnson-Odim and Margaret Strobel (Bloomington: Indiana University Press).

Hartog, J. 1968. *Curaçao*, translated by J. A. Verleun (Aruba, Netherlands Antilles: De Wit).

———. 1961. *Aruba Past and Present: From the Time of the Indians until Today*, translated by J. A. Verleun (Aruba, Netherlands Antilles: De Wit).

Hawley, Amos H. 1960. *The Population of Aruba: A Report Based on the Census of 1960.* Oranjestad, Aruba.

Henry, Frances. 1987. "Caribbean Migration to Canada: Prejudice and Opportunity." 214–22. In *Caribbean Exodus*, edited by Barry B. Levine (New York: Praeger).

Henry, Paget. 1990. "Decolonization in Antigua and Its Impact on Agriculture and Tourism." In *The Newer Caribbean*, edited by Paget Henry and Carl Stone (Institute for the Study of Human Issues).

———. 1985. *Peripheral Capitalism and Underdevelopment in Antigua* (New Brunswick, NJ: Transaction Books).

———. 1981. "Decolonization, Tourism and Class/Race Structure in Antigua." 243–63. In *Contemporary Caribbean*, edited by Susan Craig (Maracas, Trinidad and Tobago: College Press).

Heroy, William B. 1950. "The Functional Organization of the Petroleum Industry." In *World Geography of Petroleum*, edited by Wallace E. Pratt and Dorothy Good (Princeton, NJ: Princeton University Press).

Herskovits, M. J. and F. Herskovits. 1947. *Trinidad Village* (New York: Knopf).

Immanuel, Patrick A. M. 1978. *Elections and Party Systems in the Commonwealth Caribbean, 1991–1994* (Barbados, West Indies: Caribbean Development Research Services).

Inkeles, Alex and David H. Smith. 1974. *Becoming Modern: Individual Change in Six Developing Countries* (Cambridge, MA: Harvard University Press).

Jarrett, Robin L. 1994. "Living Poor: Family Life among Single Parent, African-American Women." *Social Problems* 41: 30–49.

Kalm, Florence. 1975. *The Dispersive and Reintegrating Nature of Population Segments of a Third World Society: Aruba Netherlands Antilles*. Ph.D. Diss. (Anthropology), The City University of New York (Ann Arbor, MI: Xerox University Microfilms).

Karch, Cecelia. 1981. "The Growth of the Corporate Economy in Barbados: Class/Race Factors, 1890–1977." In *Contemporary Caribbean*, edited by Susan Craig (Maracas, Trinidad and Tobago: College Press).

Kasinitz, Philip. 1992. *Caribbean New York* (Ithaca, NY: Cornell University Press).

Koot, Wim. 1981. "Socioeconomic Development and Emigration in the Netherlands Antilles." In *Contemporary Caribbean*, edited by Susan Craig (Maracas, Trinidad and Tobago: College Press).

Kritz, Mary, Lin Lean Lim, and Hania Zlotnik, eds. 1992. *International Migration Systems. A Global Approach* (Oxford: Clarendon Press; New York: Oxford University Press).

Langley, Lester D. 1989. *The United States and the Caribbean in the Twentieth Century* (Atlanta: University of Georgia Press).

Larson, Henrietta M., Evelyn H. Knowlton, and Charles Popple. 1971. *New Horizons 1927–1950: History of Standard Oil Company (New Jersey)* (New York: Standard Oil).

Layton-Henry, Zig. 1992. *The Politics of Immigration: Immigration, "Race," and "Race" Relations in Post-War Britain* (Cambridge, MA: Blackwell Publishers).

Lee, E. S. 1966. "A Theory of Migration." *Demography* 3 (1).

Levine, Barry B., ed. 1987. *The Caribbean Exodus* (New York: Praeger).

Liebow, Elliot. 1967. *Tally's Corner: A Study of Negro Street-Corner Men* (Boston, MA: Little, Brown and Company).

Maingot, Anthony P. 1994. *The United States and the Caribbean: Challenges of Asymetrical Relationships* (Boulder, CO: Westview Press).

Marshall, Dawn. 1985. "Migration and Development in the Eastern Caribbean." In *Migration and Development in the Caribbean: The Unexplored Connection*, edited by Robert A. Pastor (Boulder CO: Westview Press).

———. 1982. "The History of Caribbean Migration: The Case of the West Indies." *Caribbean Review* 11 (1) : 6–9, 52–53.

Martinez, Anibal R. 1989. *Venezuelan Oil: Development Chronology* (London: Elservier Applied Science).

Massiah, Joycelin 1989. "Women's Lives and Livelihoods: A View from the Commonwealth Caribbean." *World Development* 17 (7): 965–77.

McAfee, Kathy. 1991. *Storm Signals: Structural Adjustment and Development Alternatives in the Caribbean* (London: Zed Books).

McClelland, David C. 1961. *The Achieving Society* (New York: Van Nostrand).

Mencher, Joan P. and Anne Okongwu. 1993. "Introduction." In *Where Did All the Men Go? Female-Headed/Female-Supported Households in Cross-Cultural Perspectives*, edited by Joan P. Mencher and Anne Okongwu (Boulder, CO: Westview Press).

Miles, Robert. 1993. *Racism after "Race Relations"* (London: Routledge).

Miller, Mark J. 1986. "Introduction: Temporary Workers: Programs, Mechanisms, Conditions, Consequences." *International Migration Review* 20 (4): 740–57.

Mintz, Sidney W. 1992. "Panglosses and Pollyannas; or Whose Reality Are We Talking About?" In *The Meaning of Freedom, Economics, Politics, and Culture After Slavery*, edited by Frank McGlynn and Seymour Drescher (Pittsburgh: University of Pittsburgh Press).

Momsen, Janet H. 1993. "Development & Gender Divisions of Labour in the Rural Eastern Caribbean." In *Women & Change in the Caribbean*, edited by Janet H. Momsen (Bloomington: Indiana University Press).

Moses, Yolanda T. 1977. "Female Status, the Family and Male Dominance in a West Indian Community." *Signs* 3: 142–53.

Nash, June, Helen Safa, and Maria Patricia Fernandez-Kelly, eds. 1983. *Women, Men and the International Division of Labor* (Albany, NY: State University of New York Press).

Okongwu, Anne. 1993. "Some Conceptual Issues: Female Single-Parent Families in the United States." In *Where Did All the Men Go? Female-Headed/Female-Supported Households in Cross-Cultural Perspectives*, edited by Joan P. Mencher and Anne Okongwu (Boulder, CO: Westview Press).

Olwig, Karen Fog. 1993. "The Migration Experience: Nevisian Women at Home & Abroad. In *Women & Change in the Caribbean*, edited by Janet H. Momsen (Bloomington: Indiana University Press).

Omi, Michael and Howard Winant. 1986. *Racial Formation in the United States from the 1960s to the 1980s* (New York: Routledge and Kegan Paul).

Ong, Aihwa. 1992. "Limits to Cultural Accumulation: Chinese Capitalists on the American Pacific Rim." In *Towards a Transnational Perspective on Migration*, edited by Nina Glick Schiller, Linda Basch, and Christina Blanc-Szanton (New York: New York Academy of Sciences).

———. 1987. *Spirits of Resistance and Capitalist Discipline: Factory Women in Malaysia* (New York: State University of New York Press).

Palmer, Ransford. 1995. *Pilgrims from the Sun. West Indian Migration to America* (New York: Twayne Publishers).

Pantin, Dennis. 1994. "Techno-Industrial Policy in the Restructuring of the Caribbean: The Missing Link in Caribbean Economic Thought." In *The Caribbean in the Global Political Economy*, edited by Hilbourne A. Watson (Boulder, CO: Lynne Rienner Publishers).

Parpart, Jane L. 1990. "Wage Earning Women and the Double Day: The Nigerian Case." In *Women, Employment and the Family in the International Division of Labour*, edited by Sharon Stichter and Jane L. Parpart (Philadelphia: Temple University Press).

Parsons, Talcott. 1955. "The American Family: Its Relation to Pesonality and to the Social Structure." In *Family, Socialization and Interaction Process*, edited by Talcott Parsons and Robert F. Bales (New York: Free Press).

Patterson, Orlando. 1982. *Slavery and Social Death: A Comparative Study* (Cambridge, MA: Harvard University Press).

Pessar, Patricia R. 1995. *A Visa for a Dream: Dominicans in the United States* (Boston: Allyn and Bacon).

Phalen, John Harvey. 1977. *Kinship, Color and Ethnicity: Integrative Ideologies in Aruba, Netherlands Antilles*. Ph.D. Diss. (Anthropology), State University of New York at Stony Brook. (Ann Arbor, MI: Xerox University Microfilms).

Philipps, Ann Elizabeth. 1988. *Labour Migration in the Caribbean: British West Indian Domestic Servants in Curaçao, 1940–1960* (Leiden, Netherlands: History Dept., University of Leiden).

Philpott, Stuart B. 1973. *West Indian Migration: The Montserrat Case* (London: Athlone Press).

Popple, Charles Sterling. 1952. *Standard Oil Company New Jersey in World War II* (New Jersey: Standard Oil Company).

Portes, Alejandro. 1982. "International Labor Migration and National Develop-
     ment." In *U.S. Immigration and Refugee Policy*, edited by Mary Kritz (Boston,
     MA: D.C. Heath & Company).

Pratt, Wallace E. 1950. "The Caribbean Area as a Whole." In *World Geography of
     Petroleum*. American Geographical Society, Special Publication No. 31 (New
     York: Oxford Univeristy Press).

Proudfoot, Malcolm Jarvis. 1954. *Population Movements in the Caribbean: A Compara-
     tive Study in Methods of Development* (New York: Negro University Press).

Proudfoot, Mary. 1954. *Britain and the United States in the Caribbean: A Comparative
     Study in Methods and Development* (New York: Praeger).

Pulsipher, Lydia Mihelic. 1993. "Changing Roles in the Life-Cycles of Women in
     Traditional West Indian Houseyards." In *Women & Change in the Caribbean*,
     edited by Janet H. Momsen (Bloomington: Indiana University Press).

Reddock, Rhoda E. 1994. *Women, Labour & Politics in Trinidad & Tobago: A History*
     (London: Zed Books).

———. 1988. "Women and the Slave Plantation Economy in the Caribbean." In
     Retrieving Women's History. Changing Perceptions, edited by S. Jay Kleinberg
     (New York: Berg Publishers).

Reimers, David M. 1985. *Still the Golden Door: The Third World Comes to America* (New
     York: Columbia University Press).

Repak, Terry A. 1994. "Labor Recruitment and the Lure of Capital: Central American
     Migrants in Washington, D.C." *Gender & Society* 8 (4): 507–24.

Richardson, Bonham C. 1992. *The Caribbean in the Wider World, 1492–1992* (New York:
     Cambridge University Press).

———. 1983. *Caribbean Migrants: Environment and Human Survival on St. Kitts and
     Nevis* (Knoxville: University of Tennessee Press).

Ricketts, Erol. 1985. *The Relationship between U.S. Investment and Immigration from the
     Caribbean: Prospects for the Reagan Administration's Caribbean Basin Initiative.*
     Research Abstract (New York: City University of New York Graduate School
     and University Center).

Riviere, Bill. 1981. "Contemporary Class Structure in Dominica." In *Contemporary
     Caribbean*, edited by Susan Craig (Maracas, Trinidad and Tobago: College
     Press).

Rodman, Hyman. 1971. *Lower Class Families: The Culture of Poverty in Negro Trinidad*
     (London: Oxford University Press).

Rollins, Judith. 1985. *Between Women: Domestics and Their Employers* (Philadelphia:
     Temple University Press).

Romero, Mary. 1992. *Maid in the U.S.A.* (New York: Routledge).

Rubenstein, Hymie. 1987. *Coping with Poverty: Adaptive Strategies in a Caribbean
     Village* (Boulder, CO: Westview Press).

Safa, Helen I. 1995. *The Myth of the Male Breadwinner: Women and Industrialization in
     the Caribbean* (Boulder, CO: Westview Press).

Safa, Helen I. and Peggy Antrobus. 1992. "Women and the Economic Crisis in the
     Caribbean." In *Unequal Burden: Economic Crises, Persistent Poverty, and
     Women's Work*, edited by Lourdes Beneria and Shelly Feldman (Boulder, CO:
     Westview Press).

Sassen, Saskia. 1992. "Why Migration?" *Report on the Americas* 26 (1): 14–19.

Sassen-Koob, Saskia. 1983. "Labor Migration and the New Industrial Division of
     Labor." In *Women and Men and the International Division of Labor*, edited by

June Nash and Maria Fernandez-Kelly (Albany: State University of New York Press).

Satzewich, Vic. 1991. *Racism and the Incorporation of Foreign Labour: Farm Labour Migration to Canada Since 1945* (London: Routledge).

Scott, Rebecca J. 1987. "Comparing Emancipations: A Review Essay." *Journal of Social History* 20: 565–83.

Sealy, Neil. 1992. *Caribbean World* (New York: Cambridge University Press).

Sen, Gita and Caren Grown. 1987. *Development, Crises, and Alternative Visions: Third World Women's Perspecties* (New York: Monthly Review Press).

Senior, Olive. 1991. *Working Miracles: Women's Lives in the English-Speaking Caribbean* (Bloomington: Indiana University Press).

Small, Stephen. 1994. *Racialized Barriers: The Black Experience in the United States and England in the 1980s* (London: Routledge).

Smith, Joan, Immanuel Wallerstein, and Hans-Dieter Evers. 1984. *Households and the World Economy* (Beverley Hills, CA: Sage Publications).

Smith, M. G. 1962. *West Indian Family Structure* (Seattle, WA: University of Washington Press).

Smith, R. T. 1987. "Hierarchy and the Dual Marriage System in West Indian Society." In *Gender and Kinship: Essays Towards a Unified Analysis*, edited by Jane Fishburne Collier and Sylvia Junko Yanagisako (Stanford: Stanford University Press).

Soto, Isa Maria. 1987. "West Indian Child Fostering: Its Role in Migrant Exchanges." In *Caribbean Life in New York City: Sociological Dimensions*, edited by Constance R. Sutton and Elsa M. Chaney (New York: Center for Migration Studies).

Spensky, Martine. 1992. "Producers of Legitimacy: Homes for Unmarried Mothers in the 1950s." In *Regulating Womanhood*, edited by Carol Smart (New York: Routledge).

Stack, Carol B. 1974. *All Our Kin: Strategies in a Black Community* (New York: Harper and Row).

Stack, Carol B. and Linda M. Burton. 1994. "Kinscripts: Reflections on Family, Generation, and Culture." In *Mothering: Ideology, Experience, and Agency*, edited by Evelyn Nakano Glenn, Grace Chang, and Linda Rennie Forcey (New York: Routledge).

Stichter, Sharon. 1990. "Women, Employment and the Family: Current Debates." In *Women, Employment and the Family in the International Division of Labour*, edited by Sharon Stichter and Jane L. Parpart (Philadelphia: Temple University Press).

———. 1985. *Migrant Laborers* (New York: Cambridge University Press).

St. Victor, Rosalind. 1986. "The Family and Support Systems." In *Women of the Caribbean*, edited by Patricia Ellis (London: Zed Books).

Sunshine, Catherine A. 1994. *The Caribbean: Survival, Struggle and Sovereignty* (Washington, DC: Ecumenical Program on Central America and the Caribbean).

Sunshine, Catherine A., Philip Wheaton, and Juel Kamke, eds. 1985. *Grenada: The Peaceful Revolution* (Washington, DC: Ecumenical Program on Central America and the Caribbean [EPICA]).

Sutton, Constance R. and Elsa M. Chaney, eds. 1987. *Caribbean Life in New York City: Sociocultural Dimensions*, edited by Constance R. Sutton and Elsa M. Chaney (New York: Center for Migration Studies).

Swidler, Ann. 1986. "Love and Adulthood in American Culture." In *Family in Transition*, edited by Arlene S. and Jerome H. Skolnick (Boston: Little, Brown).

Taylor, Wayne C. and John Lindeman. 1955. *The Creole Petroleum Corporation in Venezuela* (New York: Arno Press, New York Times Co.).

Tinker, Irene. 1994. "The Urban Street Food Trade: Regional Variations of Women's Involvement." In *Women, The Family And Policy. A Global Perspective*, edited by Esther Ngan-Ling Chow and Catherine White Berheide (New York: State University of New York Press).

Trost, Jan. 1975. "Married and Unmarried Cohabitation: The Case of Sweden, with Some Comparisons." *Journal of Marriage and the Family* 37: 677–82.

Turrittin, Jane Sawyer. 1976. "Networks and Mobility: The Case of West Indian Domestics from Montserrat." *Canadian Review of Sociology and Anthropology* 13 (3): 303–20.

van Rossem, Ronan. 1996. "The World System Paradigm as General Theory of Development: A Cross-National Test." *American Sociological Review* 61 (June): 508–27.

Wall, Bennett, H. 1988. *Growth in a Changing Environment: A History of Standard Oil Company (New Jersey) 1950–1972 and Exxon Corporation 1972–1975* (New York: McGraw Hill).

Wallerstein, Immanuel. 1987. "Household Structures and Labor Force Formation in the Capitalist World Economy." In *Households and the World Economy*, edited by Joan Smith, Immanuel Wallerstein, and Hans-Dieter Evers (Beverly Hills, CA: Sage Publications).

——. 1974. *The Modern World System: Capitalist Agriculture and the Origins of the European World Economy in the Sixteenth Century* (New York: Academic Press).

Ward, Kathryn B. 1993. "Reconceptualizing World System Theory to Include Women." In *Theory On Gender/Feminism on Theory*, edited by Paula England (New York: Aldine de Gruyter).

Waters, Mary C. 1994. "Ethnic and Racial Identities of Second-Generation Black Immigrants in New York City." *International Migration Review* 28: 795–820.

West Indian Commission. 1992. *Time For Action* (Barbados, West Indies).

Williams, Eric. 1964. *History of the People of Trinidad & Tobago* (New York: Praeger).

——. 1944. *Capitalism and Slavery* (Chapel Hill: University of North Carolina Press).

Wiltshire, Rosina. 1992. "Implications of Transnational Migration for Nationalism. The Caribbean Example." In *Towards a Transnational Perspective on Migration*, edited by Nina Glick Schiller, Linda Basch, and Christina Blanc-Szanton (New York: New York Academy of Sciences).

Wong, Sau-Ling C. 1994. "Diverted Mothering: Representations of Caregivers of Color in the Age of 'Multiculturalism.' " In *Mothering: Ideology, Experience, and Agency*, edited by Evelyn Nakano Glenn, Grace Chang, and Linda Rennie Forcey (New York: Routledge).

Zinn, Maxine Baca. 1994. "Feminist Rethinking from Racial-Ethnic Familes. In *Women of Color in U.S. Society*, edited by Maxine Baca Zinn and Bonnie Thorton Dill (Philadelphia: Temple University Press).

——. 1987. "Structural Transformation and Minority Families." In *Women, Households and the Economy*, edited by Lourdes Beneria and Catherine R. Stimpson (New Brunswick, NJ: Rutgers University Press).

Zuloaga, Guillermo. 1950. "Venezuela." In *World Geography of Petroleum*. American Geographical Society, Special Publication No. 31 (New York: Oxford University Press).

Index

About the Author

PAULA L. AYMER is a professor of Sociology in the department of Sociology and Anthropology at Tufts University in Medford, Massachusetts.